How Sampling Works

THE PINE FORGE PRESS SERIES IN RESEARCH METHODS AND STATISTICS

Richard T. Campbell and Kathleen S. Crittenden, Series Editors

Through its unique modular format, this series offers an unmatched flexibility and coherence for undergraduate methods and statistics teaching. The two "core" volumes, one in methods and one in statistics, address the primary concerns of undergraduate courses, but in less detail than found in existing texts, and are both available in inexpensive, paperback editions. The smaller "satellite" volumes in the series can either supplement these core books, giving instructors the emphasis and coverage best suited for their course and students, or be used in more advanced, specialized courses.

Investigating the Social World:
The Process and Practice of Research *by Russell K. Schutt*

A Guide to Field Research *by Carol A. Bailey*

Designing Surveys: A Guide to Decisions and Procedures *by Ronald Czaja and Johnny Blair*

How Sampling Works *by Richard Maisel and Caroline Hodges Persell*

Forthcoming

Introduction to Social Statistics *by Chava Frankfort-Nachmias*

Regression: A Primer *by Richard T. Campbell and Kathleen S. Crittenden*

Experimental Design and Analysis of Variance *by Robert Leik*

Analyzing Data *by James Davis and Jere Bruner*

Applied Social Research *by Marty Jendrek*

How Sampling Works

Richard Maisel
New York University

Caroline Hodges Persell
New York University

Pine Forge Press

Thousand Oaks, California • London • New Delhi

For information, address:

 Pine Forge Press
A Sage Publications Company
2455 Teller Road
Thousand Oaks, California 91320
(805) 499-4224
E-mail: sales@pfp.sagepub.com

SAGE Publications Ltd.
6 Bonhill Street
London EC2A 4PU
United Kingdom

SAGE Publications India Pvt. Ltd.
M-32 Market
Greater Kailash I
New Delhi, 110 048 India

Production and Typesetting: Scratchgravel Publishing Services
Production Manager: Rebecca Holland
Designer: Lisa S. Mirski
Cover Design: Paula Shuhert and Graham Metcalfe

Printed in the United States of America

96 97 98 99 10 9 8 7 6 5 4 3 2 1

Library of Congress Cataloging-in-Publication Data
Maisel, Richard, 1928–
    How sampling works / Richard Maisel, Caroline Persell.
        p.   cm. — (The Pine Forge Press series in research methods
    and statistics)
    Includes bibliographical references and index.
    ISBN 0-8039-9061-8 (acid-free)
    1. Sampling (Statistics)   I. Persell, Caroline Hodges.
II. Title.   III. Series.
QA276.6.M35   1995
001.4'222—dc20   94-47987
                                                          CIP

About the Authors

Richard Maisel is a past president of the American Association of Public Opinion Research and a consultant for statistical design for many corporations and government agencies. He is an Associate Professor of Sociology at New York University, where he teaches statistics and research methods.

Caroline Hodges Persell is currently president of the Eastern Sociological Society. She is the author or co-author of numerous scholarly monographs, research articles, and eight books in sociology, including three editions of *Understanding Society: An Introduction to Sociology.* She is a Professor of Sociology at New York University, where she teaches research methods among other courses.

About the Publisher

Pine Forge Press is a new educational publisher, dedicated to publishing innovative books and software throughout the social sciences. On this and any other of our publications, we welcome your comments and suggestions.

Please call or write us at:

Pine Forge Press
A Sage Publications Company
2455 Teller Road
Thousand Oaks, California 91320
(805) 499-4224
E-mail: sales@pfp.sagepub.com

*Dedicated to all the students
who put this book to use*

Notice Regarding the ISEE Software

Please read this notice carefully before using the disk accompanying this book.

License

This software is protected by United States copyright law and international treaty provisions. This software may be used by more than one person and it may be used on more than one computer, but no more than one copy of this software may be used at the same time. Pine Forge Press authorizes the purchaser to make archival copies of the software for the sole purpose of backing up the software in order to protect against loss.

Limited Warranty

The warranty for the enclosed disk is for ninety (90) days. If, during that time, you find defects in workmanship or material, the Publisher will replace the defective item. The publisher and author have taken care in the preparation of this book, but make no expressed or implied warranty of any kind and assume no responsibility for errors or omissions. No liability is assumed for incidental or consequential damages in connection with or arising out of the use of the information or programs contained herein.

For warranty service, contact:

Pine Forge Press
2455 Teller Road
Thousand Oaks, California 91320
(805) 499-4224
Fax (805) 499-7881
E-mail: sales@pfp.sagepub.com

Contents

3 Simple Random Samples and Sampling Distributions 25

7 Making It Work   139

Series Foreword

The Pine Forge Press Series in Methods and Statistics, consisting of core books in methods and statistics and a series of satellite volumes on specialized topics, allows instructors to create a customized curriculum.The authors of the core volumes are both seasoned researchers and distinguished teachers, and the more specialized texts are written by acknowledged experts in their fields. To date, the series offers the core text in research methods and three satellite volumes focusing on sampling, field methods, and survey research. To be published soon are the core text in statistics and accompanying satellite volumes on such specific topics as regression and data analysis, as well as additional supplementary volumes in research methods.

How Sampling Works, by Richard Maisel and Caroline Hodges Persell, offers an imaginative new way for students without strong mathematical backgrounds to visualize powerful principles of statistical sampling and inference, principles that underlie the quality of knowledge in virtually every field and profession. Using the authors' pioneering ISEE software, this book facilitates the teaching and learning of these difficult principles. It is designed to be used in conjunction with Russell Schutt's core text, *Investigating the Social World,* in a basic research methods course, with Ronald Czaja and Johnny Blair's *Designing Surveys* in a course on sample survey methodology, or as a supplementary text in a basic statistic course.

Richard T. Campbell
Kathleen S. Crittenden
Series Editors

Preface

Few tools for gaining knowledge are as powerful and widely applicable as the principles of statistical sampling and inference. These principles can enhance the quality of knowledge available in virtually every field and profession. Election polling, quality control in production, social services evaluation, tests of new medical treatments, market research, crime control, and many other efforts depend on understanding statistical sampling and inference.

If understanding sampling is so valuable, why isn't it taught to everyone as they go through school? Probably because the concepts are difficult to learn. To grasp the power of sampling, one needs to understand the mathematical theory on which it rests. This theory is usually taught in undergraduate and graduate statistics courses, but even there mastery is far from certain for several reasons. Sampling theory is only one small part of most statistics courses, it is usually covered quickly (perhaps in a week or two), the material is intrinsically difficult, and the ideas are usually presented in the form of equations. Although students with a deep background in mathematics can grasp these equations with relative ease, this method of teaching presents a formidable, sometimes insurmountable, barrier to other students.

This book is aimed at the many students who tremble in the face of equations. Our goal is to help students without extensive background in mathematics understand the theoretical principles underlying statistical sampling and inference. To accomplish this goal, this book differs from a standard statistics textbook in four major ways. First, the whole book—rather than just one chapter or less—is devoted to the principles of sampling and inferences from samples. Second, the core of the book is a series of experiments that permit students to discover the principles of sampling for themselves. Third, the results of these experiments are presented visually in the form of graphs. These experiments and dynamic graphs are done on a microcomputer, which draws, tallies, and displays the results with great speed. Fourth, the book includes an original software package for IBM-compatible PCs that was developed by the authors and two professional programmers with support from the U.S. Department of Education's Fund for the Improvement of Postsecondary Education (FIPSE). The software is called ISEE to capture the idea that students will both see and understand statistical principles as they use the program. ISEE is designed to be "user friendly" for students with little or no background in computers.

By changing the conditions of sample size or variability in a population, students can see the effects of those factors on their experimental results. These visual experiences provide an alternative basis to equations for understanding the mathematical theory underlying statistical sampling. Equations are presented in this book only after students have themselves discovered and tested the underlying rules that the equations represent.

We wish we could say that this alternative approach to statistical sampling and inference makes teaching and learning the subject "a piece of cake." We can say, however, that the ISEE program and this book make it *easier* for students to learn the principles of statistical sampling. With hard work and attention this material can be learned, even by students with limited mathematical backgrounds and students who freeze at the sight of an equation.

The book opens with a series of practical problems faced by people working in business, social work, criminal justice, politics, child development, the health professions, and education. In all fields, people need good information to answer important questions with confidence, but they are often overwhelmed by the quantity of cases or data involved. Such problems can be solved, usually with a manageable expenditure of time and money, by understanding and applying the principles of statistical sampling and inference. The goal of this book is to teach those principles. Chapter 1 describes some of the uses of sampling and concludes with a list of the symbols used in the book.

Chapter 2 begins with the Martin family and their information problems and introduces some basic concepts in sampling. Chapter 3 introduces the concept of random samples and their virtues, demonstrates two methods of selecting simple random samples, introduces the concept of a sampling distribution, and shows how to use the concept for evaluating sampling results. Chapter 3 shows how to use the ISEE program to explore three other ways of selecting samples—namely, systematic random sampling, replicated sampling, and thin zone sampling.

In Chapter 4 students are guided toward the discovery of two general rules of sampling and are shown how to conduct experiments to evaluate those rules using a very small population. Chapter 5 guides students through experiments designed to test the rules with large, real populations. Chapter 5 also leads students to the discovery of a third general rule and provides an experiment for testing and evaluating that rule.

Chapter 6 develops the vital concept of a confidence interval and considers the practical issues of costs and optimum sample size, drawing on the examples from Chapter 1. Chapter 7 discusses additional concerns that need to be considered when applying sampling theory to practical situations, such as obtaining the sampling frame and using a table of random numbers.

Chapters 2 through 6 contain exercises (with answers in Appendix C) that enable students to apply what they are learning and test their understanding of the material as they proceed.

The appendixes contain directions for installing and using the ISEE program, as well as the cards and forms needed for conducting the experiments and many of the exercises. A glossary of statistical terms is combined with the index at the end of the book.

Acknowledgments

This book and the Introduction to Sampling Error Experiments (ISEE) computer program that accompanies it would not exist without the help of a great many people and institutions. Jack Bleich and Eray Ekici did the necessary extensive programming and reprogramming, and they remained both creative and careful throughout the process.

We gratefully acknowledge three years of support, totaling $124,164, from the Fund for the Improvement of Postsecondary Education (FIPSE) in the U.S. Department of Education. Without FIPSE support we never could have developed the ideas behind the program and this book. We appreciate New York University's support through the entire process of development and writing, especially the early encouragement of then-Dean Ann Burton. We value the helpful comments of our reviewers, Robbyn Wacker (University of

Northern Colorado) and Marty Jendrek (Miami University). Thanks also to Grant Blank (University of Chicago) for his help in the development of the software.

Edward Chapel of Queensboro Community College gave tirelessly of his good ideas at all stages of the development and writing process and checked the entire manuscript. He and Zvia Napthali taught in the experimental trials we conducted at several schools, and we thank them both. We also thank all the undergraduate and graduate students at various colleges and universities who tried different versions of the program—with some benefit to them, we hope—as it was being developed. Ganka Dimitrova analyzed the experimental trials conducted on an early version of the program, which we published in *Teaching Sociology* (October 1993).

The late Gloria Wentowski of Bennett College spent a wonderful summer with us in New York learning the ISEE program so she could take it home to use with students at Bennett. She was writing a paper on those experimental trials at the time of her premature death. We appreciate the chance we had to work with her, and we mourn her passing.

In Steve Rutter at Pine Forge Press we found the kind of innovative publisher who actively works to publish creative tools for improved pedagogy. His committed and careful staff, Rebecca Holland and Sherith Pankratz, were great additions to the enterprise. They contributed productively and pleasantly to the final result. Anne and Greg Draus of Scratchgravel Publishing Services produced the book in its final form and found a wonderful copy editor, Peggy Tropp, blessed with a clear mind that grasped mathematical ideas while gracefully achieving stylistic consistency in their expression.

1 Turbocharging Your Work: An Introduction to the Power of Sampling

Sampling is one of the most powerful tools available to professionals and researchers. If someone offered you a way to get ten times the gas mileage you do now, at a cost of only ten cents a gallon, would you be interested? Sampling offers such a boost for solving problems. Consider the following examples.

Problems Sampling Can Solve

In Business

You are a small software distributor. You have licensed a piece of software developed by an independent programmer. You will arrange for a disk copying center to make 50,000 copies of the software, which you will distribute. You want to be sure that the copy center is doing a good job, that the copies work, and that no viruses get on the disks you will be distributing. How do you satisfy yourself that this is the case, without testing every disk?

In Social Work

You work in a small social work agency that has handled more than 3,000 cases over the past 10 years. Your board of directors has asked what happened to the cases handled. You have no extra staff to track all those cases, but you want to answer the board's question. What can you do?

In Criminal Justice

You work in your state's criminal justice department, which has been named in a lawsuit asserting that whites and African Americans are treated differently by the criminal justice system in the state. The specific concern is that African Americans are getting stiffer jail sentences than white Americans. There are more than 56,000 inmates in the state prison system. You have a very small budget to pay some outside researchers to gather and analyze data addressing this issue. If the charge is true, one resolution of the lawsuit could be to change state court practices so that they are race-neutral. Your budget cannot begin to cover the cost of studying all 56,000 cases. How do you proceed?

In Politics

You are an elected public official who wants to stay close to your constituents. As part of this effort, you send a mail survey to everyone in your district. Since you have a participatory and well-educated district, you receive more than 7,000 replies. Your one part-time administrative assistant is overwhelmed. Not only are the questionnaires filling her apartment, but she wonders how anyone can possibly read all of them, much less figure out what they mean. What should you tell her?

In Child Development

You are thinking of starting a day-care center. You have already learned from the county how many births were registered there in each of the last three years. What you don't know is how many people need day care, what type of day care they seek, and how they might respond to the type of center you are proposing. You can't afford to contact everyone, but you want to get some idea of how much interest there might be. How can you do this?

In the Health Professions

You are a health professional trying to understand the research literature on the effectiveness of various forms of cancer treatments. Every study you read discusses the population, sample, and the sampling error associated with the results. How do you make sense of this information?

Or, you are a nurse-midwife trying to decide whether you should affiliate your practice with a local hospital or deliver babies in people's homes. You want to know, for your county, what proportion of home births with midwives present required emergency trips to hospitals. You have obtained a list of all home births in the last five years, but there are too many for you to call every single one. What do you do?

In Education

You work in a large elementary school, and you want to monitor the progress of all the students in your school. You want to assess them by using more than just a single standardized test score, since you are interested in various aspects of children's intellectual, personal, and social development. Such rich assessment materials take considerable time to prepare and time to evaluate. Given that there are more than 1,500 students in the school, this looks like an impossible task. Can you find a solution?

The Good News

Real people face problems like these all the time. In all walks of life—health, social work, public opinion, market research, criminal justice, education, business—people confront situations in which they need good information to answer important questions with confidence, but they are overwhelmed by the quantity of cases or data involved. Sometimes they are lucky enough to work for large organizations that have the resources to hire full-time researchers and statisticians. In such a situation, their job is to understand and interpret the results. Often, however, their response is to do nothing, which means they can't do their work as effectively as possible. The good news is that every one of these problems can be solved, usually with a manageable expenditure of time and money, by properly applying the principles of statistical sampling and inference.

The reason sampling theory is so powerful is that it allows us to study *some* rather than all the cases of interest, while at the same time allowing us to draw valid conclusions about all of them. This power can only be realized if we understand and apply the scientific principles underlying statistical sampling and inference. The purpose of this book is to help you to learn those powerful principles, so that you can understand and apply them to important problems. Apart from learning how to read and how to do simple mathematical calculations, sampling may well be the most vivid example of the adage "Knowledge is power."

Seven Approaches to Sampling

People trying to solve problems like the ones you've just encountered often adopt one of the following seven strategies:

1. They use a **census**.[1] In a census, data are collected on every member of some specified population. For example, a 100% testing program for all automobiles that are produced by a manufacturer would be a complete census because every member of the population is tested.

2. They use a **pseudo-census**. That is, they try to measure every member of the population, but they end up with a sample in which some members of the population are not measured. The United States Census of Population conducted every 10 years is an example of a pseudo-census. The Census tries to collect data from each household in the United States, but a small proportion of the population is not reached.

3. They use a **self-selected sample**. In this approach, they send a general message requesting everyone who reads or hears it to respond by mail or telephone. For example, some television programs will ask viewers to express their opinion on a subject by calling their number. Since there is not a 100% response, it is not a census; and since the data are requested by a general method (television broadcast) rather than by an individual approach (such as the Census, which tries to contact each household individually), it is not a pseudo-census.

4. They use a **convenience** or **haphazard sample,** which is a sample of cases that can be collected in the easiest way possible, with little cost or effort. Such a sample does not try to cover every member of the population. Examples include market research studies of the general public conducted among shoppers in a mall on a given day or psychological tests developed by professors using only students in their classes.

5. They strive to find a **typical case**. This is a sample of one or more cases thought to be typical of an entire population. For example, researchers ask what is a "typical community" in the United States and decide that it should not be a very big city or a small town, but a small to medium-sized city. They decide that it should not be in a highly distinctive region, like the South, so they select the Midwest as typical of "middle" America. It is in

---

[1]Note: **Boldface** terms in the text are defined in the Glossary/Index.

the middle geographically, it often has fewer extremes of wealth and poverty, and it is more homogeneous ethnically than the coasts. Historically, community studies such as *Middletown* reflect such a selection process. In marketing and political studies there is an expression, "Will it fly in Peoria (Illinois)?" which captures the idea of a "typical" case.

6. They use a **quota sample.** Certain general requirements are set, and any sample of cases meeting those requirements is used. An example is a telephone survey of residents in a certain city, using a sample that is 50% male and 50% female.

7. They use a **probability sample**. This is a sample selected by a random procedure that gives every member of the population a known (and nonzero) probability of selection. For example, to select a probability sample of 100 children in a school of 1000 children, we would get a list of all the children in the school and randomly select 100 students from the list. There are many different types of probability samples, and you'll learn about several of them in this book.

Deciding What to Do

To choose among these various ways of selecting a sample when we conduct a specific study, we must consider three factors.

1. *The purpose of the study*—what we want to learn and why we want to learn it. If we want to set up congressional districts of equal population size, then we must know how many people live in each city block or rural area. This means we must conduct a census or a pseudo-census. If we want to know the average age of the population, then we can select a sample of the population.

2. *The potential for error* in the way we are selecting the sample. Some methods give estimates that are widely different from the true value, while others are very close.

3. *The cost in time, money, and effort.* Some methods require large, costly samples, while others may use small, inexpensive samples.

By balancing the purpose of a study, its costs, and its potential for error, we can decide the best way to select a sample. In general, a pseudo-census that excludes information for a large part of the population and self-selected samples are very poor methods for selecting samples. When we are limited to a single case study, the typical-case method is often the best method of selecting a sample. When the goal is no error, as in an immunization program, then a census must be conducted. Note that a pseudo-census is not the same as a census, because it has a potential for error. The United States Decennial Census, for example, undercounts poorer people, members of minority groups, and people living in large cities. When we have very limited resources and can tolerate a very large error, then a convenience sample may work, but in general the best balance between controlling error and cost comes when we use probability samples.

In this book you will learn several ways of selecting probability samples. You will learn how probability samples can be selected in a very scientific way, guided by the general theory of probability. When you have learned this theory, you can also use it to better understand the potential for error in nonprobability samples.

Overview of the Book

Now, how can you use this book to learn the theory of sampling?

In Chapter 2 we outline some basic ways to think about sampling and define some technical terms needed to talk about sampling in a very precise way. These ideas provide background and definitions for the rest of the book.

In Chapter 3 you will conduct some very simple mental experiments designed to acquaint you with the concept of a sampling distribution and show you how it can be used to measure the potential error in using samples.

To understand the results of these experiments, you will have to know the meaning of a number of terms used in elementary statistics and be able to use them. These terms, listed below, are defined in the glossary to this book and are discussed in the first few chapters of any basic statistics textbook.

- **distribution**
- **frequency distribution**
- **shape of the frequency distribution**
    rectangular, unimodal, bimodal, dichotomous
    symmetrical, skewed positive, skewed negative
- **normal curve**
- **mean**

- **proportion**
- **median**
- **mode**
- **maximum value in a distribution**
- **minimum value in a distribution**
- **range**
- **standard deviation**
- **variance**

In Chapter 4 we will conduct a number of computer experiments using the ISEE program that accompanies this text. You don't have to know much about computers to conduct these experiments. You (or someone else who helps you) must know how to turn the computer on and off and how to load files from a floppy disk to a hard disk. Everything else you need to know is explained in this book. As you will see, under some conditions, most samples selected are good samples. That is, they provide a very good picture of the population. Under other conditions, you will see that many bad samples are selected. They offer a poor picture of the population. For example, you will see that larger samples usually give a better picture of the population than smaller samples.

These experiments will help you to formulate rules indicating when to expect many good or poor samples. When you finish Chapter 4, you will have a very good grasp of the statistical terms **bias** and **standard error** and will understand the equations used for measuring these two statistics.

In Chapter 5 you will conduct further computer sampling experiments designed to test these rules on much larger populations. The data for these real populations are loaded with the program. You will see that you can predict the results of the experiments conducted in Chapter 5, using the rules developed in Chapter 4. In Chapter 5 you will learn an additional rule that is required for many applications of the theory. This additional rule will also explain why the normal curve is so important in studying statistics.

In Chapter 6 you will learn how to apply the rules developed in Chapters 4 and 5 to improve sample estimates and to determine the right sample size for a study. When you finish the chapter, you will understand the statistical measure called a **confidence interval** and know how to use this measure in planning and analyzing your research.

Chapter 7 covers a number of practical issues involved in carrying out probability samples. These issues include the problems of getting and using lists for selecting samples.

To learn successfully from this book, you need to read it, learn some important definitions, and expend the concentrated effort required to conduct and study the computer experiments. In our discussions we will define a number of terms—such as *population, sample, estimate, actual error,* and so forth—in very specific ways. It is essential that you learn the specific meaning for each term.

A List of Symbols Used in This Book

Some terms appear often in this book and are used in equations. To simplify their use, we represent them with symbols.[2] For example, we use the symbol **N** to stand for the number of cases in a *population,* while the symbol n represents the number of cases in a *sample.*

We use a number of equations in this book, but we try to make it as easy as possible for you to read them. In most cases, the symbols we use will be words or abbreviations that are easy to recognize. For example, we will use the term MEAN in equations for the population mean and ST.DEV. for the standard deviation in the population. One general rule about the equations that you should remember is that terms in equations referring to the population will be written in capital letters (N, MEAN, ST.DEV.) and terms referring to the sample will be written in lowercase letters (n, mean, st.dev.). Below you will find a list of terms we will use in many equations. We will define a few other symbols later in the book.

N	= population size (the Number of cases in a population)
n	= sample size (the number of cases in a sample)
MEAN	= mean of a population
mean	= mean of a sample
TOTAL	= total of a population
total	= total of a sample

[2]When you read other statistics books, you will find that different symbols are sometimes used. Some authors use Greek letters. We use English letters, words, and abbreviations, with capital letters referring to the value in the population and lowercase letters referring to the value in the sample. We think this will help you to remember what term is being discussed and whether it is from the population or the sample.

ST.DEV. = standard deviation of a population

st.dev. = standard deviation of a sample

It would be helpful for you to copy, on a piece of paper or an index card, this list of symbols and their definitions. You can use this list for reference as you read, and add other definitions as you come across them later in the book.

To illustrate the use of these symbols, assume there is a family of five children. The family will be our population, so N = 5. Suppose the ages of the children are 1, 3, 4, 5, and 7. Then the total age of all the children in the population is TOTAL = 20, and the mean age of all the children in the population is MEAN = 4. The standard deviation of the ages of all the children in the population is ST.DEV. = 2.

Suppose we select a sample of two children in the family, ages 1 and 5, to go on a trip. Then the sample size is n = 2. The total age of the two children in the sample is total = 6. The mean age of the two children in the sample is mean = 3, and the standard deviation of the ages of the children in the sample is st.dev. = $\sqrt{8}$. (Remember, we divide by n – 1 when we calculate the standard deviation of a sample, by N for a population.)

Installing the ISEE Program

To conduct and understand the experiments described in this book, you will need the ISEE program that accompanies this book and access to a 286 or more advanced PC, with an EGA or VGA graphics card, DOS 3.0 or higher, a hard disk with at least one megabyte of free space, and the capacity to read high-density 3.5-inch diskettes.

Before continuing, you should install the ISEE program on the PC you will be using, if that has not already been done for you in your laboratory or network. See Appendix A for directions on installing the program.

Once you have installed the program, review pages 167–193 of Appendix A to get an overview of how the ISEE program operates. Then continue to Chapter 2.

2 Information, Action, and Sampling

Solving Information Problems

The Martin Family

The Martin family consists of Mr. Martin, who runs a small in-line skate manufacturing company; Mrs. Martin, who is the supervisor of the county blood banks; and their daughter, Helen, who is a student at Baytown High, the local high school. The Martins are a very friendly family, and they usually do a lot of spirited talking at meals. But one Saturday afternoon they are preoccupied and eat their lunch in silence.

When the meal is almost over Mrs. Martin says, "I don't know what is wrong with you two, but I have a problem." Both Mr. Martin and Helen look up and in a single voice respond, "So do I."

This book considers the problems the Martins are having and how they could solve their problems with sampling. Although we use many other examples in this book, we will keep returning to the Martin family and their problems.

Overview of This Chapter

The Martin family's problems illustrate some of the basic ideas underlying sampling theory. As you will see, sampling is always done as part of a larger research project in which we are trying to learn something about the world. If we do a good job of sampling, it will help us learn what we want to know. If we do a poor job of sampling, it may prevent us from finding out what we want to know. But what does it mean to do a good job? In this chapter we will define what we mean by a good job or a poor job of sampling. The central idea revolves around the concepts of a parameter, an estimate, and the error of an estimate. In particular, you will see how important it is to be able to measure the potential for error in the way a sample is selected.

When you finish this chapter, you will understand a way to think about sampling and you will know many of the technical terms that are used in the sampling literature. But now, back to the Martin family and their problems.

The Martin Family's Problems

Mrs. Martin supervises several small blood banks in the county. The newspaper recently ran an article saying that many blood banks in the United States are facing problems with the hepatitis B virus getting into the nation's blood supply. She believes her blood banks are safe, but needs to find out for sure whether any of them contains infected blood supplies. She also has to protect the blood banks from collecting infected blood during the coming year. Finally, she is very concerned about how much blood will be available if the blood banks must discard some of their current blood supply and reject a large number of donations during the coming year. What should she do?

Mr. Martin has decided to manufacture in-line skates for pre-teens, which he plans to sell to 12 sports stores located in and around Baytown. He wants to know how many pairs of skates will be sold, so he can start ordering the materials and setting up his production schedule. What should he do?

Helen Martin plays in the school band. She has been elected by the other band members to arrange a party for them and for band members from three other local schools (Chester, Hillside, and Lakeview). To make plans, she needs to know how many band members will be coming from the four schools. What should she do?

Information Problems

The problems facing the Martins are similar to ones people often face, as you saw in Chapter 1. Basically they each have a situation in which they need information in order to make a decision or take action. Such problems occur daily. We may need to know if a pot of soup requires seasoning. Or we may need to know a telephone number to make a call. Businesspeople need information to market products or set prices. Government officials constantly face information problems when they formulate laws and policies. We use the term *information problem* to refer to a problem that requires information. To solve an information problem, we must get the necessary information, often by doing some kind of research. We must taste the soup to see if it requires seasoning. We must look in a telephone book for a number. A business must conduct a survey of its customers to find out how they feel about its products and prices. Government officials must conduct studies to help them formulate policies.

The Martins' Research Projects

After some discussion, the Martins decided to do so some research to get the information they needed to solve their problems. Mrs. Martin attended a blood donors' meeting the next day at one of the five blood banks in her county. She asked the 50 people attending the meeting if they would allow their blood to be tested for the hepatitis B virus. Forty of the 50 people attending the meeting tested negative for the virus, and 10 tested positive. Given this result, Mrs. Martin decided that about 20% (10 out of 50) of all blood donors have hepatitis B. Hence, she decided that the usable supply of donated blood would drop by 20 percent, a serious prospect.

Helen knew there were 30 members in her own band. She decided to write a letter to the directors of the other three bands asking for the number of members in each one. She received return letters telling her there were 35 in the Chester band, 20 in the Hillside band, and 15 in the Lakeview band. She added up the number of band members, giving her an estimate of 30 + 35 + 20 + 15 = 100 members in the four bands. In planning the party, therefore, she reserved a room large enough for 100 and ordered dinners for 100.

After thinking about his problem, Mr. Martin realized that there was one purchasing agent for each sports store and that any purchase made by the store would be made by that agent. He decided to ask Betty Arrow and Max Braun, the purchasing agents for two of the 12 local sports stores, how many skates they might purchase. He choose these two purchasing agents because they were both good customers and close friends. This was not an actual order, but just a question to get some orientation from his friends.

Betty told Mr. Martin she thought she might order 10 pairs and Max told him he might order 30 pairs. Mr. Martin decided to project the estimates he got from Betty and Max to all 12 stores. First he calculated the average estimated number of pairs that Betty and Max might buy, which gave him an average of (10 + 30)/2 = 20 pairs. He then projected this average to all stores by multiplying the average by 12 (the number of stores). This gave him an estimate of 12 × 20 = 240 pairs of skates that he might sell to all 12 stores. Given these results, Mr. Martin decided to make 240 pairs of preteen skates.

What do you think of the research the Martins conducted to solve their problems? In the remainder of this chapter, and in the next chapter, we will try to answer this question. It might be a good idea to do Exercise 1 at the end of this chapter before going to the next section. (Answers to the exercises are in Appendix C at the end of the book).

Getting Scientific: Population Parameters, Estimates, and Errors

Before we can use sampling principles to solve information problems, we need to define some technical terms and develop a way of thinking about research and sampling. Learning definitions is slow going and not much fun. As with learning to play an instrument, in the beginning we must learn how to play the notes and chords. Only then can we play the tunes. Here, we cover concepts that are the notes and chords of sampling. If you can learn these terms, they will help you to play the beautiful tunes of statistical inference.

The Parameter

The object of any research project is to learn something. The term **parameter** refers to the actual information we want to know. For example, the object of Helen Martin's research was to find out how many band members would attend the party. For the sake of discussion, let us assume that 80 band members will actually attend the party. This means that the parameter for Helen Martin's problem is 80 band members. If 5% of all blood donors in Mrs. Martin's county actually test positive for the hepatitis B virus, then 5% is the parameter for her problem.

Parameters share certain features. They are specific (for example, 80 band members), they refer to reality, and they are unknown to us when we conduct our research. If we knew the parameter, we would not waste our time doing research. In many cases we may never know the parameter. *The strength of sampling is the way it allows us to assess or estimate the value of a parameter.*

Helen Martin could find the parameter for her problem, 80 members attending, if she counted the number of band members who actually came to the party. But she does not know the parameter when making her plans. Thus, she must conduct research to learn what the parameter might be.

Mrs. Martin doesn't know the parameter for her problem when she must decide how serious a threat the hepatitis B virus poses to the blood banks in her county, and she will not know the parameter until after the impact has been felt. Mr. Martin does not know how many skates he will sell when he starts producing them. If Mr. Martin decided not to make the skates, he would never know how many he would sell.

There are two types of parameters: quantitative and qualitative. A quantitative parameter takes the form of a number that could have been derived by some mathematical operation such as addition or subtraction and that could itself be used in further mathematical operations. A qualitative parameter does not meet the requirements for a quantitative parameter. The parameters for each of the Martin problems are numerical because we could add numbers or count to derive each one of them.

Qualitative parameters are different. Suppose we wanted to know the name of the first president of the United States or the telephone number of a friend. The parameter for the first problem would be the name George Washington, and the parameter for the second problem might be 443-5688. Neither of these is a quantitative parameter. The first parameter is not a number. The second parameter is a number, but it is not derived from or used in mathematical operations.

Defining a Quantitative Parameter as a Population Parameter

Quantitative parameters can always be defined in terms of some **set** of things we want to know about. We will call the total set of entities we want to know about the **population** and the individual case a **population member.** The population for Helen Martin's problem would be the four schools (Baytown, Chester, Hillside, and Lakeview), while any one of the schools, such as Baytown, would be a population member. Associated with each member of the population is some measure we want to know. We will call that measure a **true score,** and the set of scores associated with all members of the population a **population distribution.** For example, the true scores for Helen Martin's problem would be the number of band members who would attend from each school. Suppose the number of band members who would attend from each of the four schools was 26, 30, 14, and 10. These four numbers would be the population distribution for her problem, while 26 would be the true score for the first population member.

We can always think of the population and the population distribution as a list of all population members, each with its associated true score. For example, we can portray the population and population distribution for Helen Martin's problem as follows:

Population (name of band)	Population Distribution (number of attending members)
Baytown	26
Chester	30
Hillside	14
Lakeview	10

In the study of statistics, we learn many ways of generating summary measures that describe a distribution, such as the population distribution for the four bands listed above. These summary measures include a total, a mean, a median, a range, and a standard deviation. We refer to a summary measure of a population distribution as a **population parameter.** Thus a population mean, a population total, and a population range are all population parameters.

A quantitative parameter can always be defined as some type of population parameter, such as the population total. Both Mr. Martin and Helen Martin want to know the population total, while Mrs. Martin wants to know the population percentage that tests positive for the hepatitis B virus.

In this book we limit ourselves to the study of mathematical parameters like those needed to solve the Martins' problems. For clarity, we use the term *population parameter* to refer to the parameter we want to know. In most cases, we limit ourselves to three specific population parameters: the population total, the population mean, and the population percentage.

The Sample and the Estimate

Our goal is to discover the population parameter. To do so, we conduct some kind of research. When we complete our research, we have an idea of what the population parameter might be. We call this picture of the population parameter an **estimate.** Helen Martin's research gave her an estimate of 100 band members attending the party. Mrs. Martin's research gave her estimates of 80% testing negative for the hepatitis B virus and 20% testing positive.

There are many ways to generate an estimate. We can use our past experience or that of some expert. For example, Mr. Martin might have used his past experience in selling to the local sports stores to estimate the number of skates he might sell them. Helen might have asked a faculty member who helped to arrange prior parties how many band members might attend.

A second way, and the one used by the Martins, is to select a sample of cases and use the information from those cases to generate an estimate. In this book, we focus exclusively on estimates of a population parameter based on information obtained from a sample. We will use the term **sample** to refer to the total set of cases that we observe, and **sample member** to refer to the specific case. Mrs. Martin's sample consisted of the 50 donors who attended the meeting, and any one of them would be a sample member.

Note that our use of the term *sample* is similar to, but not quite the same as, its meaning in everyday conversation. We usually use the term in everyday conversation to mean a subset of the total population. For example, the sample in Mr. Martin's problem is a subset of the population. Our definition of the term *sample* covers such cases. Our use of the term also covers cases in which the sample is the same as the population, as in Helen Martin's study. The term *census* is often used in popular discussion when observations are made on every member of a population. From our point of view, a census is one type of sample. Our definition of the term *sample* also covers a set of observations that may (mistakenly) include sample members who are not part of the population. For example, in Mrs. Martin's study some of the people who attended the meeting and had their blood tested may not have been blood donors. They might have been friends or relatives accompanying a donor.

We use the term **observed score** to refer to the measure we obtain for each sample member, and the term **sample distribution** to refer to the set of observed scores obtained for all members of the sample. The sample distribution Helen Martin obtained from her research was a set of four numbers, 30, 35, 20, and 15, while 30 was the first observed score.

We can always think of the sample as a list of all sample members we have observed, and a sample distribution as the observed scores we obtain for these sample members. For example, the sample and its associated sample distribution for Helen Martin's problem are as follows:

Sample	*Sample Distribution*
(name of band)	*(reported number of band members)*
Baytown	30
Chester	35
Hillside	20
Lakeview	15

Many statistics can be generated from a sample distribution, including a mean, a median, a range, and a standard deviation. We use the term **sample statistic** when referring to statistics generated from a sample distribution, to distinguish them from similar measures that can be generated from a population distribution. Thus, we will talk about sample means and population means.

Every estimate that we study will be a sample statistic or some combination of sample statistics and other information. Helen Martin's estimate was a sample statistic (the sample total). Mr. Martin generated an estimate by multiplying a sample statistic (the sample mean) by another piece of information (the population size).

It may be worthwhile for you to stop at this point and do Exercises 2, 3, 4, and 5 at the end of this chapter.

Comparing the Terms Used in Defining the Population Parameter and the Sample Statistic

We use five pairs of similar terms for defining a population parameter and generating a sample statistic. The following table lists these five paired terms:

Reality	*Observation*
population member	sample member
population	sample
true score	observed score
population distribution	sample distribution
population parameter	sample statistic

In some studies the paired terms may be very similar, and in others they may be quite different. In Helen Martin's study, the population member and sample member are both bands, and the population and the sample consist of the same four bands. But the true score and the observed score are different. The *true score* is the number of members who actually attend the party, whereas the *observed score* is the number of members in the band. As a result, the population distribution and sample distribution for Helen's study are not the same.

In Mrs. Martin's study, the true score and the observed score are similar (testing positive), but the sample is quite different from the population. The population for Mrs. Martin's problem consists of 870 donors who give blood annually, whereas the sample is the 50 people attending the meeting. Most members of the population are not in the sample, and the sample may contain some people who are not in the population. Since the sample is not the same as the population, the sample distribution for Mrs. Martin's problem is not the same as the population distribution.

Evaluating the Estimate by Its Actual Error

Each estimate can be paired with the population parameter it is meant to portray. For example, Helen's 100-band-member estimate can be paired with its 80-band-member population parameter. In some ways estimates are similar to the population parameters with which they are paired, and in some ways they are very different. The estimate and the population parameter with which it is paired are similar in that both are specific and both are expressed in the same type of unit. For example, both the estimate (100) and the population parameter (80) for Helen Martin's problem are specific numbers of band members. As a result, the estimate and the population parameter could be compared to each other, and that comparison would be, at least theoretically, the best way we have of evaluating the estimate.

The estimate and the population parameter may differ, however, because the population parameter is some unknown reality that we want to know, while the estimate is an attempted approximation of that reality that is known to us as a result of our research. Since the estimate and the population parameter are not the same, we are faced with the problem of evaluating the estimate. Is it a good estimate—that is, does it give a good picture of reality—or is it a bad estimate that gives a distorted view of the real world?

We call the difference between the estimate and the population parameter the **actual error.** The actual error for Helen Martin's problem would be 100 (the estimate) minus 80 (the population parameter), or 20. If Helen uses her estimate of 100, she will have an actual error of 20. That is, she will order 20 more dinners than are needed and will get a proportionately larger than necessary room for the meeting. The actual error would be a perfect way of evaluating an estimate. However, we cannot use it precisely because the population parameter is unknown. Helen does not know that only 80 band members will attend when she makes her arrangements for the meeting.

Evaluating an Estimate by Its Potential Error

There is a second, indirect way of evaluating an estimate. By reviewing the procedure used in generating the estimate, we can see its potential for error. Helen obtained information about the number of band members in each of the four bands and calculated the total number of band members. She used this total (100) as her estimate of the number of band members who would attend the meeting (80). Assume her information is correct and there are exactly 100 members in the four bands. It seems unreasonable to expect 100% attendance. Thus, we expect her estimate to be too high. That is, we see a potential for error in her procedures that would result in an estimate that is larger than the population parameter (an overestimate). Though we cannot calculate the actual error of her estimate, we know that this potential error is there.

Measurement Error and Sampling Error

Two of the most important sources of potential error are called measurement error and sampling error. **Measurement error** occurs when there is a difference between the true score and the observed score. **Sampling error** occurs when there is a difference between the population and the sample. In our discussion of Helen Martin's estimate, we saw there was a potential for error. This error did not come from the cases she observed—the sample was the same as the population—but from the information she obtained about each case. The observed score obtained in Helen's study, the number of band members, will generally be larger than the true score she would like to know, the number of band members that will attend the party. The potential for error in Helen Martin's estimate is therefore an error in measurement.

Consider Mrs. Martin's estimate. The information she obtained may have been correct. Assuming that each of the 50 people tested was tested accurately, there would be no measurement error. But suppose the blood bank where the meeting occurred was in a drug rehabilitation center. We might expect those donors to be more likely to test positive on hepatitis B than other donors. In that case, there would be a potential for error in Mrs. Martin's estimate that would favor testing positive. The source of this error would be in the selection of cases observed; thus, it would be a sampling error. In this book we will focus on the potential for sampling error. (At this point you may find it helpful to work on Exercise 6 at the end of this chapter.)

Two Uses of Potential Error

We can use our understanding of the potential error in two different ways, one before and the other after we have conducted our research. First, we can use it in designing a study. We might have advised Helen Martin, on the basis of our understanding of the potential error in her procedure, to ask the band leaders a different question. She might have asked them "How many members of your band will attend?" rather than "How many members are there in your band?" We might have suggested to Mrs. Martin that she test a more representative sample of donors and that she make sure that everyone tested was a donor.

Second, after we have conducted a study, we can use our understanding of the potential error to adjust an estimate. For example, we might have suggested to Helen that she adjust her estimate of 100 attenders based on the total number of all band members. She might lower her estimate by multiplying it by .9 (meaning we assume 90% of the band members will attend). This would give her a new estimate of 90 attenders, which would have reduced her actual error from 20 to 10.

One broad method of selecting a sample, called probability sampling, allows us to measure very precisely the potential for sampling error. This measure of potential error can be used in both of the ways just described. First, we can measure the potential for error in the various types of probability samples we might select, enabling us to choose the optimum sample design. Second, after we have selected the probability sample, we can use its measure of potential error to adjust the estimate to take the potential for error into account. Because probability sampling can measure the potential for sampling error, help develop optimum sample designs, and adjust estimates, it has become the standard approach to scientific sampling. The next chapter describes one type of probability sampling, called a simple random sample, and shows how we can evaluate its potential for error.

EXERCISES

The answers to these exercises are in Appendix C.

1. What type of sample did each of the Martins select? (Use the classification of the seven types of samples given in Chapter 1.)

2. Reread the section of this chapter called The Martin Family's Problems, and answer the following questions about Mr. Martin's problem:

   A. What is a population member, and what is a true score?

   B. What are the population and the population distribution?

   C. What is the population parameter Mr. Martin wants to know, and how would it be calculated?

3. Reread the section called The Martin Family's Research Projects, and answer the following questions about Mr. Martin's research:

   A. What are the sample member and the observation?

   B. What are the sample and the sample distribution?

   C. What sample statistic was used?

   D. What estimate was generated, and how was it generated?

4. Following is a list of the population for Mr. Martin's problem (the name of the purchasing agent in each of the local department stores) and the population distribution (the number of pairs of skates each agent would purchase).

Population (name of purchasing agent)	Population Distribution (number of pairs would purchase)
1. ARROW B.	10
2. BRAUN M.	5
3. BROWN G.	15
4. ELF G.	10
5. GRAY C.	0
6. HART R.	10
7. JONES J.	20
8. KRAUS K.	10
9. KRIM E.	10
10. RALT V.	5
11. TIMM E.	15
12. VELT R.	10

Use this population and population distribution to answer the following questions:

A. What is the name of the population parameter, what symbol will we use to represent this parameter in equations, and what is the value of this parameter for Mr. Martin's population distribution?

B. What are the values of the following population parameters: N, TOTAL, MEAN, ST.DEV., MEDIAN, MODE, MAXIMUM VALUE, MINIMUM VALUE, RANGE?

If you cannot answer Exercise 4B, review these parameters in an elementary statistics book before continuing your work here.

5. Refer once again to The Martin Family's Research Projects.

A. Generate a list for Mr. Martin's sample with its associated sample distribution.

B. What are the values of the following sample statistics for Mr. Martin's sample distribution: n, total, mean, st.dev., median, maximum value, minimum value, range?

3 Simple Random Samples and Sampling Distributions

In the last chapter you met the Martin family and learned about their information problems. Mr. Martin, you will remember, wanted to know how many pairs of in-line skates he could sell to 12 local stores. He selected a convenience sample of his two best customers and asked them to estimate how many skates they would buy. Mr. Martin then projected the average of his two best customers to all 12 stores. We cannot know for sure if his estimate is a good one or a bad one. But we have reason to think it is much too large, because his two best customers will probably purchase more skates than the average customer. We call his estimate biased because we think it will err on the side of being too large. In this chapter, you will discover a better way to select a sample of stores, called a simple random sample.

In this chapter you will learn (1) what it means to say a sample is *random*, (2) how to generate two kinds of simple random samples, (3) why random sampling is such a powerful tool and why it usually has less error than samples of convenience like Mr. Martin's, (4) how to use sampling distributions to measure two kinds of potential error in estimates based on samples, (5) how the measure of the total error allows us to compare different methods of drawing samples to see which is better, and (6) how to apply what you've learned to information problems like Mr. Martin's. If you want to learn more about other ways of selecting samples, you can read our discussion of stratified random samples at the end of this chapter and use the ISEE program to explore three other methods of drawing samples. These methods include systematic, replicated, and thin zone sampling. Each of these, as well as stratified sampling, builds on the same general rules that simple random sampling does.

We begin by conducting a mental experiment to illustrate how to select a simple random sample of a small population.

Experiment 3.1: Selecting a Simple Random Sample Without Replacement

Let's start by simplifying Mr. Martin's problem. Suppose there are only four stores instead of 12 in his population; we will call these stores A, B, C, and D. To conduct the experiment, assume that we take four blank 3-by-5 index cards and write A on the first card (to represent Store A), B on the second card, C on the third card, and D on the fourth card. Suppose we now take the four index cards, make a deck of them, hold the deck face down so we cannot read the store labels, and give the deck a very thorough shuffle. We will shuffle the deck of four index cards until we have no idea which card is on the top, in the middle, or on the bottom.

After we shuffle the deck, we take the card on the top and turn it face up. The store named on the top card will be the first member of our sample. Next, we turn over the card that is now on the top of the deck. The store named on this card is the second member of our sample. *We have just selected a simple random sample of size n = 2, without replacement,* from the population of four stores.

Notice that there are six possible combinations of two different population members: AB, AC, AD, BC, BD, and CD. Each of these six combinations could have been selected as our sample in two different ways. For example, the sample AB could have been selected with A as the top card and B the second card, or with B as the top card and A the second card. Every possible combination of two population members has the *same chance* of being selected as our sample. We shall soon see that selecting a simple random sample is a better procedure than Mr. Martin's convenience sample because it gives an unbiased estimate of the population mean, with a smaller potential error. But first let's consider another way of selecting a simple random sample, called *a simple random sample with replacement.*

Experiment 3.2: Selecting a Simple Random Sample With Replacement

In this experiment, we use the same population of four stores (A, B, C, and D) and the same deck of four index cards from the previous experiment. Once again we give the deck a thorough shuffle and turn the top card over to get our first sample member. But now we do something a little different. Instead of turning the next card over to get our second sample member, we *return* the first card to the deck and shuffle it again. Then we turn the top card over to get the second sample member.

Notice the difference in how we selected the sample in these two experiments. In this experiment, we put the first population member we selected back in the deck, making it available for the next selection. Hence this method of selection is called a simple random sample *with replacement*. In Experiment 3.1, after we selected the first population member, we did not put it back in the deck and so it could not be selected a second time. Hence the sample we selected in Experiment 3.1 is called a simple random sample without replacement.

In simple random sampling without replacement, a member of the population can be selected only once as a sample member, while in simple random sampling with replacement, a sample member can be selected more than once. For example, in this experiment we might select store D as the first sample member and then select store D again as the second sample member. If this happened, our sample would be DD.

Selecting with replacement and samples that include the same case more than once may seem a bit strange, but you will understand this idea better after you have worked with it for a while.[1] First, it is important to realize that the sample size is still n = 2, even if both sample members are the same case, as in the DD sample. When a case is selected for the sample more than once, it is treated as a separate case for each appearance it makes in the sample. For example, suppose we selected a simple random sample of three stores with replacement and selected the sample DDA. Suppose that when we collected the data on potential skate sales from the stores in this sample (D and A), we found that Store A would purchase 30 skates and store D would buy 60 skates. Then the average number of purchases would be

$$\text{mean} = (D + D + A)/3 = (60 + 60 + 30)/3 = 50$$

Notice that case D was used twice in calculating the mean. The sample size used in calculating the mean was 3, the number of selections made, and not 2, the number of stores selected. We will return to sampling with replacement in the next chapter. In the rest of this chapter, we talk only about simple random sampling without replacement.

---

[1]The difference between sampling with and without replacement is missed in many statistics courses and books. However, failing to understand this difference contributes to many errors in practice, so it is an important distinction to keep in mind.

Sampling Distributions: Measuring the Potential Error of Sample-Based Estimates

Consider two different ways Mr. Martin could have selected a sample of two stores from a reduced population of four stores (A, B, C, and D). Assuming the two best customers are stores C and D, the two ways of selecting the sample are

- the convenience sample of the two best customers. We will call this a CON sample. There is only one way he could select the CON sample of the two best customers, C and D.

- a simple random sample of two stores, selected without replacement from the deck of four stores, as described in Experiment 3.1. We will call this an SRS sample. Any combination of two stores could be the SRS sample, and each combination of the two stores has the same chance of being selected. This gives us six possible SRS samples: AB, AC, AD, BC, BD, and CD.

Which procedure should Mr. Martin use? He will lose a lot of money if he estimates wrong. Therefore, he should use the procedure that will give him the best estimate of the population mean.

There is no way we can be certain how good an estimate will actually be when selecting a sample, but we can judge the potential for error associated with each estimate. One of the most valuable features of a random sample is that we can measure its potential error. If you are like most people, your first reaction may be that you don't want to know about potential error. After all, isn't error bad? In fact, however, it is much better to know the potential for error than not to know it. If you drive a car, you learn (or you depend on a mechanic who knows) that after a certain number of miles your brakes may begin to wear out and need checking. Just as your knowledge of your brakes' potential for error can save your life, a knowledge of sampling error allows you to assess the chances of being wrong when you make an estimate based on a sample.

Let's measure the potential for error in the estimates Mr. Martin might get from the CON or the SRS samples that he could select. We can then recommend that Mr. Martin use the method whose estimate has the smallest potential for error.

To assess the potential error, imagine what the population distribution of the four stores might be. We will assume that stores C and D, which have in the past have been the best customers, will buy more skates than stores A and B, which in the past have not been as good customers. Exhibit 3.1 contains a population distribution,

Exhibit 3.1

The Four-Store Population and the Four-Store Population Distribution

Population	Population distribution
A	30
B	60
C	90
D	120
MEAN	75

which we will call the four-store population distribution. In this four-store population distribution, we assume that Store A will buy 30 pairs of skates, Store B will buy 60, and so forth. Note that Stores C and D each purchase more than Stores A and B, which satisfies our assumption that C and D are the better customers. Also note that the mean of the assumed four-store population distribution is MEAN = 75.

Assuming this four-store population distribution, we can calculate the mean of each of the samples we could select. Exhibit 3.2 shows the samples that could be selected as the CON or the SRS samples, with the means of these samples. It is essential that you

Exhibit 3.2

The Sampling Distributions for the Convenience (CON) and Simple Random (SRS) Samples, Given the Four-Store Population Distribution

Samples		Sample means (sampling distribution)		Errors	
CON	SRS	CON	SRS	CON	SRS
.	AB	.	45	.	−30
.	AC	.	60	.	−15
.	AD	.	75	.	0
.	BC	.	75	.	0
.	BD	.	90	.	15
CD	CD	105	105	30	30
mean		105	75	30	0

check Exhibit 3.2 to make sure that you understand how it was derived and that we haven't made any mistakes. First, check to make sure we have listed every sample that could be selected for each sample type. Next, using the four-store population distribution in Exhibit 3.1, check to see that we have calculated the correct mean for each sample.

The set of means associated with the set of samples that could be selected from some population by some method of sample selection is called a sampling distribution of a mean. For simplicity we call the sampling distribution of a mean a **sampling distribution**. The sampling distribution for the CON sample is a single mean, 105. The sampling distribution for the SRS sample is a set of six means: 45, 60, 75, 75, 90, and 105. We will see in the next section how the sampling distribution can be used to measure the potential error in an estimate. But first note the following features of a sampling distribution:

- A sampling distribution is a set of one or more numbers; therefore it has a mean, a standard deviation, and a shape.
- A sampling distribution is determined by
  - the population distribution from which it is selected
  - the way the sample is selected from the population distribution
  - the sample size
- There is one and only one sampling distribution for a given population distribution, sample size, and method of sampling.

Using our four-store example, these features can be illustrated as follows:

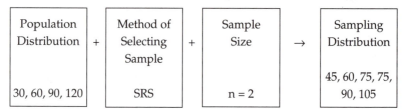

Population Distribution	+	Method of Selecting Sample	+	Sample Size	→	Sampling Distribution
30, 60, 90, 120		SRS		n = 2		45, 60, 75, 75, 90, 105

Measuring Potential Error by the Sampling Distribution

Many information problems, like Mr. Martin's, require us to use a sample mean rather than the real mean of a population. We want to see how much error there may be when we base our estimate on a sample, to see how far off the mark we might be and if we can live with that amount of error. We do this with that elusive but vital concept, the sampling distribution.

We know that the mean of the four-store population distribution is MEAN = 75. By subtracting 75 from each sample mean, we can measure the error resulting from using the mean of that sample as an estimate of the population mean. For example, the mean of sample AB that could be selected as an SRS sample is 45. If we used this sample mean as an estimate of the mean of the four-store population, we would make an error of 45 – 75 = –30. The errors associated with each sample mean are given in the last two columns of Exhibit 3.2. Check to make sure that we have calculated the error correctly for each sample.

Now we can use the results in Exhibit 3.2 to evaluate the potential error for the CON and SRS samples. If Mr. Martin uses his CON sample, then he will select the sample CD and he must make an error. If he selects an SRS, then four of the six samples he might select (AB, AC, BC, and BD) would result in an error and two would not (AD and BC). His chance of making an error is 4/6 or 2/3 if he uses the SRS and 1/1 = 1 for the CON sample. Thus, his chance of making an error is reduced by one-third if he uses the SRS sample. In this example, the potential for error is smaller for the SRS sample and greater for the CON sample.

Biased and Unbiased Estimates and Systematic Error

If you look at the error distributions for SRS and CON samples in Exhibit 3.2, you will see another reason why the SRS sample is better. The errors for the SRS sample are balanced: for every possible positive error there is a comparable negative error. When the potential for a positive error is balanced by the potential for a negative error, we call the estimate **unbiased**. Our goal is to get unbiased estimates. Now look at the error distribution of the CON sample. You will see that potential for error is not balanced; it is all on the positive side. Thus, we would expect the mean of the CON sample to overestimate the number of skates Mr. Martin will sell. An estimate in which the potential for negative and positive errors is not balanced is a **biased** estimate. If the potential for a positive error is greater, as in the CON sample, we say the estimate has a **positive bias**. If the potential for a negative error is greater, we say the estimate has a **negative bias**.

It is very useful to measure the size of the bias. The best way to do this is to calculate the mean of the sampling distribution, which is called the **expected value**, and then subtract the population mean from the expected value. We will use the abbreviation *EXP.VAL.*, (read "expected value of the mean") to stand for the mean of the sampling distribution. The formula for measuring bias is: *BIAS = EXP.VAL. – MEAN.*

From Exhibit 3.2 we can see that the expected values are 105 for the CON sample and 75 for the SRS. Since the mean of the four-store population distribution is 75, the bias for the two samples is as follows:

For CON Sample: *BIAS = EXP.VAL. – MEAN* = 105 – 75 = 30

For SRS Sample: *BIAS = EXP.VAL. – MEAN* = 75 – 75 = 0

This measure of bias confirms our observation of the error distributions in Exhibit 3.2:

- The SRS is an unbiased estimate; its bias measure is 0.

- The CON estimate has a positive bias; its bias measure is 30.

Another term for bias is **systematic error**. The measure of bias tells how much of the potential for error is due to systematic causes. *Because the SRS is randomly selected and gives each member of the population the same chance of being selected,* it has no potential error due to systematic causes. The CON sample was selected for convenience to be the two best customers. The bias measure shows the potential for error in systematically selecting the best customers.

Random Error

Now consider the SRS samples. In the previous section, we saw that there was no potential for systematic error in the SRS sample: Its measure of bias was zero. Yet we know from Exhibit 3.2 that there is some error in the SRS. In fact, if we select an SRS sample, the chances are 2 out of 3 that the sample mean will be different from the population mean. This tells us there must be another type of error. This type of error is called random error. **Random error** is any source of error that is not systematic or predictable. For example, suppose we were to select the simple random sample AB and use its mean of 45 as an estimate of the population mean. We would have an error of 45 – 75 = –30. What caused this error? The selection of the AB sample. What caused the AB sample to be selected? Just the luck of the draw. The selection of the AB sample was a chance event. Thus, the error associated with it had nothing systematic about it; it was random error.

How large is the potential for random error? It depends on the variability of the sample means. If there is no difference in the sample means, as in the CON sample, then it doesn't matter which sample we select. There is no random error. But in the case of the SRS sample, in which the sample means differ, the error will depend on the specific sample selected. The potential for error is determined by the size of the difference between the sample means.

We can use the standard deviation of the sampling distributions in Exhibit 3.2 to measure the variability of the CON and SRS sample means, which then becomes our measure of random error. We will call the standard deviation of the sampling distribution its **standard error**. Note, we use the expected value, which is the mean of the sampling distribution, to calculate the standard error. (Also note that we divide by the number of samples and not the number of samples minus one.) We use the abbreviation *ST.ERR.* to stand for the standard error.

For CON sample: $ST.ERR. = \sqrt{\dfrac{(105 - 105)^2}{1}} = 0$

For SRS sample: $ST.ERR. = \sqrt{\dfrac{(45 - 75)^2 + \cdots + (105 - 75)^2}{6}} = 19.4$

The sampling distribution for the CON has no variations. Therefore, it contains no potential random error, and its standard error is zero. The sampling distribution of the SRS sample has considerable variation. It has a potential for random error that is equal to 19.4 pairs of skates.

The Total or Root Mean Error (RME)

The total potential for error comes from the systematic plus the random error. These two sources of error are not related to each other, so we can measure the total potential for error by adding the systematic error and the random error. The best way to get this combined or total error is something called the **root mean error**. We use the symbol RME to stand for the root mean error, which is calculated as follows:

- Square the bias measure.
- Square the standard error.
- Add the bias squared and the standard error squared.
- Take the square root of the sum.

The formula for the root mean or total error is:

$$RME = \sqrt{BIAS^2 + ST.ERR.^2}$$

Since there is no random error in the CON sample, its total error is equal to its systematic error. For the CON sample, RME = BIAS = 30. Since there is no systematic error for the SRS sample, its total error is equal to its random error. For the SRS sample, RME = ST.ERR. = 19.4. This shows that the SRS has a smaller potential for total error than the CON sample.

We have covered considerable material, so it would be a good idea for you to work on Exercises 1 to 4 at the end of this chapter before going on to the next section. These exercises will give you a chance to review the ideas we have covered so far in this chapter. Exercises 5 and 6 may be helpful but are not required.

Applying the Results to Mr. Martin's Problem

Now let's return to Mr. Martin's problem, which involved 12 stores, not four. We could select a simple random sample of two stores by making a deck of 12 cards labeled A, B, C, . . . , K, and L (one for each of the 12 stores), shuffling the deck, and taking the top two cards. Would the two-store SRS sample of the 12 stores still be better than the CON sample of the two best customers? We could reproduce Experiment 3.1 for the 12-store population

- by assuming stores K and L are the two best customers, and
- by generating a population distribution of sales to the 12 stores using any numbers we want, as long as the sales for K and L are greater than the sales for the other 10 stores.

It would be a lot more work than Experiment 3.1, but our results would be the same. No matter what values we used for the population distribution, as long as the sales we assign K and L are larger than the sales given the other 10 stores, we would find the following:

- The CON sample gives a biased estimate, while the SRS sample is unbiased.

- The SRS sample has a potential random error, while the CON sample does not.
- The total potential for error using the SRS sample is smaller than the total potential for error using the CON sample.

Given our results, we would advise Mr. Martin to select an SRS rather than the CON sample. Would he get better results if he used the SRS? He probably would, but we cannot be absolutely certain. On this occasion, the two best customers in the past might buy exactly the same number of skates in this case as the average customer, and our simple random sample might select two stores that purchase more or less than the average customer. The odds are that the SRS would be better, but the odds never give you absolute certainty in every individual case. In the long run, however, we will do better to keep the odds on our side, even though we may occasionally do better when they are not.

But our goal is to select samples from both large and small populations and to measure the potential error even when we do not know the population distribution. How can we do this? In the next three chapters, you will learn how to describe and use the sampling distribution for simple random samples even when you do not know the population distribution. You can skip now to the chapter summary and go on to the next chapter, or if you want to learn more about other ways of selecting samples, you can continue with the next section.

Stratified Sampling

There are many ways of selecting a probability sample. In this section, we will describe stratified sampling in some detail. In the next section, we will show you how the ISEE program can be used to learn more about systematic random sampling, replicated sampling, and thin zone sampling.

To select a stratified sample, we first divide the population into two or more parts, called **strata**, in such a way that every member of the population is in one and only one stratum.[2] We then select a simple random sample, or some other type of probability sample, from each stratum.

To illustrate stratified sampling, we will conduct another mental experiment with the four-store population and its population

[2]The term *strata* is plural. One layer or part is called a *stratum*.

distribution. Since Mr. Martin knows his customers, we will use his knowledge to divide the population into two strata of equal size (although strata do not have to be of equal size). In the first stratum we put the better customers, which we have assumed are stores C and D. In the second stratum we will put the poorer customers, which we have assumed are stores A and B.

We now randomly select one store from each stratum. We can make the selection using a deck of index cards or a table of random numbers. Exhibit 3.3 shows the stratified samples we could select and the sampling distribution of the mean for these samples.

The expected value of the sampling distribution for the stratified sample is 75. The population mean is 75, so the bias measure is *BIAS* = *EXP.VAL.* − MEAN = 75 − 75 = 0. This tells us that the mean of the stratified sample is an unbiased estimate of the population mean. The standard error of the sampling distribution for the stratified sample (the standard deviation of the sampling distribution) is *ST.ERR.* = 10.6.

Since the mean of the stratified sample is an unbiased estimate, its potential for error is the same as its random error. Thus the RME = 10.6. Earlier we calculated the RME for the SRS sample and found it was 19.4. Thus, the stratified sample has a lower potential for error than the SRS in this example. Mr. Martin could reduce his potential error by using a stratified sample rather than an SRS.

It is instructive to analyze the difference between the SRS and the stratified estimate. At first glance the two methods of selecting the sample may seem similar. Both types are samples of size two that are randomly selected. Note, however, that the AB sample consists of two poor customers and the CD sample consists of two good customers. Both of these samples should give poor estimates of the mean. The mean of the AB sample is too small, since it contains only poor customers (mean = 45 with an error of −30), while the mean of

Exhibit 3.3

The Stratified Samples and Their Sampling Distributions

Samples	Sample means (sampling distribution)
AC	60
AD	75
BC	75
BD	90

the CD sample is too big, as it contains only good customers (mean = 105 with an error of 30). Both the AB and CD samples can be selected as SRS samples, but both are eliminated as stratified samples. Thus, the stratification in this example has reduced the potential for random error by eliminating samples that are likely to overestimate and underestimate the mean.

In stratifying we are using Mr. Martin's knowledge of his customers as a resource to help reduce the random error. In general, stratifying will reduce the random error if the strata differ from each other on the measure we are using. Besides reducing the random error, stratified samples are particularly useful when you are interested in comparing two groups of members that you know are not equally present in the population. For example, suppose you want to study the mental health of men and women in the United States military, and you know that there are many more men than women. By stratifying your population into men and women and then drawing two equal-sized samples from each group, you can be sure to have enough women to be able to make meaningful comparisons.

Other Types of Sample Design

You can learn about three other methods of sampling, called systematic random, replicated, and thin zone sampling, as well as more about stratified and simple random sampling, from the SAMPLE DESIGN module in the ISEE program. The information in the SAMPLE DESIGN module is not required for work in the remaining chapters, but it can enhance your understanding of the relative advantages of using various methods of drawing samples.

Installing the ISEE Program

If you have not done so already, install the ISEE program on your hard disk and read Appendix A up to the section on the SETUP option. Note that there are two ways to issue commands in the ISEE program: by keyboard or by mouse. The experiments in this text are described for the keyboard. To use the keyboard, load the program by typing the command, ISEE /NOMOUSE and then pressing the ENTER key. Remember, if you use WINDOWS, be sure to exit WINDOWS and return to DOS before typing the ISEE /NOMOUSE command.

Setting Up the Computer

When the ISEE program is loaded, you will see the MAIN MENU in the lower left corner of the screen. The first three options in the

MENU will load the operating modules for conducting experiments. Option 4, SETUP, is used for customizing the computer for the various ISEE applications. Read the SETUP section in Appendix A, and then activate the SETUP option by placing the cursor on it and pressing the ENTER key. When the SETUP menu appears in the lower left corner of the screen, it should read as follows:

```
Music   YES
Sounds  NO
Printer (set to your printer)
Port (set for the port you are using)
Numbers Fixed 2
```

If necessary, change the SETUP so that it corresponds to these settings. Remember to put the cursor on UPDATE and press the ENTER key after you make any changes in the SETUP menu.

After you have completed any changes in the SETUP menu, return to the MAIN MENU by pressing the ESC key.

The Sample Design Module

To learn more about different methods of selecting a probability sample, activate the SAMPLE DESIGN option by placing the cursor on it and pressing the ENTER key. When the SAMPLE DESIGN module is activated, your screen display will be divided into four sections. The lower left corner of the screen contains a SAMPLE DESIGN menu listing the options in this module. Options 1–5 illustrate five different methods of selecting a sample. (Option 6 illustrates how a sampling distribution is generated.)

To study any of the five sample designs listed in the SAMPLE DESIGN menu (1–5), read the instructions in Appendix A for the SAMPLE DESIGN module. Remember, you can print any screen display by pressing the ALT + P keys, and you can exit the program by pressing the ALT + X keys.

Summary

In this chapter you have learned how to:

• select a simple random sample by using a shuffled deck of cards.

• list the samples that could be selected from a small population for a simple random sample with replacement and a simple random sample without replacement.

- generate a sampling distribution for the samples we have listed when you know the population distribution.

- measure the potential error for each sample design by using the sampling distribution.

You have learned that simple random sampling means that every member of a population has an equal chance of being selected. This method of sampling can eliminate bias in a sample, and it has a smaller potential for error than an estimate derived from a convenience sample.

If you continued through the section on stratified sampling, you learned how stratified random samples can reduce random error. If you used the ISEE SAMPLE DESIGN module, you were able to see three other methods of selecting samples on your computer screen. You have learned the meaning of the statistical terms *expected value, standard error, bias* (or *systematic error*), *random error,* and *total error* (*root mean error*).

Do you feel as though you are starting to make a little music?

EXERCISES

The answers to these exercises are in Appendix C.

1. If we selected the sample in Experiment 3.1 by taking the bottom two cards in the deck instead of the top two cards, would the potential for error in using the sample mean as an estimate of the population mean be greater, smaller, or the same? Assume the four-store population distribution and use the sampling distribution to answer this question.

2. The results of Experiment 3.1 were based on our use of the four-store population distribution. Would we get the same results (that is, would the SRS sample have a smaller error than the CON sample) if we used a different population distribution? In this exercise, you will redo Experiment 3.1 using your own population distribution for the four stores (A, B, C, and D). You can use any numbers you want, but the numbers you assign stores C and D (the good customers) must be larger than the numbers you assign stores A and B. (You will find the required calculations are a little easier if you use even numbers and make the sum of the

four numbers divisible by four.) After you have generated your population distribution, calculate the following:

A. the population mean (MEAN)

B. the sampling distribution for the CON and SRS samples

C. the expected value (*EXP.VAL.*) for the CON and SRS sampling distributions

D. the BIAS measure for the CON and SRS samples (*EXP.VAL.* – MEAN)

E. the standard error (*ST.ERR.*) of the CON and SRS sampling distributions

F. the total or root mean error (RME) for the CON and SRS sampling distributions

Were the results using your population distribution the same as the results obtained in Experiment 3.1?

3. Suppose we selected the top three cards in the deck in Experiment 3.1 instead of the top two cards. The mean of the three cards should have a smaller potential for error than the mean of the two-card sample. Assume the four-store population distribution and prove that the potential error for the three-store sample would be smaller than the potential error for the two-store sample. Use the root mean error (RME) as the criterion for measuring the potential error. Would the three-store sample give an unbiased estimate of the population mean?

4. The CON sample in Experiment 3.1 has a systematic error but no random error, while the SRS sample in Experiment 3.1 has a random error but no systematic error. In this exercise, we will study an estimate that has both systematic and random error.

Suppose we were to select a sample from the four-store population (A, B, C, D), with the four-store population distribution (30, 60, 90, 120) assumed in Experiment 3.1, but that Store A is unwilling to provide the required information. In this case, we would have to substitute the third card in the deck for Store A, if Store A were the first or second card in the deck. Given this condition, there are three possible samples we could select: BC, BD, and CD. Calculate the following for the sample design described in this exercise:

A. its sampling distribution

B. its expected value, *EXP.VAL.*

C. its systematic error, *BIAS*

D. its random error, *ST.ERR.*

E. its total error, RME

5. In this chapter, we conducted two experiments in which we selected simple random samples of two stores from the four-store population. In Experiment 3.1 we selected a simple random sample without replacement, and in Experiment 3.2 we selected a simple random sample with replacement. We then analyzed the potential for error in using the mean of the SRS selected without replacement. We found that the mean of the SRS without replacement was an unbiased estimate with a total potential error of 19.4 pairs of skates. In this exercise, you should analyze the potential error in using the mean of the SRS at size n = 2 selected with replacement from the four-store population. Would the mean of the SRS selected with replacement be an unbiased estimate of the population mean? Which way of selecting the sample, with or without replacement, has the smallest potential for error?

To answer this question, you must generate the sampling distribution of the SRS selected with replacement and calculate the *BIAS* and RME for this sampling distribution. When you generate the sampling distribution, list both ways of selecting the samples of two different sample members. Thus, you should list the AB sample on one line and BA sample on a different line. (When we listed the samples for the SRS selected without replacement, we listed the AB and BA samples together on the same line.) You should list 16 different samples that could be selected with replacement.

6. Suppose Mr. Martin wished to select a simple random sample of two stores from his population of 12 stores, using the procedure described in Experiment 3.1. There are 66 possible simple random samples that he could select. List the 66 samples using the letters A, B, C, D, E, F, G, H, I, J, K, and L for the 12 stores.

4 The Rules of the Game

In the Indiana Jones movie *Raiders of the Lost Ark,* the hero and the villains both want to find the lost ark because they think it contains some secret keys to power. This chapter contains some secret keys to power as well. Just as it was for Indiana Jones, the quest is challenging. In this chapter you will formulate two general rules, conduct some experiments to see if the rules are true under a variety of conditions, and then decide if you can trust the rules to guide your quest for better knowledge.

In the last chapter you learned how to generate a sampling distribution and use it to measure the potential for error in a sample estimate. It was easy to generate the sampling distribution because

- the population size was very small,
- the sample size was very small, and
- the population distribution was known.

In actual practice, however, the population and sample sizes are usually quite large, which makes it impractical to list all the possible samples that could be selected. For example, suppose there are 870 blood donors in Mrs. Martin's district. The number of simple random samples that could be selected grows astronomically with the population size. Exhibit 4.1 shows the number of simple random samples that could be selected, without replacement, from 870 donors, for samples of size one through five.

Imagine trying to list the four trillion plus samples of size five that could be selected from Mrs. Martin's population of 870 donors. But that is only the first problem. Even if we could list all the samples, we couldn't generate the sample means because we don't know the population distribution.

However, we can take another approach that allows us to describe the sampling distribution. We can generate a set of rules about

Exhibit 4.1

The Number of Simple Random Samples That Could Be Selected Without Replacement from the 870 Donors in Mrs. Martin's District

Sample size	Number of samples that could be selected
1	870
2	378,015
3	109,372,000
4	23,706,460,000
5	4,105,958,000,000

the sampling distribution, and these rules will enable us to measure the potential error without generating a list of all the possible samples and the means associated with those samples. In the last chapter we saw that the mean of a simple random sample selected from the four-store population was an unbiased estimate of the population mean. Let's call this Rule I. Suppose Rule I were always true. Then we would have a rule that says no matter how large the size of the sample or the population and no matter what the shape of the population distribution, the mean of a simple random sample selected from that population will be an unbiased estimate of the population mean. If this rule is true, then we know that the potential for error, when we use the mean of a simple random sample as an estimate of the population mean, comes solely from random error.

We need two types of rules. Rule I tells how to measure the potential for systematic error, or bias, in a sampling distribution. Rule II tells how to measure the potential for random error (the standard error) of a sampling distribution.

Rules I and II were developed by applying the mathematical theory of probability. When developed this way, the rules are expressed in a series of equations. For example, Rule I, which says that the mean of a simple random sample is an unbiased estimate of the population mean, can be expressed by the equation

$EXP.VAL. = MEAN$ (the expected value equals the population mean)

or

$EXP.VAL. - MEAN = 0$

These equations can be applied in many ways to find the most efficient sample design and to adjust sample estimates. They are the basis for the scientific theory of sampling you want to learn, and you will find them in most statistics textbooks. We will examine these equations in this book, but we will generate the rules in an approximate way through a series of experiments. These experiments may seem like a roundabout way to learn the equations, but you will find it much easier to understand, learn, and apply the equations after you have conducted the experiments.

Each experiment has three parts. First, we formulate the problem being tested in the experiment. Second, we conduct the experiment, and third, we analyze the results. Each part is important. The first two parts are usually quite easy, although conducting the experiments may require some work. The third part of each experiment may be the most difficult, though it is the most exciting. Be sure you understand the lesson to be learned from each experiment before going on to the next one.

When you finish the experiments, you will be pleased and surprised to see how easy it is to learn and use the equations. In fact, you may even see a kind of beauty and elegance in these equations that might otherwise have escaped you. In this chapter we restrict ourselves to experiments in which we sample from Mr. Martin's population of 12 stores using the SIMPLE SAMPLE module in the ISEE program and the 12-store deck of cards in Appendix B.

The Testing Approach

The basic idea behind the experiments is very simple. If you select many samples from a population, the means of those samples should approximate the sampling distribution.[1] If you vary the conditions under which the samples are selected, you can see how the sampling distribution is affected by these conditions. For example, suppose you select many simple random samples from different population distributions using many different sample sizes. Suppose that in every experiment you find the expected value (the mean) of the selected sample means is equal to the population mean. Then you will have evidence supporting Rule I (*EXP.VAL.* = MEAN).

---

[1]If you select an infinite number of samples, the means of those samples will be the sampling distribution.

To study the sampling distribution through a series of tests, you must select thousands of samples. You could select those samples of the 12-store population by hand, using a deck of cards, as we did in Chapter 3, but this would require days! The same tests can be done in a few minutes on a computer using the ISEE program. We begin by learning how the SIMPLE SAMPLE module works.

Experiment 4.1: Introduction to SIMPLE SAMPLE

This experiment will be conducted two ways. First, you will select five simple random samples, with and without replacement, from the 12-store deck of cards in Appendix B. Then you will replicate this experiment using the SIMPLE SAMPLE module. By doing this, you will learn how to use the SIMPLE SAMPLE module, and by comparing the two methods, you will see what the program is doing.

Part 1 of the experiment is carried out in four steps:

- Using Form 4.1 to record the results
- Analyzing the population
- Selecting samples and calculating their means
- Analyzing the sample means

Using Form 4.1

Take Form 4.1 from Appendix B. The top half is for listing and analyzing the population, the bottom part for recording and analyzing the sample means. The experiment is described briefly at the top of the form. You'll use this form to analyze the results of the experiment and to record your work, so you can review it later.

Now examine the cards in the 12-store deck in Appendix B. Each card represents one of the 12 local stores in Mr. Martin's population. One side of each card is blank. On the other side is a number (from 1 to 12), followed by a name. The number identifies a specific store, and the name is the purchasing agent for that store. For example, the card marked 1. Arrow, B. represents Store 1, whose purchasing agent is Betty Arrow. Betty Arrow, you will remember, was a good friend of Mr. Martin's and one of the two purchasing agents in his convenience sample. The names of the agents are listed next to their store numbers at the top of Form 4.1. Below the store number and purchasing agent name is another number, which ranges in value from

36 to 60. This is the number of pairs of in-line skates that each store will purchase. Record this number on the row for that store on Form 4.1, under the column heading V1. V1 stands for **Variable** 1, which is simply the number of pairs of skates each store will buy. The set of 12 numbers representing the number of pairs of skates being purchased by each store is called *the population distribution for V1.*

Analyzing V1

To analyze V1, calculate the following population parameters of V1 and record the results on the upper right part of Form 4.1:

N (population size)   STANDARD DEVIATION

MEAN   MINIMUM VALUE

MEDIAN   MAXIMUM VALUE

Next, record the frequency distribution for V1 as a **histogram,** using the HISTOGRAM V1 form on Form 4.1, by filling in the boxes over the scale values. For example, if two stores have V1 values of 44, then fill in the bottom two boxes right over the value of 44 on the scale. Check your work against Exhibit 4.2. From our analysis of V1, we can see that Mr. Martin's sales would have varied from 36 to 60 pairs of skates, with an average of 48 per store. Notice that the median number of skates sold is equal to the mean. When the median of a distribution is equal to its mean, the distribution must be symmetrical.

Exhibit 4.2

Recording the Population Analysis on Form 4.1

	NAME		V1
1.	Arrow	B.	52
2.	Braun	M.	40
3.	Brown	G.	48
4.	Elf	G.	36
5.	Gray	C.	56
6.	Hart	R.	52
7.	Jones	J.	48
8.	Kraus	K.	60
9.	Krim	E.	44
10.	Ralt	V.	48
11.	Timm	E.	48
12.	Velt	R.	44

N	12	ST. DEV.	6.32
MEAN	48	MINIMUM	36
MEDIAN	48	MAXIMUM	60

HISTOGRAM V1

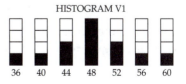

36   40   44   48   52   56   60

From the histogram you can see that the distribution of V1 is symmetrical and unimodal, with the mode located at 48 skates. The mode, the mean, and the median are the same, which always occurs with symmetrical, unimodal distributions.

Conducting Experiment 4.1, Part 1

To conduct Part 1 of this experiment, you will select five simple random samples of size four, without replacement, from the 12-store deck. First, copy the pages in Appendix B containing the 12-store deck and cut out each card. Next, take the deck of 12 cards. Shuffle it and draw one card. Record the number of pairs of skates given on that card onto Form 4.1 (SAMPLE 1, CASE 1, WITHOUT REPLACE-MENT). Do not replace the first card, but shuffle the remaining 11. Draw a second card and record the number of pairs of skates on FORM 4.1 (SAMPLE 1, CASE 2, WITHOUT REPLACEMENT). Repeat this process two more times to get a sample of four (SAMPLE 1, CASES 3 AND 4, WITHOUT REPLACEMENT). Then draw four more samples exactly the same way and record the observed scores in CASE columns 1–4, using rows 2, 3, 4, and 5 (WITHOUT RE-PLACEMENT) on Form 4.1. After you select each sample, calculate the mean of the sample and record it on Form 4.1, in the column marked "mean" (12-STORE DECK, WITHOUT REPLACEMENT). Remember, you must return the four cards selected for each sample to the deck and give all 12 cards a thorough shuffle before selecting the next sample.

Next repeat the work you have just done, this time selecting five simple random samples of size four from the deck *with replacement.* Record the observed scores for these samples in the CASE columns, using rows 1–5 under the heading WITH REPLACEMENT. Calculate the means of the five samples and record them on Form 4.1 in the column marked "mean" (12-STORE DECK, WITH REPLACE-MENT). Remember, the same population member may be selected two or more times in a sample with replacement.

Analyzing Experiment 4.1, Part 1

Next calculate, and record in the "mean" columns of Form 4.1, the following parameters for the five means selected without and with replacement:

- *EXP.VAL.* (expected value, or the mean of the five sample means)

- *BIAS (EXP.VAL. – MEAN)*
- *ST.ERR.* (the standard error, or standard deviation, of the sample means; use N = 5)

An Overview of SIMPLE SAMPLE

Next we will repeat Experiment 4.1 using the SIMPLE SAMPLE module. If you have not installed the ISEE program on your hard disk or did not use it when you read Chapter 3, you should read Appendix A from the beginning through the section on SETUP and also read pages 37–38 in Chapter 3. If necessary, install the ISEE program on your hard disk and make sure the SETUP menu is as described in Chapter 3, page 38. You may, if you wish, change the Music option from YES to NO.

Load the ISEE program and select option 2, SIMPLE SAMPLE, from the MAIN MENU (type 2). Remember, you can exit the ISEE program by pressing the ALT + X keys, and you can print any screen display by pressing the ALT + P keys.

When the SIMPLE SAMPLE module is loaded, you will see a screen display that has four windows. These four windows are always present while you are in the SIMPLE SAMPLE module:

- The MENU is in the lower left corner of the display. The MENU lists eight options (numbered 1–8) that are available for use in this module. Note the small ball that appears before option 1. This ball tells which option the program has just executed. Also note the box that surrounds option 1. This box is called the cursor. You can move the cursor using the ARROW keys or a mouse, and use it to activate commands in the program.
- The POPULATION is in the upper left corner of the display, which lists the population and four population distributions, called V1, V2, V3, and V4. You may enter or change the values in these four population distributions at any time during a SIMPLE SAMPLE session, although in this module you are limited to using values between 36 and 60. These limits greatly facilitate our ability to display the results of the experiments.
- The RESULTS of any options executed by the module are displayed in the upper right corner of the screen.
- The COMMANDS are in the lower right corner. They describe the options available in the MENU or list commands that are available in the various options. We use the COMMANDS to conduct and analyze experiments.

Look now at the POPULATION window. It has 12 rows, numbered 1 through 12. Each row in the POPULATION window stands for one of the local stores in Mr. Martin's population. After each row number is the name of the purchasing agent. The store numbers and names are the same as the ones in the 12-store deck. At the top of the POPULATION window you will see four column headings: V1, V2, V3, and V4. These column headings are the names of four population distributions that are available for us to sample. Under V1 you will see a column of numbers that is the same as the distribution V1 you found on the cards in the 12-store deck and listed on Form 4.1. Check the names and the values of V1 in the POPULATION window against the names and values of V1 you listed on Form 4.1. You will use the V1 distribution in the POPULATION window to replicate Part 1 of Experiment 4.1.

Under V2, V3, and V4 in the POPULATION window, you will see a column of asterisks. An asterisk here means missing data. There are no population distributions for V2–V4 when the SIMPLE SAMPLE module is loaded. Later you will learn how to enter your own population distributions in V2–V4.

Look at the eight options in the MENU. The first four options (1–4) allow us to analyze the population distributions V1–V4. Options 5 and 6 permit us to enter, delete, or change the values in population distributions V1–V4. Option 7 is used to conduct experiments in which we select samples from population distributions V1–V4. Option 8 prints the current screen display. You can view the results of SIMPLE SAMPLE experiments on the screen or print them, but there is no way to save the results in a machine-readable form.

Now we will replicate Part 1 of this experiment using SIMPLE SAMPLE. This part of the experiment has three steps:

- Analyzing the population distribution V1 in the POPULATION window
- Conducting the experiment
- Analyzing the experiment

Analyzing V1 in the POPULATION Window

We begin by analyzing V1. Since V1 in SIMPLE SAMPLE and V1 in the 12-store deck are the same, they should have the same parameters and the same histogram. To check the parameters we use option

1, Parameters, in the MENU. Since this option was activated when ISEE was loaded, you can see the parameters of V1 in the upper right. Check the parameters reported for V1 against those on Form 4.1. The two sets of parameters should be the same. If they are not, check the values listed on Form 4.1 for V1 against the values listed for V1 in the POPULATION window and then check your calculation of the parameters on Form 4.1. Since there were no data for V2–V4, there are asterisks (missing data) for the parameters of these distributions.

Next we compare the SIMPLE SAMPLE histogram for V1 with the histogram recorded for V1 on Form 4.1. Use the ARROW keys to move the cursor down until it surrounds option 3. Press the ENTER key to execute option 3. After you press the ENTER key, the ball moves to option 3, indicating that option 3 is now active. The upper right corner of your screen will display four small rectangles, labeled Variable 1 for V1, Variable 2 for V2, and so forth. Three of the rectangles—those labeled Variable 2 (V2), Variable 3 (V3), and Variable 4 (V4)—are marked EMPTY SET because V2, V3, and V4 have no values entered. The Variable 1 rectangle displays the histogram for V1, which should look like HISTOGRAM V1 on Form 4.1. Note the thin vertical line in the center of the histogram on the screen. This thin line shows the value of the population mean (48 for V1).

Conducting Experiment 4.1, Part 2

Now move the cursor so that it surrounds option 7, Experiments, and press the ENTER key. Two lists will appear in the lower right corner, and the cursor will move onto the Select label. The list on the left is used to specify the details of an experiment you wish to conduct. The list on the right is used to analyze your most recent experiment. The results of an experiment are available for analysis until a new experiment is conducted or you leave the SIMPLE SAMPLE module.

Look at the list on the left. You will see four rows, labeled C1, C2, C3, and C4. Each row stands for an experimental **condition** (C1 = Condition 1, C2 = Condition 2, and so forth) that you may or may not use, depending on the experiment you wish to conduct. To use a condition, we must specify:

- the variable number (1, 2, 3, or 4) of the population distribution from which samples will be selected (first column in the menu, labeled Var).

- the type of sample to select (second column in the menu, labeled Type). We can choose one of three types of samples:

    SRSW = simple random sample with replacement

    SRSN = simple random sample without (no) replacement

    SYS = systematic random sample

- the size of the sample to be selected (third column in the menu, labeled Size).

The fourth column of the menu, labeled Mis. (for missing data), is optional and is used to specify a population member that will be excluded from any sample.

To complete the specification of an experiment, you must type in the number of samples (from 1 to 9999) you want the program to select on the last row of the menu. The number of samples specified on the bottom row of the menu will be selected for each condition specified in the menu. Different samples are selected for each condition.

To specify an experiment, use the ARROW keys to move around the Experiment menu. To illustrate the procedure for specifying an experiment, you will reproduce Part 1 of Experiment 4.1, in which you selected five simple random samples of size four, without and with replacement, from the V1 population distribution. You will use Condition 1 (sampling without replacement) and Condition 2 (sampling with replacement) for this experiment. You could use any two of the four conditions for this experiment.

Begin by putting the cursor in the first column (Var) of the C1 row. If the number 1 does not appear under the cursor, clear the box by pressing the BACKSPACE key until an asterisk appears and then type 1. This specifies V1 as the population distribution from which samples will be selected for Condition 1. Now move the cursor to the second column (Type) on the C1 row. If the entry SRSN (simple random sample no replacement) does not appear, keep pressing the SPACE bar until it does.

Now move the cursor to the third column (Size) on the C1 row. If the number 4 does not appear in the third column, press the BACKSPACE key until an asterisk appears and then type 4 (for samples of size four). If the last column on the row for C1 (Mis.) does not contain an asterisk, move the cursor to the fourth column and press the BACKSPACE key until one appears. This completes the specification of C1.

Now move the cursor to the first column in the row for C2 and specify the following experimental condition: sample from the V1 variable, select simple random samples with replacement (SRSW), and select samples of size four. Use the SPACE bar to change the entries in the Type column. Make sure there is an asterisk (no specification) in the last column of C2 and an asterisk in the Var column on the rows for C3 and C4, because an asterisk in the Var column eliminates that condition from an experiment.

To complete the specification of the experiment, tell the program to select five samples for each experimental condition. Do this by moving the cursor to the bottom row of the EXPERIMENT MENU, pressing the BACKSPACE key until the Number of Samples box contains an asterisk, and then typing the number 5. You have now specified an experiment that duplicates Part 1 of Experiment 4.1. Check to see that the Experiment menu on the screen display looks exactly like the Experiment menu in Exhibit 4.3. If it does not, change the entries in the Experiment menu on the screen so that they are the same as those in Exhibit 4.3.

You are now ready to conduct the experiment. Move the cursor to the Select label in the upper left corner of the Analysis menu. When you press the ENTER key (do not press it yet), the program will carry out the experiment you have specified. In this experiment, the program will do exactly what you did with the 12-store deck. That is, it will select five simple random samples of size four, without replacement, from V1, calculate the mean of each sample, and store the means in its memory under C1. The program will then repeat the process, selecting five simple random samples of size four with replacement from V1, calculate the means of these samples, and store them under C2 in its memory.

Now press the ENTER key and look at the EXPERIMENTS window, where four rectangles will appear, one for each of the four experimental conditions (Condition 1, Condition 2, and so forth).

Exhibit 4.3

The Specification of Experiment 4.1, Part 2

	Var	Type	Size	Mis.
C1	1	SRSN	4	*
C2	1	SRSW	4	*
C3	*	SRSN	*	*
C4	*	SRSN	*	*
Number of Samples:		5		

Above each rectangle appears the label of the condition it portrays. When you press the ENTER key to activate the Select option, you will see a message appear in each rectangle. If you have specified a condition (in this case, Condition 1 and Condition 2), the message will say PREPARING SET, which tells you it is preparing the selection you specified. If you have not specified the details for a condition (Conditions 3 and 4 in this experiment), the message will say EMPTY SET, which means nothing is done for that condition.

After the preparation is completed, the program will generate the sampling distribution for each experimental condition. Then it will draw a histogram of the sampling distribution. In this example, it will draw a histogram of the five sample means selected without replacement in the rectangle for Condition 1. It will draw a second histogram of the five sample means selected with replacement in the rectangle for Condition 2.

Note the thin vertical line in the center of each histogram. This line shows the mean of the population (48) from which the samples were selected. The more the histogram clusters around that vertical line, the more closely the sample means resemble the population mean.

For small experiments such as this one, the preparation time is minimal. In fact, it may have happened so fast that you couldn't see the preparation message. In more extensive experiments, it may take several minutes or longer to complete the preparation. If you wish to stop an experiment while the preparation message appears on the screen, hit the ESC key.

If you wish to observe the display again, press the ENTER key while the cursor is on the Select label. Conduct the experiment as many times as you wish, but remember the program selects different samples each time you press the ENTER key. When you finish observing the results, press the ENTER key one more time while the cursor is resting on the Select label. This provides the experimental results you will analyze.

Analyzing Experiment 4.1, Part 2

To analyze this experiment, move the cursor down to the List label, but don't press the ENTER key yet. Look at the column listing the conditions (C1, C2, C3, C4) on the right MENU. There should be a small ball to the left of the C1 entry in this column. This small ball marks the condition that will be listed.

If the ball is not in front of the C1, move the cursor over the C1 label and press the ENTER key. This will move the ball next to C1 and allow you to list the sample means for the C1 condition. Return the cursor to the List label and press the ENTER key. The EXPERI-MENTS window will now list the means of the five samples it has selected for Condition 1. A "C1" should appear above these five means, which tells you the means are for Condition 1. Copy these five sample means onto Form 4.1, using the column for SIMPLE SAMPLE mean (WITHOUT REPLACEMENT).

Next list the sample means for C2 by moving the cursor over the C2 label (right side of the MENU) and pressing the ENTER key. This will move the ball from C1 to C2, which directs the program to list C2. The program will now list the five sample means for C2 in the EXPERIMENTS window. (Note the "C2" above the list of five means.) Copy these five means onto Form 4.1, using the SIMPLE SAMPLE mean (WITH REPLACEMENT) column.

Next calculate the expected value, bias, and standard error for each set of five means generated by SIMPLE SAMPLE and record these measures on Form 4.1. (Use 5, the number of samples in the denominator, when you calculate the standard error.) Finally, draw a histogram on Form 4.1 for the five SIMPLE SAMPLE means se-lected without replacement, using the sample means you have listed on Form 4.1.

Now move the cursor to the Param. option in the right list and press the ENTER key. The EXPERIMENTS window will display 12 parameters, numbered 1 to 12, for each experimental condition. At present you are interested only in the following four parameters for C1 and C2:

- 1. Population Parameter. This is the population parameter of in-terest—namely, the mean of V1. Check the value for this param-eter against the value of the MEAN on Form 4.1. Both should be 48.

- 3. Expected Value – Ob. This is the expected value (observed) of the sample means. Check the values of this parameter for C1 and C2 against the expected values you calculated for the SIMPLE SAMPLE sample means. The values of *EXP.VAL.* for C1 and C2 should be equal to the values of *EXP.VAL.* that you have recorded for the SIMPLE SAMPLE means on Form 4.1.

- 5. Bias – Ob. (3 – 1). This is the bias in the five sample means, which is equal to *EXP.VAL.* (Param. 3) – MEAN (Param. 1). Check the bias measure for C1 and C2 against the bias measure you recorded for the SIMPLE SAMPLE means on Form 4.1. The two measures of bias should be the same.

- 8. Standard Error – Ob. This is the standard error (*ST.ERR.*) of the five sample means selected for C1 and for C2. Check to see if the values of the standard error for C1 and C2 are the same as those you recorded for the *ST.ERR.* (SIMPLE SAMPLE mean) on Form 4.1.

If the values you have recorded for *EXP.VAL.*, *BIAS*, or *ST.ERR.* on your form differ from those in the EXPERIMENTS window, check the values you have entered for the SIMPLE SAMPLE means (use the List option) and your calculations.

As a final step check the histogram of the SIMPLE SAMPLE sample means (without replacement) on Form 4.1 by using the Hist.1 option. Move the cursor to the Hist.1 label and press the ENTER key. The EXPERIMENTS window will show the histograms of the five sample means selected for Condition 1 (without replacement) and Condition 2 (with replacement). Check the histograms for C1 in the EXPERIMENTS window against the histogram on Form 4.1. The histograms should be the same.

Summary of Experiment 4.1

In Experiment 4.1, working with the SIMPLE SAMPLE module, you have learned how to:

- use Parameters and Histograms to examine the V1–V4 population distributions in the POPULATION window.
- specify experiments with up to four experimental conditions (C1–C4).
- use List, Param., and Hist.1 to analyze the experiments you conduct.[2]

You have also learned that there is nothing mysterious or difficult about the program. It does exactly what you did using the 12-store deck, nothing more and nothing less. The reason for using the program is to save time.

---

[2]The program has many more features that are not covered in this experiment, and there are several different ways to move the cursor and issue commands. See Appendix A for different ways of issuing commands and for additional features of the program not covered in this text.

One final note about this experiment. You may have noticed that the results obtained in Part 1 were different from the results in Part 2. This difference is not due to using the deck or the program but was caused by the small number of samples selected. If you had selected a large number of samples in each part of the experiment, the results of Part 1 and 2 would have been very similar. The larger the number of samples, the more similar the results of Part 1 and 2 would be.

You may also find that the expected value of your five samples is not equal to the population mean. This should not be taken as evidence against Rule I (EXP.VAL. – MEAN = 0), again because the experiment is based on such a small number of samples. In our experiments we must select thousands of samples to get reliable results. Even then, our results will only closely approximate the true value of the expected values and standard error.

Experiment 4.2: Samples of Size One

Next you will select 9999 samples of size one from four different populations. It may seem surprising that we can learn anything from something as simple as a sample of one. In actual practice you will rarely, if ever, select a sample that small. Nonetheless, a sample of one is a perfectly legitimate sample, and its simplicity makes it very easy to see how a sampling distribution is formed. It also gives a useful base from which to develop rules about the standard error.

When you conduct these experiments using SIMPLE SAMPLE, think about how you would do it using the 12-store deck. You would shuffle the deck and select the top card. That would be a sample of size one. The value of the one card we select as a sample would also be the mean of that sample. Thus, if we selected card number 5, which has a value of 56 skates purchased, then the mean for that sample would also be 56. Note that there is no difference between sampling with and without replacement, because there is no second selection and hence no need to replace the first card selected.

Someone once said that the secrets of the whole world can be found within a single raindrop. Well, the secrets of sampling can be seen in simple random samples of size one. There are five steps in this experiment:

• Using Form 4.2 for recording the results

- Entering three new population distributions, V2, V3, and V4, in the POPULATION window
- Analyzing the four population distributions, V1–V4
- Selecting 9999 samples of size one from each of the four distributions, V1–V4
- Analyzing the means of the samples selected from the four distributions, V1–V4

Using Form 4.2

Begin this experiment by taking Form 4.2 from Appendix B. On the top left side of Form 4.2 are four population distributions, called V1–V4, that will be used in the experiment. On the upper right side is a table for recording the parameters of the four distributions. In the center of the form are four scales for drawing histograms of the four distributions. At the bottom is a table for recording your experimental results.

Entering V2, V3, and V4

Begin by loading the SIMPLE SAMPLE module. If you are already in SIMPLE SAMPLE, exit and reenter the module by pressing the ALT and M keys and typing Y. (We begin every experiment by reentry, unless otherwise specified, as this ensures that the screen display will be the same as that described here.)

The four population distributions for this experiment are listed in the upper left corner of Form 4.2 in the columns labeled V1, V2, V3, and V4. The V1 distribution on Form 4.2 is the V1 distribution in the POPULATION window. Your first task is to load the three other distributions, V2, V3, and V4. Activate option 6, Data, by moving the cursor to option 6 and pressing the ENTER key.

The cursor will move to the POPULATION window, over the entry in the first row of the V1 column. Move the cursor to the first entry in the second column (V2) and type the value 36, which is the value of V2 in row 1, Form 4.2. Now go down the V2 column, entering the V2 distribution as it appears on Form 4.2. Then follow the same procedure and enter V3 and V4. When you finish entering the population distributions, the POPULATION window should show the same values for V1 to V4 as Form 4.2 does. (If you need to make any corrections, place the cursor on the entry that you wish to change, press the BACKSPACE key until an asterisk appears, and then type in the correct entry.) When you are sure the entries under V1, V2, V3, and V4 in the POPULATION window are the same as those on Form 4.2, press the F6 key. This will save the four distributions V1–V4 for future use.

Analyzing V1–V4

When you press the F6 key, the program will display the histograms of the four distributions in the EXPERIMENTS window: Copy these histograms onto Form 4.2, over the scales for V1–V4. You will see that the four distributions are quite different, though they share three common features: Each distribution has 12 true scores. The mean of each distribution (shown on the histogram by the vertical line) is 48. Each distribution is symmetrical around its mean. The shapes of the distributions are:

- V1: unimodal (same mean, median, and mode)
- V2: dichotomous, with two values of 36 and 60
- V3: similar to a uniform distribution but with a gap at the mean value (48)
- V4: bimodal, with modes at 36 and 60 and a gap at the mean value (48)

Next you need to know the parameters of the four distributions. You could calculate these values, but it is easier to let the program do it for you. Press the ESC key, which will return you to the MENU, and activate option 1, Parameters. The parameters of the four distributions will appear in the EXPERIMENTS window. Copy the parameters into the table on the upper right side of Form 4.2. Note, as we saw in the histograms, that the mean of each distribution is 48. The median equals the mean, which is the test for a symmetrical distribution. The four distributions differ in their variability, with V1 being the most homogeneous (ST.DEV. = 6.32) and V2 the most heterogeneous (ST.DEV. = 12.00). When you finish this step, Form 4.2 should look like Exhibit 4.4. Check to see that the histograms and parameters on Form 4.2 and Exhibit 4.4 are the same.

Conducting Experiment 4.2

To conduct Experiment 4.2, move the cursor to option 7, Experiments, and press the ENTER key. Then use the Experiment menu to specify an experiment in which the program will select 9999 simple

Exhibit 4.4

How Your Completed Form 4.2 Should Look, Showing Parameters and Histograms of V1 to V4

NAME	V1	V2	V3	V4
1. Arrow B.	52	36	36	36
2. Braun M.	40	36	36	36
3. Brown G.	48	36	40	36
4. Elf G.	36	36	40	40
5. Gray C.	56	36	44	40
6. Hart R.	52	36	44	44
7. Jones J.	48	60	52	52
8. Kraus K.	60	60	52	56
9. Krim E.	44	60	56	56
10. Ralt V.	48	60	56	60
11. Timm E.	48	60	60	60
12. Velt R.	44	60	60	60

	V1	V2	V3	V4
N	12	12	12	12
MEAN	48	48	48	48
MEDIAN	48	48	48	48
ST. DEV	6.32	12.00	8.64	9.79
MINIMUM	36	36	36	36
MAXIMUM	60	60	60	60

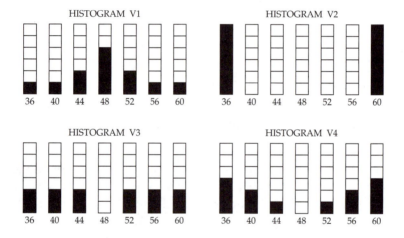

random samples with replacement (SRSW) of sample size one from V1, V2, V3, and V4. Assign V1 to C1, V2 to C2, V3 to C3, and V4 to C4. When you finish specifying the experiment, check your specification against Exhibit 4.5.

Before you conduct the experiment, see if you can predict the results. If Rule I (*EXP.VAL.* − MEAN = 0) is right, then you should find that the expected value in each condition is equal to the population mean (48).

What else would you expect to find in the sampling distributions that you will generate for C1–C4? You have no other rules as yet, but what do you think the sampling distributions for samples of size one will look like?

Exhibit 4.5

Specifications for Experiment 4.2

	Var	Type	Size	Mis.
C1	1	SRSW	1	*
C2	2	SRSW	1	*
C3	3	SRSW	1	*
C4	4	SRSW	1	*

Number of Samples: 9999

When you have completed specifying the experiment and thinking about the results, move the cursor to the Select label and press the ENTER key.

Analyzing Experiment 4.2

When the program has selected the samples and stored the results, it will display a histogram of the sampling distribution for each of the four experimental conditions. Look at the histograms in the EXPERIMENTS window. Where have you seen these histograms before? If you don't remember, check the histograms for V1–V4 on Form 4.2.

The histograms of the sampling distributions for samples of size one, C1–C4, look very much like the population distributions, V1–V4, from which they were selected. Did you guess that? Check and you will see that the histogram for C1 has the same unimodal, symmetrical shape as V1, the population distribution from which it was selected. C2 has the dichotomous shape of V2, with half its values at 36 and the other half at 60. C3 has V3's uniform shape with the gap at 48, and C4 has the same bimodal shape as V4 with a gap at 48.

Why does the sampling distribution of sample size one have the same shape as the population distribution from which it was selected? You may have figured this out already. Consider C2, in which the program was selecting samples of size one from V2. The mean of each sample selected was the observed score of the sample member selected. There is no population member in V2 with a score of 40 to 56, so no sample in C2 can have a mean of 40 to 56. Since the only scores for population V2 are 36 and 60, the only means for C2 would be 36 and 60. Our method of selecting samples gives every population member the same chance of being selected, so we would expect each population member to be selected as often as any other population member. Since there are 12 population members, we would expect each population member to comprise about one-twelfth of the samples. Since half the population members of V2 have a score of 36 and half a score of 60, we would expect half the samples to have means of 36 and half to have means of 60. That is exactly what we see in the histogram for C2.

The preceding argument leads us to expect the same mix of cases in the sampling distribution of size one as there is in the population from which the samples are selected. If the mix of cases in the population and sampling distributions are the same, the distributions should have the same mean and standard deviation. This gives us a new Rule IIA,[3] which tells us that the standard deviation of the sampling distribution (the standard error) for samples of size one is equal to the standard deviation of the population distribution from which the sample was selected. Rule IIA may be expressed in the form of an equation:

$$ST.ERR.(1) = ST.DEV.$$

where $ST.ERR.(1)$ is the standard error for simple random samples of size one. The mean of the sampling distribution for samples of size one ($EXP.VAL.$) must be equal to the population mean (MEAN), which verifies our existing Rule I ($EXP.VAL. - $ MEAN $= 0$) for samples of size one.

The histograms of C1–C4 suggest that Rule I must be true, as each one is evenly balanced around the mean of the population (the vertical line). This tells us that the chances of overestimating are equal to the chances of underestimating, or that $EXP.VAL. - $ MEAN $= 0$. We can get a more precise test of Rule I and a test of Rule IIA by using the Param. option in the Experiment menu: Move the cursor to the Param. label and press the ENTER key. From the table of parameters that appears in the EXPERIMENTS window, copy the values of

Row 3	Expected Value
Row 5	Bias
Row 8	Standard Error

---

[3]This is called Rule IIA because it is a special case of the rule, based on a sample of one. The more general rule will follow.

for C1–C4 into the table at the bottom of Form 4.2. You should find that the expected values are very close to the population mean of 48 and the bias is near zero, which shows that Rule I is true. The standard error for each condition should be very close to the standard deviation of the variable sampled in that condition (C1–V1, C2–V2, and so forth), which is what we would expect from Rule IIA. The results should be close but not exact. If we were to select millions of samples, they would come so close we could not observe a difference.

This completes Experiment 4.2. It would be a good idea for you to do Exercises 1 and 2 at the end of this chapter before reading the summary. (The answers to all exercises appear at the end of the book.)

Summary of Experiment 4.2

The results of this experiment further confirm Rule I and suggest a new rule, which we have called IIA. We now have two rules for describing sampling distributions:

Rule I.   The mean of a simple random sample is an unbiased estimate of the population mean ($EXP.VAL.$ – MEAN $= 0$).

Rule IIA.   The standard error for samples of size one is equal to the standard deviation of the population from which the sample was selected ($ST.ERR.(1) = $ ST.DEV.).

Now let's see what happens to the sampling distribution when you increase the size of the sample.

Experiment 4.3: Doubling the Sample Size

In this experiment you will select 9999 samples of sizes one, two, four, and eight with replacement from V2 used in Experiment 4.2. Note that each sample size is twice as large as the one that preceded it. The first goal of this experiment is to see the effect of doubling the sample size on the expected value of the sampling distribution. A second and even more important goal is to see the effect of doubling the sample size on the standard error. We would expect the standard error to decline as the sample size grows larger (the potential error should decrease as the sample size increases), but will doubling the sample size cut the error in half?

The answer to this question has tremendous practical implications. Larger samples cost more time and money. These costs need to be weighed against the increased precision of a larger sample. This experiment will increase your understanding of the relationship between sample size and the size of the potential error in a sample estimate.

You will select simple random samples with replacement because it is easier to identify the effect of sample size on the standard error when you sample with replacement. (In the next, optional experiment you will see how to adjust the rules for sampling without replacement.) There are four steps in this experiment:

- Using Form 4.3 to record the results of the experiment
- Entering the V2 population from Experiment 4.2 (if necessary)
- Conducting the experiment
- Analyzing the experiment

Using Form 4.3

Begin by taking Form 4.3 from Appendix B to record your results. The mean and standard deviation of V2 are already recorded on it.

Entering V2

If the V2 distribution used in Experiment 4.2 is currently listed as V2 in the POPULATION window, you may skip this step. If not, load the SIMPLE SAMPLE module and use option 6, Data, to load the V2 distribution from Experiment 4.2. Remember to press the F6 key after you enter V2 and press the ESC key to return to the MENU.

It is a good idea to review V2 before proceeding. Look at the histogram of V2 on Form 4.2 or on your computer screen. You will see that it is a symmetrical dichotomy with six scores equal to 36 (12 fewer than the mean of 48) and six scores of 60 (12 more than the mean of 48). The median equals the mean (48), which confirms our visual impression that V2 is symmetrical. The standard deviation is 12.

Conducting Experiment 4.3

Next you will conduct an experiment in which you select 9999 simple random samples, with replacement, of sizes one (C1), two (C2), four

(C3), and eight (C4) from V2. Activate option 7, Experiments (by placing the cursor on option 7 in the MENU and pressing the ENTER key), and specify the experiment. (It is easier to interpret the results when you use C1 for n = 1, C2 for n = 2, C3 for n = 4, and C4 for n = 8). Check your specification for this experiment against the specification given in Exhibit 4.6.

Exhibit 4.6

Specifications for Experiment 4.3

	Var	Type	Size	Mis.
C1	2	SRSW	1	*
C2	2	SRSW	2	*
C3	2	SRSW	4	*
C4	2	SRSW	8	*
Number of Samples: 9999				

Spend a moment thinking about the experiment you are about to conduct. From Rule I we would predict *EXP.VAL.* − MEAN = 0, so the expected value for C1 should be 48. From Rule IIA we would predict that the standard error of C1 will equal the standard deviation of V2, so the standard error of V2 should be 12. But what will happen to the sampling distribution as we increase the sample size? Will the shape of the distribution change, and if so, what shape will it take? Think about the change in the sampling distribution as the sample size increases. Try to imagine how the sampling distribution will look for samples of sizes two, four, and eight. If you don't come up with any good ideas, just make a guess. When you finish thinking about the experiment, move the cursor to the Select label and press the ENTER key.

Analyzing Experiment 4.3

Look at the histograms of C1–C4 in the EXPERIMENTS window. You can see them better by activating the Hist.1 option (by moving the cursor to the Hist.1 label and pressing the ENTER key). Begin with the histogram for C1, based on a sample size of n = 1. As expected, the sampling distribution of C1 looks like V2, with half the sample means at 36 and the remaining half at 60.

What happens to the shape of the sampling distribution as the sample size increases? Look at the histograms for C2, C3, and C4.

Does the shape change? Yes, the shapes are obviously quite different. How can we describe the change? The simplest way is to say that as the sample size increases (C1 to C4), the distribution clusters more and more tightly around the population mean (the vertical line). This clustering around the population mean suggests a new rule, which we will call Rule IIB. As the sample means pile up more tightly around the population mean, the variability of the sample means and the potential error in using a sample mean as an estimate of the population mean should decrease.

For example, consider the difference between the C1 and C2 histograms. Half the sample means in C1 ($n = 1$) are 36, which would give an error of −12 pairs of skates in estimating the population mean of 48. The remaining half of the samples in C1 would give sample means of 60, making an error of +12 pairs in estimating the population mean. The C2 ($n = 2$) distribution has about one-fourth of the sample means at 36, with a potential error of −12, one-fourth at 60, with a potential error of +12, and the remaining half at 48, with a zero error. Thus, as we move from C1 to C2, half the samples move from an error of plus or minus 12 to an error of zero. As a result, the potential error in using the mean of sample size $n = 2$ (C2) is less than the potential error in the mean of a sample of one (C1). Later you will examine the sampling distributions in the histograms of C1–C4, so copy the histograms on the scales provided on Form 4.3.

Now use the Param. option to test the question about the effect of doubling the sample size on the expected value (Rule I) and the standard error (Rule IIB). Move the cursor to the Param. label and press the ENTER key. Copy the values shown in the EXPERIMENTS window for the expected value (row 3), bias (row 5), and standard error (row 8) for C1 to C4 onto Form 4.3.

First, examine the bias measure for each condition. Each measure of bias should be very close to zero, which confirms Rule I. The mean of a simple random sample is an unbiased estimate of the mean of the population from which the samples were selected. You could drive the bias measure down to zero if you selected millions of samples.

Next examine the standard errors. As expected from Rule IIA, the standard error for C1 ($n = 1$) is close to 12, which is the standard deviation of the population ($ST.ERR.(1)$ = ST.DEV. = 12). The standard error should get smaller as we move from C1 to C4, verifying Rule IIB.

Does doubling the sample size cut the standard error in half? If so, as you go from C1 to C4 each standard error should be half the size of the preceding one. We can write this idea as a set of equations in which *ST.ERR.* (n) is read "standard error for sample size n." For example, *ST.ERR.* (4) would be read "standard error for sample size four" and *ST.ERR.* (8) would be read "standard error for sample size eight." The equations are:

$$ST.ERR. (2)/ST.ERR. (1) \quad = 1/2 = .5$$
$$ST.ERR. (4)/ST.ERR. (2) \quad = 1/2 = .5$$
$$ST.ERR. (8)/ST.ERR. (4) \quad = 1/2 = .5$$

Test the doubling rule by dividing each standard error you have recorded on Form 4.3 by the standard error of the preceding condition (C2/C1, C3/C2, and C4/C3). Record these **ratios** on Form 4.3 in the column for testing the doubling rule, using the rows for C2, C3, and C4. You will find that the doubling rule does not work. Doubling the sample size does not cut the standard error in half, but reduces it to about .71 of what it was.

The fact that the ratio of the standard errors is the same (.71) as we go from one condition to the next tells us there must be some kind of a rule, but it is not the doubling rule we expected. Now let's try something a little different. Let's see if increasing the sample size by a factor of 4 cuts the standard error in half. If so, we should find:

$$ST.ERR. (4)/ST.ERR. (1) \quad = 1/2 = .5$$
$$ST.ERR. (8)/ST.ERR. (4) \quad = 1/2 = .5$$

Test the 4-times rule by dividing the standard error for C3 (n = 4) by the standard error for C1 (n = 1), and record the ratio on Form 4.3, row C3, in the column for testing the 4-times rule. Next divide the standard error of C4 by the standard error of C2 and record the ratio on the row for C4 in the same column. Hurray, it seems to work! Increasing the sample size by a factor of 4 cuts the standard error in half. Now let's push the 4-times rule a little further.

Rule II

Be patient as we go through this section, think through every step very carefully, and you will come out with a very basic rule for measuring the standard error. Assume the 4-times rule is true, that every time we increase the sample size by a factor of 4 we cut the standard error in half. What should happen if we increase the sample size by a factor of 16—for example, going from a sample size of 1 to a sample size of 16? Well, 16 is 4 times 4. So increasing the sample size by 16 is like increasing the sample size 4 times (1 to 4) and then increasing the sample size by 4 once again (4 to 16). The first increase, from 1 to 4, should cut the standard error in half, and the second increase, from 4 to 16, should cut it in half once again. So, increasing the sample size by a factor of 16 should cut the standard error by a factor of 4 ($1/2 \times 1/2 = 1/4$).

By the same logic, if we increase the sample size by 64, which is 4 $\times 4 \times 4$, we should cut the sampling error by $1/2 \times 1/2 \times 1/2$, or by a factor of 8 ($1/2 \times 1/2 \times 1/2 = 1/8$). The 4-times rule therefore gives the following results:

Increasing the sample size by a factor of	*cuts the standard error by a factor of*
4	2
4 * 4 = 16	4
4 * 4 * 4 = 64	8

What connection is there between the increase in the sample size and the decrease in the standard error? What rule links the factor by which the sample increases and the factor by which the standard error is cut? Ask yourself, what is the relationship between 2 and 4, 4 and 16, and 8 and 64? If you see the connection, you will be on the edge of a great discovery.

If you don't see the connection between 2 and 4, 4 and 16, and 8 and 64, divide the second member of the pair by the first and what do you get? Well, $4/2 = 2$, $16/4 = 4$, and $64/8 = 8$. So $4 = 2 \times 2$, $16 = 4 \times 4$, and $64 = 8 \times 8$. The relationship between the increase in sample size and the decrease in the standard error is the square root: 2 is the square root of 4, 4 is the square root of 16, and 8 is the square root of 64.[4] In other words, *the standard error shrinks by the square root of the increase in the sample size.*

The connection between the increase in the sample size and the reduction in the standard error suggests a general square root rule, which says if we increase the sample size by a factor of k, then we will cut the standard error by the square root of k. For example, if k = 4, then increasing the sample size by 4 should cut the standard error by a factor of $\sqrt{4}$, or 2. If k = 9, then increasing the sample size by a factor of 9 should decrease the standard error by a factor of $\sqrt{9}$, or 3.

---

[4]Remembering back to your basic math instruction, the square root of a number is the number which, when multiplied by itself, produces that number.

Consider two sample sizes, 1 and n, where n can be any positive number. For example, n could be 9. Then n is n times greater than 1; for example, 9 is 9 times greater than 1. According to the square root rule, the standard error of sample size n should be equal to the standard error of sample size one divided by $\sqrt{n}$, which we write as

$$ST.ERR.\ (n) = ST.ERR.\ (1) * (1/\sqrt{n}) = ST.ERR.\ (1)/\sqrt{n}$$

We can go one step further, because Rule IIA tells us that the standard error of a sample of one is equal to the standard deviation of the population from which the sample is selected. Using Rule IIA, we can put $ST.ERR.\ (1)$ = ST.DEV. into the equation for the square root rule. This gives us Rule II for the standard error:

$$ST.ERR.\ (n) = ST.ERR.\ (1)/\sqrt{n} = ST.DEV./\sqrt{n}$$

We read Rule II as follows: "The standard error for a simple random sample of size n, selected with replacement, is equal to the standard deviation of the population from which the sample is selected, divided by the square root of the sample size."

Now let's test Rule II using the results of Experiment 4.3, in which you selected sample sizes of one, two, four, and eight from a population distribution V2 with a standard deviation of 12. According to Rule II, the standard error for these sample sizes should be

C1:	n = 1	$ST.ERR.\ (1)$ = ST.DEV./$\sqrt{n}$ = $12/\sqrt{1}$	= 12.00
C2:	n = 2	$ST.ERR.(2)$ = ST.DEV./$\sqrt{n}$ = $12/\sqrt{2}$	= 8.48
C3:	n = 4	$ST.ERR.(4)$ = ST.DEV./$\sqrt{n}$ = $12/\sqrt{4}$	= 6.00
C4:	n = 8	$ST.ERR.(8)$ = ST.DEV./$\sqrt{n}$ = $12/\sqrt{8}$	= 4.24

Compare these predicted results for the standard error with the results you actually found in Experiment 4.3. The predicted results should be close to the actual results of your experiment. So, Rule II explains the standard errors you obtained in Experiment 4.3.

Having completed Experiment 4.3, it would be a good idea for you to work on Exercises 3–6 at the end of this chapter before reading the summary.

Summary of Experiment 4.3

On the basis of Experiments 4.2 and 4.3, you have developed two very general rules (I and II) that describe the sampling distribution based on simple random samples selected with replacement. These rules are:

Rule I.   The mean of a simple random sample is an unbiased estimate of the population mean (*EXP.VAL.* – MEAN = 0).

Rule II.   The standard error is equal to the standard deviation of the population from which the sample is selected, divided by the square root of the sample size (*ST.ERR.* = ST.DEV./$\sqrt{n}$).

When you selected a sample of size one, the sampling distribution was the same as the population distribution from which it was selected. This tells you that the sampling distribution has the same shape, same mean (expected value), and same standard deviation (standard error) as the population distribution.

As the sample size grows larger, the sampling distribution clusters more and more around the population mean. As the sample means cluster around the population mean, the variability of the sample means (standard error) decreases by the square root of the sample size ($1/\sqrt{n}$), but the sample mean remains an unbiased estimate of the population mean.

These rules reveal a great deal about the sampling distribution, but two questions remain:

• Are they true for simple random sampling without replacement?

• How do you use these rules to design a sample and adjust your sample estimates?

In the next, optional experiment you can explore whether the rules are true for simple random sampling without replacement. If you decide to skip this section, continue with the following section, which covers the symbols that are used in other statistics texts for expressing Rules I and II.

Experiment 4.4: Sampling Without Replacement

In this experiment you will repeat Experiment 4.3, this time selecting the samples without replacement. Thus, you will see if Rules I and II need to be changed when we sample without replacement. There are four steps in this experiment:

• Using Form 4.4 to record the results

• Entering the population distribution V2 of Experiment 4.2 (if necessary)

- Conducting the experiment
- Analyzing the results

Using Form 4.4

Take Form 4.4 from Appendix B to record your experimental results. The mean and standard deviation of V2 are already recorded on Form 4.4.

Entering V2

If the V2 distribution used in Experiment 4.2 is currently listed in the POPULATION window, you may skip this step. If it is not, load the SIMPLE SAMPLE module and use option 6, Data, to load the V2 distribution from Experiment 4.2. Remember to press the F6 key afterwards to save your entry and press the ESC key to return to the MENU.

Before proceeding, let's review V2. Look at the histogram of V2 on Form 4.2. You will see that it is a symmetrical dichotomy with six values equal to 36 (12 less than the mean of 48) and six values of 60 (12 more than the mean of 48). The median equals the mean (48), which confirms our visual impression that V2 is symmetrical. The standard deviation is 12 pairs of skates.

Conducting Experiment 4.4

You will now select 9999 simple random samples *without replacement* of sizes one, two, four, and eight from V2. This experiment is the same as Experiment 4.3 in all respects except that you are selecting the samples without replacement. Activate option 7, Experiments (by placing the cursor on option 7 in the MENU and pressing the ENTER key), and specify the experiment. (It is easier to interpret the results when you use C1 for $n = 1$, C2 for $n = 2$, C3 for $n = 4$, and C4 for $n = 8$.) Check your specifications for this experiment with those given in Exhibit 4.7.

Spend a moment thinking about the experiment you are about to conduct. If Rules I and II work for sampling with replacement, this is what you should find:

- The histograms for C1–C4 should be balanced around the population mean of 48 (the thin vertical line in the histogram), and the bias measure should be close to zero for each condition (Rule I).

Exhibit 4.7

Specifications for Experiment 4.4

	Var	Type	Size	Mis.
C1	2	SRSN	1	*
C2	2	SRSN	2	*
C3	2	SRSN	4	*
C4	2	SRSN	8	*
Number of Samples: 9999				

- The histograms should cluster closer and closer to the population mean as you go from C1 to C4, and the standard errors should be almost equal to STD.DEV./ $\sqrt{n}$ = 12/ $\sqrt{n}$ (Rule II).

Now move the cursor to the Select label and press the ENTER key. It takes the program a little longer to select samples without replacement, so it will take longer to complete this experiment than Experiment 4.3.

Analyzing Experiment 4.4

First, examine the histograms by moving the cursor to the Hist.1 label and pressing the ENTER key. The histograms are balanced around the population mean. As the sample size increases, they cluster more and more around the population mean. The histograms suggest that Rules I, IIA, and IIB may be true for sampling without replacement. Copy the histograms for C1–C4 onto the scales for these conditions on Form 4.4.

Next activate the Param. option by placing the cursor on the Param. label and pressing the ENTER key. Copy onto Form 4.4 the values of the expected value from row 3, bias from row 5, and standard error from row 8 for C1 to C4 in the EXPERIMENTS window. The value of the bias for each condition should be close to zero, which confirms Rule I for sampling without replacement.

Now compare the standard errors from Experiments 4.3 and 4.4. Remember that the two experiments are the same, except that we sampled with replacement in 4.3 and without replacement in 4.4. Take Form 4.4 and write in the standard errors you got in Experiments 4.3 and 4.4. Compare your results to the values in Exhibit 4.8. The results for the two experiments should be similar but not exactly the same.

Exhibit 4.8

A Comparison of the Standard Errors in Experiments 4.3 and 4.4

	n	Standard errors	
		Exp. 4.3	Exp. 4.4
C1	1	12.00	12.00
C2	2	8.48	8.09
C3	4	6.00	5.11
C4	8	4.24	2.55

First, you should see that the standard error for Experiment 4.4 becomes smaller as the sample size increases. Increasing the size of a simple random sample, selected without replacement, reduces the standard error. But once the sample size is greater than one, the standard errors for Experiment 4.4 (selecting without replacement) are smaller than those for Experiment 4.3 (selecting with replacement).

If reducing the size of the standard error while using the same size sample is really important to you—and it often is, since you usually want to increase precision without increasing cost—you can see from this experiment that sampling without replacement is the better path to follow. In fact, you will usually sample without replacement.

However, Rule II ($ST.ERR. = ST.DEV./ \sqrt{n}$), which fit the data for Experiment 4.3, does not quite fit the data in Experiment 4.4. The standard errors for conditions C2–C4 in Experiment 4.4 are somewhat smaller than those predicted by Rule II. Some kind of adjustment must be made in Rule II to reduce the standard error for sampling with replacement.

Think for moment about the reduction factor needed in Rule II so that it will fit the data for sampling without replacement. First, look at the standard errors for sample size $n = 1$. The standard errors are the same for sample size one when we sample with and without replacement. So the adjustment factor should not change Rule II for sample size $n = 1$. For sample size $n = N$ (when we select the total population as the sample), there can be no variation in sample means no matter how many samples we select. If we select 10,000,000 samples of size 12, without replacement, from a population of size 12, then every one of the 10,000,000 samples must be exactly the same, and each one must have a mean equal to the population mean. Thus, the adjustment factor must make the standard error for sampling without replacement equal to zero when n = N.

Because you have seen that the sampling error is smaller when you sample without replacement, it is important to understand how to modify the rule you have learned so that you can use it to compute the sampling error for samples drawn without replacement. This discussion is a bit technical, but worth following because sampling without replacement can give you more precise results for the same sample size and costs. It is particularly critical when a sample represents a significant proportion of an entire population. For example, suppose you were studying a population of 3000 patients who had been in a particular hospital in the past month and you selected a sample of 500 patients. Because 500/3000 represents one-sixth of the population, sampling without replacement becomes very important under such conditions.

Statisticians have developed an adjustment factor called the **finite population correction factor, or fpc.** The formula for it is

$$\text{fpc} = \sqrt{\frac{N - n}{N - 1}}$$

The numerator in this formula is the population size minus the sample size, and the denominator is the population size minus 1. The square root of this ratio is the fpc required to adjust Rule II for sampling without replacement.

The expanded Rule II for simple random samples, then, is the following:

The standard error for simple random sampling with replacement is equal to the standard deviation of the population divided by the square root of the sample size.

The standard error for simple random sampling without replacement is equal to the standard deviation of the population times the fpc, divided by the square root of the sample size.

$ST.ERR.$(with replacement)　　= $ST.DEV. / \sqrt{n}$

$ST.ERR.$(without replacement) = $ST.DEV. * \text{fpc} / \sqrt{n}$

Note that we simply multiply the standard error with replacement by the fpc to get the standard error without replacement. When the sample size is n = 1, the fpc = 1, so it does not change the standard error for sample size one. When n = N, the fpc = 0, so if n = N the standard error for sampling without replacement will be zero.

Exhibit 4.9

Calculating the Standard Error for Experiment 4.3 (With Replacement) and Experiment 4.4 (Without Replacement)

		With replacement			Without replacement			
(1)		(2)	(3)	(4) = (2)/(3)	(5)	(6)	(7)	(7)*(4)
n		ST.DEV.	$\sqrt{n}$	ST.ERR.	(N − n)	(N − 1)	fpc	ST.ERR.
C1	1	12	1.00	12.00	11	11	1.00	12.00
C2	2	12	1.41	8.51	10	11	0.95	8.08
C3	4	12	2.00	6.00	8	11	0.85	5.10
C4	8	12	2.83	4.24	4	11	0.60	2.54

Let's see how Rule II applies to the results of Experiments 4.3 and 4.4. Exhibit 4.9 gives the calculations for the standard error, using Rule II, for the results of Experiment 4.3 and 4.4.

The standard error with replacement is calculated exactly as you calculated it for Experiment 4.3 (column 4) and should be very close to the results you obtained in that experiment. To adjust the standard error for sampling without replacement, first calculate the fpc (column 7) and then multiply the standard error with replacement (column 4) by the fpc. The results in the last column of Exhibit 4.10 should be very close to the results you actually got in Experiment 4.4.

This completes optional Experiment 4.4. Although it may have seemed complex, by breaking down your computations into small, clear steps you have learned how to calculate the standard error for samples selected without replacement. If you wish to attain further mastery of sampling without replacement, you might find it helpful to do Exercises 7–10 at the end of this chapter before reading the summary of Experiment 4.4.

Summary of Experiment 4.4

In this optional experiment, you found that Rule I does not have to be changed for simple random sampling without replacement. The mean of a simple random sample, selected with or without replacement, is an unbiased estimate of the population mean. Rule II must be adjusted by the use of the fpc when applied to sampling without replacement, particularly when the sample represents a significant proportion of the total population.

There are several things you should have noticed about sampling without replacement.

- The fpc will always be less than one, except for the unusual sample size of $n = 1$, so the standard error for sampling without replacement is smaller than the standard error for sampling with replacement. Therefore, in practice we usually select samples without replacement.

- The difference between using the formula for the standard error with and without replacement is very small when the sample is a small part of the population. If (n/N) is less than .05, the two formulas give just about the same results. Therefore, in practice you can use either formula when (n/N) is less than .05.

- Most statistics texts give the formula for the standard error for sampling with replacement because the mathematics involved in using it are much simpler. If you use the formula for sampling with replacement that you find in most statistics books, when you sample without replacement and n/N is more than .05, you will have greater precision or more significant results than your statistical test suggests.

We will focus on sampling with replacement, since the theory we want to study is basically the same for sampling with and without replacement but the details are easier to understand for sampling with replacement.

Other Ways of Representing Statistical Terms

The symbols we have been using in our equations are not the same as those used in other statistics books. (The exceptions are the symbols N and n for the population and sample size, which are used in almost all statistics books.) If you wish to study more about Rules I and II in other texts, you will have to understand the symbols that are used in the other texts. In this section we will outline the major ways in which other texts represent the six major terms we have used. If you do not wish to know the symbols used in other texts, you can skip this section. It is not required for the remainder of this book.

We have used the words "MEAN" and "mean" to represent the population and sample means. There are five commonly used approaches in statistics texts for the symbols used to represent the population and sample mean.

Population mean = μ μ_Y $\overline{Y}$ M M_Y
Sample mean = m m_y $\overline{y}$ m m_y

Notice that the population mean is always represented by Greek letters (μ for m) or capital roman letters, while the sample mean is always represented by lowercase roman letters. The letter X or x may be used instead of, or in addition to, the letter Y or y. Note also that the five usages are paired: μ goes with m, M_Y goes with m_y, and so on.

There are four ways in which the population standard deviation is represented, and these are paired with two ways of representing the sample standard deviation.

Population standard deviation = σ σ_Y S S_Y
Sample standard deviation = s s_y s s_y

The same general conventions are used in distinguishing between the population and sample standard deviations. Greek and/or capital roman letters are used for the population, and lowercase roman letters are always used for the sample. As with the means, some texts will use X and x instead of, or in addition to, Y and y.

The expected value and standard error can be represented in three ways.

Expected value = $E(\overline{y})$ $E(m)$ $E(m_y)$
Standard error = $\sigma_{\overline{y}}$ σ_m σ_{m_y}

All three forms of the expected value use the letter E, and all three forms of the standard error use the Greek letter σ (sigma). The form used for the sample mean is then added to the E or sigma to complete the symbol. Some texts will use x instead of, or in addition to, y.

The set of symbols given in this section will help you translate the rules given in this text to the usage of most other statistics books. You will find on occasion, however, that other sets of symbols are used. If you encounter another set of symbols, you will usually find a legend or description of the symbols given in the text.

Summary

In this chapter we formulated a general rule, which we called Rule I, to the effect that the mean of a simple random sample is an unbiased estimate of the population mean (*EXP. VAL.* – MEAN = 0). If Rule I is true, then the mean of a simple random sample is an unbiased estimate of the population mean under any conditions we can imagine.

- It would be true for any type of population distribution no matter what its shape or size.
- It would be true for any size sample from $n = 1$ to $n = N$.
- It would be true for samples selected with and without replacement.

We conducted experiments using different kinds of population distributions, different sample sizes, and sampling with and without replacement. Every test we conducted confirmed Rule I. Therefore, we have every reason to believe that Rule I is true. If so, all the potential for error in using the mean of a simple random sample as an estimate of the population mean comes from random error.

In Chapter 3 you learned that you can measure random error by calculating the standard deviation of the sampling distribution, which we called the standard error. The larger the standard error, the greater the variability of the sample means and the greater the potential for random error. In this chapter we formulated a general rule, Rule II, for measuring the standard error. According to Rule II, the standard error for simple random samples selected with replacement is equal to the standard deviation of the population from which the sample is selected, divided by the square root of the sample size ($ST.ERR. = ST.DEV./ \sqrt{n}$).

An optional section on sampling without replacement showed that the standard error for simple random samples selected without replacement is equal to the standard error with replacement times the fpc ($ST.ERR. = ST.DEV. * fpc/ \sqrt{n}$).

Rule II allows us to measure the random error associated with simple random sampling

- from any population distribution regardless of its size or shape.
- for any sample size.
- when sampling with or without replacement.

You conducted several tests using different populations and sample sizes and should have found that Rule II was true for all of them. Therefore, you should have reason to believe that you can use Rule II to measure the potential for random error when you use the mean of a simple random sample as an estimate of the population mean.

All these experiments were conducted on small samples from artificial populations. In Chapter 5 you will test Rules I and II using large, real populations. You will also develop a new Rule III, which describes the shape of the population distribution.

EXERCISES

The answers for these exercises are in Appendix C.

1. Below are two population distributions V1 and V2:

       V2 – 36, 36, 36, 36, 36, 36, 60, 60, 60, 60, 60, 60
       V3 – 36, 36, 36, 60, 60, 60, 60, 60, 60, 60, 60, 60

   The V2 distribution is the same as the V2 distribution we used in Experiment 4.2. The V3 distribution is one we have not used before. Use option 6, Data, in SIMPLE SAMPLE to load V2 and V3 into the POPULATION window. Remember the following three points about using the Data option:

   • To change an entry, clear it by pressing the BACKSPACE key until an asterisk appears.

   • To save the data you have entered press the F6 key.

   • To return to the MENU, press the ESC key.

   After you have loaded V2 and V3, use options 1, Parameters, and 3, Histograms, to analyze V3.
       Record the results of this exercise on Form 4, Exercise 1. (All forms related to Chapter 4 will be found in Appendix B.)
       In what ways are the V2 and V3 distributions the same? In what ways are they different? In particular, how would you describe in a few words the major difference in the shape of the two distributions?

2. In this exercise you should test the two rules we found for samples of size one by using a population distribution of your own choosing. Remember, the program will limit you to scores in the range 36 to 60. You must use scores divisible by four (36, 40, 44, 48, 52, or 60) to draw the histogram of the sampling distribution on Form 4, Exercise 2. Use Form 4, Exercise 2 to record this exercise.
       Begin by recording the population distribution you have decided to use in the V2 column at the top left of the form. Then use

option 6, Data, to enter this population distribution as V2 in the POPULATION window. Analyze V2, and record its parameters and histogram on Form 4, Exercise 2.

A. Specify an experiment in which you use condition C1 to select 9999 simple random samples with replacement (SRSW) of size one from V2. Make sure an asterisk appears in the Var column for C2–C4 and in the Mis. column for C1–C4. Check your specifications against those given in the answer for Exercise 2A before you conduct the experiment.

B. Conduct the experiment you specified in Exercise 2A. Then analyze the experiment in the same way you analyzed Experiment 4.2. Record the results on Form 4, Exercise 2.

- Was the histogram of sampling distribution C1 the same shape as the histogram of the population distribution V2?
- Was the expected value almost equal to the mean of the population distribution: *EXP.VAL.* = MEAN (Rule I)?
- Was the standard error of the sampling distribution in C1 almost equal to the standard deviation of V2: *ST.ERR.*(1) = *ST.DEV.* (Rule IIA)?

3. In testing the doubling rule in Experiment 4.3, we found that doubling the sample size did not cut the standard error in half (.50) but reduced it by .71. We found:

$$\frac{ST.ERR.(2)}{ST.ERR.(1)} = \frac{ST.ERR.(4)}{ST.ERR.(2)} = \frac{ST.ERR.(8)}{ST.ERR.(4)} = .71$$

How might we explain the fact that doubling the sample size cuts the standard error by .71 and not by .50?

4. In Experiment 4.2 you entered population distribution V4 into the POPULATION window. This V4 distribution had a standard deviation of 9.79 (check Form 4.2). Given Rule II, what would you expect the standard error to be for simple random samples, selected with replacement from V4, for sample sizes n = 1, 3, 6, and 9?

Make sure you know the answer to this question before working on Exercise 5.

5. In this exercise you will test Rules I and II using population distribution V4 (Experiment 4.2) and sample sizes of n = 1, 3, 6, and 9.

A. Specify 9999 simple random samples with replacement from V4. Record the results of your experiment on Form 4, Exercise 5. There is no need to analyze V4 as its parameters and histogram will be found on Form 4.2, but it may be helpful to review the histogram and parameters before you conduct the experiment. Check the specification of your experiment against the answer to 5A before you conduct the experiment.

B. Conduct the experiment you specified in Exercise 5A. Do the results of this experiment confirm Rules I and II? Record the parameters of the sampling distribution on Form 4, Exercise 5. Check the histograms for C1–C4 to see if the sample means cluster closer to the population mean as the sample size increases. You do not have to copy the histograms. Explain your answer. Your answer to Exercise 4 gives you the criteria for testing Rule II.

6. In this exercise you should test Rules I and II using any population distribution you want to use and any four sample sizes that increase in value from C1 to C2 to C3 to C4. Select 9999 simple random samples with replacement. Record the results on Form 4, Exercise 6.

First record the population distribution you want to use as V2 and the sample sizes for C1–C4 on Form 4, Exercise 6. Then enter the same population distribution as V2 in the POPULATION window. Use the 1. Parameter option to calculate the parameters of V2 and record them on Form 4, Exercise 6. Next specify an experiment in which you select 9999 simple random samples with replacement from V2, using the sample sizes you have recorded on Form 4, Exercise 6. Conduct the experiment and analyze it using the Param. and Hist. 1 options. Check the histograms for C1–C4 to see if the sample means cluster closer to the population mean as the sample grows larger. (You do not have to copy the histograms onto the form.) Copy the parameters of the sampling distribution of C1–C4 onto Form 4, Exercise 6.

Do the results of this experiment show that

- the mean of a simple random sample is an unbiased estimate of the population mean (Rule I)?
- the standard error is equal to the standard deviation of the population from which the sample is selected divided by the square root of the sample size (Rule II)?

7. A. Calculate the fpc for the 12-store population used in SIMPLE SAMPLE (N = 12) for sample sizes 1, 2, and so on up to 12 (n = 1, 2, . . . 11, 12) and record the results of your calculations on Form 4, Exercise 7.

B. Draw a graph that pictures your calculations on Form 4, Exercise 7. Looking at your calculations and graph, answer the following questions.

- Does the fpc decline in value as the sample size gets closer and closer to the population size?
- Does the fpc = 1 when n = 1?
- Does the fpc = 0 when n = N?
- What general conclusion might you draw on the basis of this exercise about the fpc and its effect on the standard error?

8. Use Rule II to calculate the values of the standard error for samples of sizes one, two, four, and eight selected without replacement from the population distribution V4 (ST.DEV. = 9.79) in Experiment 4.2. Make sure you know the answer to this question before working on Exercise 9.

9. A. Specify an experiment that is the same as Experiment 4.4, except select the samples from population distribution V4 of Experiment 4.2. Use Form 4, Exercise 9, to record the results of this experiment. You do not have to analyze population distribution V4, as you have already analyzed it in Experiment 4.2. It might be helpful to review the shape and parameters of V4 on Form 4.2.

Check your specification for this experiment against the answer to 9A before you conduct the experiment.

B. Conduct the experiment you specified in Exercise 9A. Do the results of this experiment confirm the use of the fpc in adjusting Rule II for sampling without replacement?

10. A. Suppose we were to select a sample of size two from a population distribution of size N = 2 with values of 36 and 60. What size standard error would we predict from Rule II

- if the sample were selected with replacement?
- if the sample were selected without replacement?

Check your answer to this question before continuing.

B. How is it possible for there to be any error when using the mean of a simple random sample of size n = N?

5 Sampling Large Populations and the Normal Curve

Introduction

In Chapter 4 we developed two rules describing the sampling distribution and tested them on a small hypothetical population of 12 stores. Will the rules we developed work equally well for large, real populations, where the time and cost of conducting a census is prohibitive? In this chapter you will test these rules on a population of 951 large U.S. cities and several other large populations. We will also develop Rule III, which describes the shape of the sampling distribution. As you will see in Chapter 6, the shape of a sampling distribution is critical for the application of Rules I and II in practical situations. It can be used to increase greatly the precision of sample estimates.

The general approach in this chapter will be familiar. You will conduct experiments by selecting samples from known population distributions using the ISEE program. But you will use the UNIVARIATE module instead of the SIMPLE SAMPLE module. The UNIVARIATE module resembles SIMPLE SAMPLE, but it allows us to sample from much larger populations.

In SIMPLE SAMPLE we were limited to a single population of 12 stores with four population distributions (V1 to V4). The UNIVARIATE module will store up to 17 different populations, each of which can have up to 17 population distributions (V1 to V17). The size of the populations (N) you use in the UNIVARIATE module is limited by the storage capacity of your computer. Six populations are loaded with the UNIVARIATE module. You can load your own populations by using the procedure described in Appendix A.

The procedures for specifying and analyzing experiments in the UNIVARIATE and SIMPLE SAMPLE modules are similar. The general appearance of the screen display and the rules for moving around the screen and giving commands in the two modules are very similar. The major difference between the SIMPLE SAMPLE and UNIVARIATE modules, apart from the population sizes they will accommodate, are

- the procedures for selecting a population
- the procedures for analyzing population distributions
- the automatic storage of all experiments conducted in the UNI-VARIATE module

We begin with the ISEE setup required for this chapter and a brief overview of the UNIVARIATE module.

Setup and a Brief Overview of the UNIVARIATE Module

Use the ISEE SETUP described in Chapter 4 for the experiments in this chapter. Load the ISEE program and activate the UNIVARIATE module (by typing 3 when the cursor is in the MAIN MENU).

When the UNIVARIATE module is loaded, you will see a screen display with three windows. The two lower windows are very similar to the windows in SIMPLE SAMPLE. The lower left UNIVARIATE window contains a menu with four options. The lower right part is where we specify and analyze experiments. When we activate options or issue commands, the histograms, parameters, and other information requested will appear in the top two-thirds of the screen.

Now look at the menu in the UNIVARIATE window. It lists four options:

1. Population
2. Variables
3. Experiments
4. Print

The first option, Population, is used to add or delete populations or to change the name assigned to a population. It is also used, as we will explain shortly, to select a specific population for a specific experiment. The second option, Variables, is used to generate the parameters and histograms of the variables in the selected population. These variables may be used as population distributions in experiments. Option 3, Experiments, and option 4, Print, are very similar to the Experiment and Print options in SIMPLE SAMPLE, except the results from a UNIVARIATE experiment are automatically stored in your computer's memory so you can review them at a later time. Now let's conduct an experiment.

Experiment 5.1: Testing the Rules With a Large Population

In this experiment you will test Rules I and II using a large population called U.S. Cities. This population consists of all cities in the United States with 25,000 or more people in 1980. You will use the average monthly electric bill of these cities as the population distribution from which the samples will be selected. The average monthly electric bill is for residential use and is measured in dollars. In the experiment you will select 5000 simple random samples, with replacement, of sizes 1, 4, 16, and 64 from the Monthly Electric Bill distribution. This experiment will also teach you how to use the UNIVARIATE module.

The experiment is conducted in five steps:

• Select the population called U.S. Cities for use in the experiment.
• Analyze the Monthly Electric Bill variable that will be used as the population distribution in this experiment.
• Conduct the experiment.
• Analyze the results of the experiment.
• Name the experiment for later recall.

Take Form 5.1 from Appendix B to record the results of the experiment. You will get the parameters (COUNT, MEAN, ST.DEV., SKEW) and histogram when you analyze the population distribution.

Selecting the U.S. Cities Population

Notice the small ball before option 1, Population, in the UNIVARIATE window. This indicates that the Population option was activated when the UNIVARIATE module was loaded. When the Population option is activated:

• The Population List is displayed in the top window. This list has 17 rows, numbered 1 to 17, in which the names of the currently loaded populations appear. Six populations are loaded with the module; their names appear in the first six rows.

- The cursor moves into the POPULATION LIST window, where it surrounds one of the rows (row 1 when the module is loaded).

- A set of six available commands is listed in the lower right part of the screen.

- The small ball moves to option 1, Population, in the UNIVARIATE window, indicating it is the active option.

Every population stored for use in the program is assigned a line in the Population List, where it is given a name and assigned the row number on which it is listed. We can add new populations, delete populations (except #1), or change the name of any population using the procedures described in Appendix A.

The Population List also tells the **size** of the population (the number of cases in it), the number of variables (Var.) in it, and the number of experiments (UniVar.) currently stored in computer memory that have used that population as a base for sampling. You will find additional information about the six populations in the README.POP file (in the ISEE directory).

You may conduct experiments with any of the populations listed, but you must first select the one you wish to use. You can tell which population is selected by the number in the upper right corner of the UNIVARIATE window. When the module was loaded the program chose 1, Population Models. Therefore, you see a small number 1 in the upper right corner of the UNIVARIATE window.

In this chapter you will use population 4, U.S. Cities, for most of your experiments. From the Population List you can see that there are 951 such cities (Cases) and 17 variables (Var.) in this population. (However, do not enter 951 as the value of N on Form 5.1.) You can use any of these 17 variables as the population distribution in an experiment. If this is the first time you have used the UNIVARIATE module, there will be zero experiments recorded for 4, U.S. Cities, in the UniVar. column.

To select the U.S. Cities population for this experiment, move the cursor to row 4 in the Population List and press the ENTER key. The number 4 will now appear in the upper right corner of the UNIVARIATE window and the cursor will return to the Population option in that window. The U.S. Cities Data population will remain the selected population until you select a different one or leave this module.

Analyzing the Variables in the U.S. Cities Population

Next you will use option 2, Variables, to study the variables in the U.S. Cities population. Before proceeding, make sure that 4, U.S. Cities, is the selected population and the cursor is in the UNIVARIATE window. Now activate option 2, Variables, by placing the cursor on that option and pressing the ENTER key. When you activate the Variables option:

- The Variable List for population 4 will appear in the upper window, showing the name, number, and parameters of each variable.

- The cursor will move to the first row of the Variable List.

- A list of four available commands will appear on the lower right side of the screen.

- The small ball will move to the left of option 2, Variables, in the UNIVARIATE window, indicating it is the active option.

The Variable List shows the name and row number of the 17 variables in the U.S. Cities population. You can refer to a variable by its name, number, or both. Sometimes we refer to a variable by placing a V in front of its number. In this experiment you will use the variable listed on the 17th row, which we call the Monthly Electric Bill or V17.

The Variable List also shows the count (N), the mean (MEAN), the standard deviation (ST.DEV.), the skew index, and the minimum (Min.) and maximum (Max.) value for each variable in the selected population. From the Variable List you can see that the Monthly Electric Bill varied from a low of $21.77 (Min.) to a high of $88.62 (Max.). The mean Monthly Electric Bill for all cities was $57.09, with a standard deviation of $11.19. Copy the values of the mean and standard deviation onto Form 5.1 for future use.

Two of the parameters on the Variable List, the count and the skew, require further discussion. The **count** tells us the number of population members for which there are data on a variable. If there are data for every member of the population on a variable, then the count for that variable will equal the population size, as it does for most variables in the U.S. Cities population (N = 951). On some variables, such as the Monthly Electric Bill, data may be missing for one or more members of the population and the count for that variable will be less than the population size. Four cities lack data on the Monthly Electric Bill (V17), so the count for V17 is 951 − 4 = 947, not 951.

The program eliminates any member of a population that lacks data on a variable when that variable is used as a population distribution in an experiment. As a result, the population size for an experiment is equal to the count for the variable from which the sample is selected. The population size for this experiment, which uses V17, is 947 (the V17 count) and not 951 (the population size). Therefore, you should record 947 as the value of N (COUNT) on Form 5.1.

The **skew index** tells us the degree to which a variable has a skewed distribution. If the skew index is zero, the distribution is symmetrical. The greater the absolute value (ignore the sign) of the skew index, the more skewed is the distribution. The sign of the skew parameter tells us the direction of the skew. From the Variable List we see that the skew measure for V17 is −.08, which is close to zero. This tells us that V17 is an almost symmetrical distribution. The skew index will help us later in the chapter, when we develop Rule III to describe the shape of a sampling distribution. Copy the skew index value of −.08 onto Form 5.1.

You may find it helpful to have a copy of the Variable List for the U.S. Cities population. If you have the facilities for printing, use the ALT + P command to print the variable list.

The Histograms Display

When you are in option 2, Variables, with the Variable List displayed, you can see the histograms of each variable by pressing the F10 key. When you press the F10 key:

- The upper screen will divide into two parts. The left section will contain the list of variable names and numbers for the selected population, and the right section will contain four empty rectangles in which histograms can be displayed.
- The cursor will move to the first row in the list of variables on the upper left.
- The three commands you may use while the Histograms display is on the screen appear in the lower right window.

To see the histogram for any variable on the list, move the cursor to the row for that variable and press the ENTER key. Test the histogram procedure using variable V17. You saw above that V17 had a skew measure of −.08, suggesting it has a nearly symmetric distribution. Move the cursor to row 17 in the VARIABLES window and press the ENTER key. The histogram for V17 will appear in the upper left rectangle of the HISTOGRAMS window. The thin vertical line in the middle of the histogram locates the population mean, whose value appears in the middle of the scale under the histogram. The variable's name appears above its histogram.

As its skew measure indicates, V17 is a relatively symmetric curve. The histogram also shows that V17 has a complex shape, with a major mode at the mean value and two less pronounced modes above and below the mean.

If you have the facilities for printing, use the ALT + P command to print the screen display of the V17 histogram. If you print the histogram, write "SEE HISTOGRAM PRINTOUT" above the scale for the histogram on Form 5.1 and staple the printout behind Form 5.1. If you do not print the histogram, make a rough sketch of the histogram for V17 on Form 5.1. To make the sketch, place a dot at the appropriate height above each scale value. Start with the modes and then work your way down to the lower values then up to the higher values. After you have placed a dot above each value on the scale, connect them to form a polygon.

Conducting Experiment 5.1

To conduct Experiment 5.1, move the cursor to the UNIVARIATE window (if it is not already there) and activate option 3, Experiments (by placing the cursor on that option and pressing the ENTER key). After you press the ENTER key:

- The Experiment List for population 4, U.S. Cities, will appear at the top of your screen. This list describes the UNIVARIATE experiments (if any) that are currently stored in the program for population 4 (the selected population). Since this is your first experiment, the list should be empty.

- The cursor will move into the EXPERIMENT LIST window, where it will rest on the first row.

- The four available commands will appear in the lower right window.

If the cursor is not on the first row of the Experiment List, move it there and press the ENTER key. The program will store the experiment you are about to conduct and later list it here.

Press the ENTER key, and two menus will appear in the lower right window. What we call the experiment menu appears on the left, and an analysis menu appears on the right. Both these menus work the same way they did in SIMPLE SAMPLE. The cursor will move to the first row (C1), first column (Var), in the experiment menu. Now specify an experiment in which 5000 simple random samples will be selected with replacement (SRSW) from V17 with sample sizes 1 (C1), 4 (C2), 16 (C3), and 64 (C4). Use the experiment menu for specifying the experiment exactly as you did in SIMPLE SAMPLE. Limit the number of samples selected to 5000, rather than the 9999 samples selected in the SIMPLE SAMPLE experiment, because the larger sample sizes used in the UNIVARIATE module increase the time required to select and process the samples. Check your specifications for Experiment 5.1 against those given in Exhibit 5.1.

Exhibit 5.1

Specifications for Experiment 5.1

Condition	Var	Type	Size
C1	17	SRSW	1
C2	17	SRSW	4
C3	17	SRSW	16
C4	17	SRSW	64
Number of Samples: 5000			

Before you conduct the experiment, think about the likely results:

- If Rule I is true, the histograms of the sampling distributions in C1–C4 should be evenly balanced around the population mean of V17 ($57.09), and the bias measure in the parameter table for the experiment should be near zero for each of the four conditions.

- The sampling distribution for C1 with size = 1 should be the same as the population distribution from which it was selected (V17). As the sample size increases, the sampling distribution should cluster more and more around the population mean.

- If Rule II is true, the standard error for C1 with a sample size of 1 should be very close to $11.19, the standard deviation of V17. Since the sample size for each condition is four times as large as the one that precedes it, the standard error should be cut in half as we go from one condition to the next. Thus, we should expect to find the standard errors observed in the parameter table for the experiment to be:

$$C1 \quad n = 1 \quad \textit{ST.ERR.} = \text{ST.DEV.}/\sqrt{1} \ = 11.19/1 = 11.19$$

$$C2 \quad n = 4 \quad \textit{ST.ERR.} = \text{ST.DEV.}/\sqrt{4} \ = 11.19/2 = \ 5.60$$

$$C3 \quad n = 16 \quad \textit{ST.ERR.} = \text{ST.DEV.}/\sqrt{16} = 11.19/4 = \ 2.80$$

$$C4 \quad n = 64 \quad \textit{ST.ERR.} = \text{ST.DEV.}/\sqrt{64} = 11.19/8 = \ 1.40$$

Now conduct the experiment by placing the cursor on Select and pressing the ENTER key.

Analyzing Experiment 5.1

When you press the ENTER key:

- The EXPERIMENT 1 window displays four rectangles, one for each experimental condition's histogram.
- A note "Preparing" appears on the screen, indicating that the program is preparing to conduct the experiment.
- The notice will disappear and the program will begin selecting samples for the C1 condition and recording the means of these samples in its memory under C1. The screen will indicate the number of the sample it has selected in the rectangle for C1. When the last sample for C1 has been selected, a histogram of the sample means selected for C1 will appear in the rectangle for Condition 1.
- The program will then move to the other conditions, selecting the required samples, indicating the sample number selected, and displaying the histograms of the sampling distributions.

From the histograms you can see that the sampling distributions for each condition are balanced around the population mean (the small vertical line at the top), which seems to confirm Rule I. The shape for C1 based on a sample size of one is similar to the shape of V17, the Monthly Electric Bill, from which it was selected (see Form 5.1).

All the histograms for C1–C4, however, seem to spread out about equally around the population mean. This appears to contradict our findings in SIMPLE SAMPLE, where we always found the sample means clustering more tightly around the population mean as the sample size increased. This apparent contradiction is due to an optical illusion.

In SIMPLE SAMPLE we restricted the data to values between 36 and 60. Because of this restricted range, every histogram in SIMPLE

SAMPLE could use the same scale, which was from 36 to 60. This meant we could examine the spread in the sampling distributions by simply comparing the histograms visually.

In the UNIVARIATE module, however, there is no restriction on the type of data and its range of values. In the U.S. Cities population, for example, the size can range from 1.50 to 30.90 for deaths per 1000 population (V11) to 23,070 to 7,262,750 for population size (V2). Because of the unrestricted range of values in the UNIVARIATE module, two different types of histograms are required.

The first type of histogram appears right after the samples are selected and is called the Hist.1 option. These histograms use a scale based on the standard error of the sampling distribution in each condition, which gives a good picture of the shape of each sampling distribution. But these histograms will probably have different size scales for each condition, which distorts the visual presentation of the spread in the different conditions. Look at the upper and lower scale values under each histogram and you will see that the range decreases as you go from one condition to the next. The range decreases by a factor of two because the standard errors decrease by a factor of two. Thus the scale drops from about 31.25 to 82.92 for C1 to about 53.87 to 60.32 for C4.

The second set of histograms, which is activated by the Hist.2 option, uses a common scale for each condition based on the largest standard error in the four conditions. These histograms may distort the shape of the curves under some conditions, but they give a good comparative picture of the spread in each condition relative to the others. Move the cursor to the Hist.2 command and press the ENTER key. You will see a new set of histograms which uses the same scale (from about 31.25 to 82.92) for all four conditions. On this common scale you can see the clustering of the sample means from C1 to C4. Thus the tighter dispersion around the population mean is vividly clear as we go to bigger samples. However, the shape of the curves (except for C1) is not as clear as it was in the initial set of histograms.

In Experiment 5.1, Hist.1 shows that the sample means in each condition are balanced around the population mean, a finding that supports Rule I. Hist.2 reveals that the sample means cluster more tightly around the population mean as the sample size increases.

If you have facilities for printing, use the ALT + P command to print first Hist.1 and then Hist.2 and write "SEE ATTACHED PRINTOUTS" above the scale for the histograms of C1–C4. Staple both printouts to Form 5.1. (The small ball to the left of Hist.1 or Hist.2 will tell you the type of histogram displayed in the printout.)

If you do not have facilities for printing, sketch the histograms of C1–C4, Hist.2 option, on Form 5.1.

To complete your analysis of this experiment, move the cursor to the Param. command and press the ENTER key. The parameter table for C1 through C4 will appear in the EXPERIMENT 1 window. Copy the values in rows 3 (Expected Value – Ob.), 5 (Bias – Ob.), and 8 (Standard Error – Ob.) onto Form 5.1. You should find the bias measure for each condition to be close to zero, which confirms Rule I. You should find the standard error for the C1 condition (n = 1) to be close to 11.19, which is the standard deviation of the population. The values of the standard error should drop by a factor of about two for each of the succeeding conditions. In C2 the standard error should be around 5.6, in C3 around 2.8, and in C4 around 1.4, which confirms Rule II.

Naming Experiment 5.1

The program will automatically save the experiment you just conducted and assign it to the first row in the Experiment List for population 4, U.S. Cities, with the name Experiment 1. Check this by activating option 3, Experiments, in the UNIVARIATE window (by pressing the ESC key, placing the cursor on option 3, and pressing the ENTER key). The Experiment List for population 4, U.S. Cities, will appear, and the first row will list Experiment 1, the experiment you have just conducted. Note that the Experiment List gives the complete specification of the experiment. To change the name of the experiment to Experiment 5.1:

- Place the cursor on the row for Experiment 1 (if it is not there already).
- Press the F8 key.
- Type in the new name, Experiment 5.1.
- Press the ENTER key.

The name is now Experiment 5.1.

If you wish to review the results of this experiment or conduct it a second time, just place the cursor on the row for Experiment 5.1 and press the ENTER key. The specifications for Experiment 5.1 will reappear below the histograms. To analyze the experiment, use the commands in the right portion of this window. If you wish to conduct the experiment again, place the cursor on the Select command and press the ENTER key.

This completes Experiment 5.1. It would helpful for you to do Exercises 1, 2A–E, 3, and 4 at the end of this chapter before reading the summary section that follows. Exercises 2F and 5 are optional.

Summary of Experiment 5.1

From Experiment 5.1 you have seen that Rules I and II are true for the Monthly Electric Bill distribution in the U.S. Cities population. You have also learned how to use the UNIVARIATE module of ISEE. Before we can put Rules I and II to work, however, we must develop one more rule about sampling distributions. We turn now to the development of Rule III, which describes the shape of the sampling distribution.

The Normal Distribution

One of the first things you encounter in any statistics course is the **normal distribution** (Exhibit 5.2), which forms a unimodal, symmetric curve, with two tails and a bell-like shape.

Exhibit 5.2
The Normal Curve

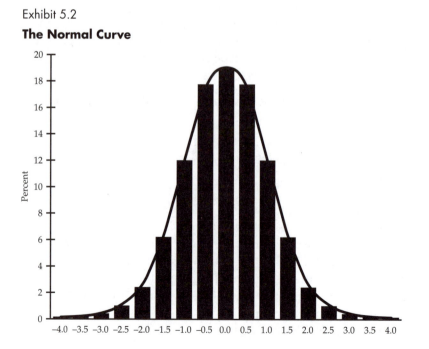

A normal curve, like any symmetric unimodal curve, has a mean equal to its median and mode. Since the curve is symmetric, half the area under the curve is above the mean and the remaining half is below it. In many of the experiments you have conducted you may have noticed that the sampling distribution begins to look like the normal curve pictured in Exhibit 5.2 as the sample size grows larger.

For example, consider the histograms in Experiment 5.1. If necessary, activate the UNIVARIATE module in the MAIN MENU and load the Experiment List for population 4, U.S. Cities, by placing the cursor on option 3, Experiments, in the UNIVARIATE window and pressing the ENTER key. Put the cursor on the first row (Experiment 5.1) of the Experiment List and press the ENTER key. The histograms for Experiment 5.1 should now be displayed in the EXPERI-MENT 1 window.

Notice that the histogram for Condition 1, with sample size one, has the trimodal shape of the Monthly Electric Bill distribution. The histogram for Condition 2, with sample size n = 4, has begun to look like a normal curve, and the histograms for Condition 3 (n = 16) and Condition 4 (n = 64) look very much like the normal curve in Exhibit 5.2. If you review the forms for Experiment 4.3 and 4.4 conducted in the last chapter, you will see the same type of change in the sampling distributions. As the sample size increases, the sampling distributions look more and more like a normal curve.

These changes in the sampling distribution suggest a third rule, Rule III, which relates the shape of the sampling distribution to the sample size. But our experiments also tell us that we must consider the shape of the population distribution in developing Rule III.

We know the sampling distribution for samples of size one has the same shape as the population distribution from which it was selected. Therefore, if the population distribution is normal, the sampling distribution for samples of size one is normal. In Experiment 5.1, in which you selected samples from a symmetric but trimodal population distribution, you can see it takes sample sizes of 16 or more before the sampling distribution begins to assume a normal shape.

These findings suggest a very important insight. The sample size required before the sampling distribution takes on a normal shape *depends on the degree to which the population distribution resembles a normal curve.* The more closely the population distribution resembles a normal curve, the smaller the sample size required before the sampling distribution takes on a normal shape.

For this reason, we must find a systematic way to measure the shape of a population distribution and its effect on the shape of the sampling distribution. In the next experiment, we will focus on the skew in a population distribution and the effect of that skew on the shape of the sampling distribution. Once we understand the effect of skew in the population distribution, we will be able to formulate a more complete rule about the sample size required for a normal-shaped sampling distribution.

Experiment 5.2: Sampling From a Skewed Population Distribution

Most of the experiments you have conducted so far were based on symmetric population distributions. It is easy to see why the sampling distribution might assume a normal shape when we sample from a symmetric population. The piling up of the sample means around the population mean that occurs with large sample sizes should be balanced when the samples are selected from a symmetric population. This symmetry in the clustering of the sample means around the population mean should result in a curve shaped like a normal curve.

But what happens when you select samples from a skewed population? Will the clustering of the sample means give a symmetric, normal shape, or will the sampling distribution take the same skewed shape as the population distribution? In Experiment 5.2 you will select samples from V5 of the population 4, U.S. Cities. Variable 5 is the percentage of the city's population that was white in 1986. It is a negatively skewed distribution, with a skew index of –1.58. You will select 5000 simple random samples, with replacement, of sizes 1, 2, 4, and 40 from V5. Your primary focus here will be on the shape of the sampling distribution. In particular, you want to learn *whether the sampling distributions will begin to resemble a normal curve as the sample size increases.* You will conduct the experiment in four steps:

• Analyze V5, the skewed population distribution from which you will select the samples.

• Conduct the experiment.

• Analyze the experiment.

• Name the experiment.

Take Form 5.2 from Appendix B to record the results of Experiment 5.2.

Analyzing V5, the Percent of White Population in a City

Load the UNIVARIATE module and select population 4, U.S. Cities. Activate option 2, Variables, in the UNIVARIATE window. From the Variable List you will see that there are data on V5 for every city (Count = 951) and that the percent white ranges from a low of 4.16 to a high of 99.48. The mean percent white is 83.27, with a standard deviation of 16.32%. The skew index for V5 is –1.58, which tells us that V5 has a pronounced negative skew.

From the Variable List copy the values of the Count, Mean, Standard deviation, and Skew for V5 onto Form 5.2.

Give the Histograms command (by pressing the F10 key) and generate the histogram for V5 (by placing the cursor on V5 and pressing the ENTER key). You will see that the histogram for V5 is negatively skewed. Its mode is at the highest value. As the percent white decreases, the number of cases drops down continuously toward the lower values. We could describe the histogram of V5 as a one-sided J-shaped curve. From the histogram you can see that most of the cities have more than the 83.27% white population of the average city. Another way of saying this is that more than half the area under the curve is above the mean.

If you have facilities for printing, use the ALT + P command to print the histogram of V5. If you print the histogram, write "SEE HISTOGRAM PRINTOUT" above the scale for Histogram V5 on Form 5.2 and staple the printout to Form 5.2. If you do not print the display, draw a rough sketch of the V5 histogram above its scale on Form 5.2.

Conducting Experiment 5.2

Activate option 3, Experiments, in the UNIVARIATE window. When the Experiment List appears at the top of your screen, if necessary move the cursor to the first empty row (most likely row 2) and press the ENTER key. This instructs the program to store Experiment 5.2 in that row.

Specify an experiment using V5 that selects 5000 SRSW samples of sizes 1, 2, 4, and 40. Check your specification against Exhibit 5.3. Then move the cursor to the Select command and press the ENTER key.

Exhibit 5.3

Specifications for Experiment 5.2

Condition	Var	Type	Size
C1	5	SRSW	1
C2	5	SRSW	2
C3	5	SRSW	4
C4	5	SRSW	40
Number of Samples: 5000			

Analyzing Experiment 5.2

When the program has selected and processed the samples, histograms (of type 1) will appear in the EXPERIMENT 2 window. What do you see in these histograms? Focus on the *shape* of the histograms. Is the skew of V5 permanent in the histograms, or is the skew of V5 gradually replaced by the symmetry of a normal curve?

Start with Condition 1, since it used a sample size of one. The histogram for Condition 1 should look very much like the histogram for V5. It should be the same single-sided J-shaped curve as V5, with its mode at the highest value and a single tail pointing toward the lower values. Now look at the histogram for Condition 2, based on samples of size two. The mode has probably moved over to the second highest category and the curve is probably beginning to develop a second side to the right of its mode. Next consider the histogram for Condition 3 with samples of 4. It is still a skewed distribution, but its mode has moved closer to the center of the histogram and the second side to the right of the mode has grown larger. Finally, look at the histogram for Condition 4, based on samples of size 40. The distribution has its mode in the center and has two clearly developed tails. The Condition 4 histogram has lost all resemblance to the J-shaped distribution of V5 from which it was selected and has begun to look very much like a normal curve.

From Experiment 5.2 you can see how the shape of the sampling distribution for small sample sizes is skewed in the same direction as the population distribution from which it is selected. However, as the sample size gets larger, it overcomes any skew in the population distribution and its sampling distribution takes on a more normal shape.

If you have the facilities for printing, use the ALT + P command to print the histograms. If you print the histograms, write "SEE

HISTOGRAM OUTPUT" over the scales of the C1–C4 histograms on Form 5.2 and staple the printout to Form 5.2. If you cannot print the display, draw a rough sketch of the C1–C4 histograms (Hist.1) on Form 5.2.

Naming Experiment 5.2

The last step in the experiment is to assign it the name Experiment 5.2. Return to the UNIVARIATE window (by pressing the ESC key) and activate option 3, Experiments. Place the cursor on the row in the Experiment List where this experiment is listed. (If necessary, use the description of the experiment to locate the right row.) Next press the F8 key, type in the name Experiment 5.2, and then press the ENTER key.

This completes Experiment 5.2. It would be helpful for you to do Exercises 6 and 7 at the end of this chapter before reading the summary section that follows.

Summary of Experiment 5.2

In this experiment you saw how the skew in a population distribution can affect the shape of the sampling distributions selected from it. *The more skewed the population distribution, the larger the sample size required before the sampling distribution takes on the shape of a normal curve.*

Rule III

We would like to have a very precise rule (like Rules I and II) that tells us exactly what size sample is required for a normal-shaped sampling distribution. We use the symbol n' to represent the sample size needed for a normal sampling distribution. Our previous experiments have shown that n' (the required sample size) depends on the shape of the population distribution. If the population distribution has a normal shape, then we know a sample size of one ($n' = 1$) will have a normal sampling distribution. If the population distribution is not normal but is symmetrical, then a small sample size (n' is small) will have a normal sampling distribution. If the population distribution is highly skewed, then large sample sizes (n' is large) are required before the sampling distribution becomes normal. Thus, the rule that tells us the value of n' (the required sample size for a normal sampling distribution) must take the skew of the population distribution into account.

There is, unfortunately, no single, precise rule for n′ that can be used for all kinds of population distributions. However, the following rule, which we call Rule III, works reasonably well for **interval scales** with five or more categories.

Rule III

The sampling distribution of the mean for simple random samples will approximate a normal distribution if

- the population distribution has a skew index in the range of +1 to −1 and the sample size is n′ = 25 or more.
- the population distribution has a skew index outside the range of +1 to −1 and the sample size equals n′ = 25 * SKEW^2.

To apply Rule III, first check to see that there are at least five categories in the population distribution. Next, calculate the skew index (explained in the final section of this chapter) and use it to calculate the required sample size.

We can illustrate the use of Rule III with the UNIVARIATE module. Load the UNIVARIATE module and select population 4, U.S. Cities. Activate option 2, Variables, in the UNIVARIATE window, which will display the Variable List for population 4. Suppose you wanted to know the required sample size for a normal sampling distribution for V9 (birth rate per 1000 population) and V14 (annual rainfall in inches).

Before using Rule III, you need to check to see if there are at least five categories for V9 and V14 in the U.S. Cities population. You can check the number of categories by looking at the histograms of the two variables. Press the F10 key to activate the Histograms option. Then generate the required histograms by placing the cursor on the rows for V9 and V14 and pressing the ENTER key. From the histograms you can see that there are more than five categories in V9 and in V14, so you know that can use Rule III for these two distributions.

Next return to the Variable List (by pressing the F10 key). Here you can see that the skew index for V9 is 1.56 and for V14 is −0.17. Using Rule III:

- V9, the birth rate per 1000, has a skew index of 1.56, which is outside the range of +1 to −1. Therefore, n′= 25 * 1.56 * 1.56 = 61.
- V14, annual rainfall in inches, has a skew index of −0.17, which falls within the range of +1 to −1. Therefore, n′= 25.

Now we will test Rule III for V14, Annual Rainfall, in the U.S. Cities population.

Experiment 5.3: Testing Rule III

In this experiment you will select 9999 simple random samples of size 1 and 25, with replacement, from V14 of population 4, U.S. Cities. The variable, as its name suggests, measures the amount of rain that falls in an average year in the U.S. Cities population. If Rule III is true, then according to our calculations in the previous section, a sample size of 25 selected from V14 should have a sampling distribution that approximates a normal curve.

There will be four steps in this experiment:

- Analyze the V14, Annual Rainfall, distribution.
- Conduct the experiment.
- Analyze the experiment.
- Name the experiment.

Take Form 5.3 from Appendix B to record the results of Experiment 5.3.

Analyzing V14, Annual Rainfall Distribution

Activate the UNIVARIATE module and select population 4, U.S. Cities. Activate option 2, Variables, in the UNIVARIATE window. The Variable List shows that the annual rainfall varies from 2.65 to 64.64 inches in the 951 cities. The average city has 33.95 inches of rain, and the standard deviation of the distribution is 13.56 inches. The skew index for the Annual Rainfall distribution is –0.17 which tells us that the distribution is relatively symmetrical but has a slight negative skew.

Copy the count (N), mean, standard deviation, and skew index for V14 onto Form 5.3. Next, with the cursor in the Variables window, activate the Histograms command (F10 key) and generate the histogram for V14 (by placing the cursor on the row for V14 and pressing the ENTER key). You will see that the histogram for V14 has an unusual, trimodal shape, with its dominant mode at the mean value of 33.95 and somewhat smaller modes above and below the mean.

Print the histograms or copy them on Form 5.3.

Conducting Experiment 5.3

Activate option 3, Experiments, in the UNIVARIATE window. Place the cursor on the first empty row in the Experiment List and press the ENTER key. Now use the Experiment menu to specify an experiment using V14 to select 9999 SRSW with sample sizes of 1 (C1) and 25 (C2). Check your specification against Exhibit 5.4.

Exhibit 5.4

Specifications for Experiment 5.3

Condition	Var	Type	Size
C1	14	SRSW	1
C2	14	SRSW	25
C3	*	SRSN	*
C4	*	SRSN	*

Number of Samples: 9999

Before you conduct the experiment, think about what the results should be according to the rules we have developed. Focus here on the shape of the sampling distribution of C1 and C2. According to your previous experiments, the sampling distribution of C1 with sample n = 1 should have the trimodal shape of V14, with a dominant mode at the mean value of 33.95 inches. In the previous section you found, using Rule III, that V14 should have an approximately normal-shaped sampling distribution for samples of size n = 25. In C2, samples of size 25 are selected from V14. Therefore, if Rule III is true, the sampling distribution for C2 should look like a normal curve.

Now place the cursor on the Select command and press the EN-TER key.

Analyzing Experiment 5.3

From the histograms that appear you will see:

- The histogram for C1, sample size n = 1, has the expected trimodal shape of V14 with a dominant mode at its mean.
- The histogram for C2, sample size n = 25, has the expected normal-looking appearance.

Rule III thus seems to work for V14.

We must always remember that, unlike Rules I and II, Rule III is not very precise. Rather, it gives a general feel for the sample size required. In some cases, particularly when the skew measure is small, you may find that a smaller sample size than the one specified by Rule III will have a sampling distribution that resembles a normal curve. In many cases, the sampling distribution for the sample size specified by Rule III will not be a normal curve but will only approximate it.

Print the Hist.1. histograms or copy them on Form 5.3.

Naming Experiment 5.3

The last step is to name your work Experiment 5.3. Return to the UNIVARIATE window (by pressing the ESC key) and activate option 3, Experiments. Place the cursor on the row in the Experiment List where your last experiment is listed. If necessary, use the description of the experiment to locate the row. Then press the F8 key, type in the name Experiment 5.3, and press the ENTER key.

This completes Experiment 5.3. It would helpful for you to do Exercises 8 and 9 at the end of the chapter before reading the summary section that follows.

Summary of Experiment 5.3

We have now developed three rules for describing the sampling distribution for simple random samples. We have found that for samples of size $n = 1$, the sampling distribution will have the same shape as the population distribution from which it was selected. This means that for samples of size $n = 1$:

- The mean of the sampling distribution will equal the mean of the population. The sample mean is thus an unbiased estimate of the population mean (*EXP.VAL.* – MEAN = 0).
- The standard error is equal to the standard deviation of the population (*ST.ERR.* = ST.DEV.).
- The shape of the sampling distribution is the same as the shape of the population distribution.

As the sample grows larger, the shape of the sampling distribution changes, as follows:

- The expected value continues to equal the population mean. According to Rule I, $EXP.VAL. - MEAN = 0$. This rule tells us that the sample mean is an unbiased estimate of the population mean for any size simple random sample, selected with or without replacement, from any population. This rule also tells us that the potential error in using the mean of a simple random sample as an estimate of the population comes from random and not systematic error.

- The sample means cluster closer and closer around the expected value, which tells us that the random error in using the sample mean declines with each increase in the sample size. Our experiments have shown that the standard error, which measures the random error, drops by a factor of $1/\sqrt{n}$ for simple random sampling with replacement and by a factor of $fpc/\sqrt{n}$ for simple random sampling without replacement. Thus, according to Rule II, $ST.ERR. = ST.DEV./\sqrt{n}$ for simple random samples with replacement, and $ST.ERR. = ST.DEV. * fpc/\sqrt{n}$ for simple random sampling without replacement.

- The shape of the sampling distribution comes to look more like a normal curve as the sample size grows larger. The more the population distribution resembles a normal curve, the smaller the sample size required before the sampling distribution will be a normal curve. In a rough way we can expect, according to Rule III, that the sampling distribution will be normal if the skew index is between +1 and –1 and the sample size is 25 or more, or if the skew index is outside the limits of +1 to –1 and the sample size is larger than $25 * SKEW^2$.

In the next chapter you will see how these three rules can help you in planning and analyzing your samples. They also provide guidance in deciding on the proper sample size for research on populations with different characteristics.

If you would like to see how the skew index is calculated, read the last section in this chapter. This section is not required for the two chapters that follow.

Calculating the Skew Index

The skew index we use in Rule III was created by Sir Ronald A. Fisher in 1932 and is often called G1. Many statistical packages for the computer will calculate this measure, but the formula for calculating G1 will rarely be found in statistics textbooks. In this section you will see how to calculate G1.

To illustrate how SKEW (G1) is calculated, we use a test distribution of five numbers: 1, 3, 4, 5, and 7 (N = 5). The mean, median, and standard deviation of our test distributions are: MEAN = 4, MEDIAN = 4, ST.DEV. = 2. Note that the mean of this distribution equals the median, which tells us that the distribution must be symmetric. Therefore, SKEW (G1) of our test distribution should equal zero.

To calculate SKEW, we can use the following formula:

$$SKEW = (A - B + C)/ST.DEV.^3$$

The formula tells us that SKEW is a ratio. The denominator of the ratio is the standard deviation cubed—that is, the standard deviation multiplied by itself three times. In our example, the standard deviation is 2. So the denominator of SKEW for our test distribution would be

$$ST.DEV. * ST.DEV. * ST.DEV. = 2 * 2 * 2 = 8$$

The numerator of the ratio is the sum of two numbers, A and C, minus a third number, B. To calculate the skew index, we must first calculate A, B, and C as follows:

A = the sum of all the values in the distribution, cubed, divided by the number of values (N). For our test distribution, the value of A would be

$$(1^3 + 3^3 + 4^3 + 5^3 + 7^3)/5 = 560/5 = 112$$

B = three times the mean, times the sum of all values in the distribution, squared, divided by the number of values (N). For our test distribution, the value of B would be

$$3 * 4 * (1^2 + 3^2 + 4^2 + 5^2 + 7^2)/5 = 3 * 4 * 100/5 = 240$$

C = two times the mean of the distribution cubed. For our test distribution, the value of C would be

$$2 * 4^3 = 2 * 64 = 128$$

If we put all these calculations, based on our symmetric test distribution, into the formula for SKEW, we have

$$SKEW = (A - B + C)/ST.DEV.^3 = (112 - 240 + 128)/8 = 0$$

You can practice calculating the SKEW (the skew index) in Exercise 10 at the end of this chapter.

EXERCISES

The answers to these exercises are in Appendix C.

1. Use the UNIVARIATE module to answer the following questions:

   A. What name did the program assign to population 2?

   B. What is the number assigned to the population called Lower East Side 1900?

   C. How many variables are in the population called U.S. County Data?

   D. What is the name of the variable that has the largest mean in the U.S. County population?

   E. What is the variable number of the variable with the smallest standard deviation in the U.S. County population?

   F. What is the range (Max.–Min.) of variable V4, Skewed: Extreme, in the Population Models population?

   G. Rank the variables in population 3 in order from the variable with the largest skew to the variable with the smallest skew. Check your results by looking at the histograms of the variables, from the variable with the most skew to the one that is least skewed. You should be able to see how the curves for the variables become more symmetrical as the skew index gets closer and closer to zero.

   H. Which of the variables in population 4, U.S. Cities, have more than one mode?

   Check your answers to this exercise before doing Exercise 2. If you have any difficulty answering these questions, review the UNIVARIATE Overview and Experiment 5.1 of this chapter.

2. Suppose we were to select a simple random sample of size 100 with replacement from population 3, U.S. Places 2500 (or more in population). This would give us a sample of size 100 for each of the six variables in population 3. It would also give a sampling distribution of the means for each of these six variables based on a sample size 100. Assume Rules I and II are true for these six sampling distributions.

   A. Which variable would have the sampling distribution with the largest expected value, and what would the expected value of that sampling distribution be?

   B. Which of the variables would have biased sampling distributions?

C. Which of the variables would have the sampling distribution with the largest standard error, and what would the standard error of that sampling distribution be?

D. Which of the variables would have the largest potential for error (RME) in using its sample mean to estimate its population mean?

E. Suppose we want to cut the potential error (RME) in half for each of the variables. How large a sample would we have to select?

F. How would your answers to questions 2A through 2D change if the sample had been selected without replacement?

3. In this exercise, conduct Experiment 5.1 using V17 (Percent HS Ed. or more) of population 2 (U.S. County Data). Use Form 5, Exercise 3 to record the results of this experiment. Check the answers to each part of the exercise before going on to the next part.

A. Analyze V17 (parameters and histogram) and record the results on Form 5, Exercise 3.

B. Specify an experiment like Experiment 5.1 using V17 of population 2. Do not conduct the experiment until you are instructed to do so.

C. If Rule II is correct, what standard errors would expect to get for conditions C1–C4?

D. Conduct the experiment as specified in 3B. Analyze the results of the experiment and record the expected values, bias, and standard errors of C1–C4 on Form 5, Exercise 3. Print the histograms (Hist.2) for C1–C4, or copy them onto Form 5, Exercise 3.

Are the results of this experiment the same as in Experiment 5.1?

• Is the shape of the sampling distribution in C1 the same as the shape of the population distribution from which it was selected?

• Are the sampling distributions of C1–C4 balanced around the population mean?

• Do the sampling distributions cluster more around the population mean as the sample size increases?

• Are the expected values and the bias measures for C1–C4 what they should be according to Rule I?

• Are the standard errors for C1–C4 what they should be according to Rule II? (See your answer to 3C.)

4. In this exercise, conduct Experiment 5.1 using any variable in any population except V17 in population 2 (U.S. County Data) or V17 in population 4 (U.S. Cities Data). We will refer to the variable you choose for this exercise as the Test Variable. Use Form 5, Exercise 4 to record the results of this experiment.

   A. Record the variable and population number of the Test Variable in the description of the experiment on Form 5, Exercise 4. The description of the experiment is on the line below the title of the form.

   B. Analyze the Test Variable (parameters and histogram) and record the results on Form 5, Exercise 4.

   C. Specify an experiment like Experiment 5.1 using the Test Variable. Do not conduct the experiment until you are instructed to do so.

   D. If Rule II is correct, what standard errors would expect to get for conditions C1–C4?

   E. Conduct the experiment as specified in 4C. Analyze the results of the experiment and record the expected values, bias, and standard errors of C1–C4 on Form 5, Exercise 4. Print the histograms (Hist.2) for C1–C4, or copy them on Form 5, Exercise 4.

   F. Are the results of this experiment the same as in Experiment 5.1?

      • Is the shape of the sampling distribution in C1 the same as the shape of the population distribution from which it was selected?

      • Are the sampling distributions of C1–C4 balanced around the population mean?

      • Do the sampling distributions cluster more around the population mean as the sample size increases?

      • Are the expected values and the bias measures for C1–C4 what they should be according to Rule I?

      • Are the standard errors for C1–C4 what they should be according to Rule II? (See your answer to 4D.)

5. In this exercise, conduct an experiment like Experiment 5.1 using the same variable, V17 (Monthly Electric Bill) of population 4 (U.S. Cities Data), but select the samples without replacement (SRSN). Use Form 5, Exercise 5, to record the results of this ex-

periment. Check the answers to each part of Exercise 5 before continuing.

A. Analyze V17 (parameters and histogram) and record the results on Form 5, Exercise 5.

B. Specify an experiment like Experiment 5.1, but select the samples without replacement. Do not conduct the experiment until you are instructed to do so.

C. If Rule II is correct, what standard errors would you expect to get for conditions C1–C4?

D. Conduct the experiment as specified in 5B. Analyze the results of the experiment and record the expected values, bias and standard errors of C1–C4 on Form 5, Exercise 5. Print the histograms (Hist.2) for C1–C4, or copy them on Form 5, Exercise 5.

E. Are the results of this experiment the same as in Experiment 5.1?

- Is the shape of the sampling distribution in C1 the same as the shape of the population distribution from which it was selected?

- Are the sampling distributions of C1–C4 balanced around the population mean?

- Do the sampling distributions cluster more around the population mean as the sample size increases?

- Are the expected values and the bias measures for C1–C4 what they should be according to Rule I?

- Are the standard errors for C1–C4 what they should be according to Rule II? (See your answer to 5C.)

6. Repeat Experiment 5.2 using V9 (Births per 1000 population in 1984) of the U.S. Cities population. Use Form 5, Exercise 6, to record the results of this experiment. Check the answers to each part of Exercise 6 before continuing.

A. Analyze V9 (parameters and histogram) and record the results on Form 5, Exercise 6.

B. Specify an experiment like Experiment 5.2 using V9 of population 4.

C. Conduct the experiment as specified in 6B. Analyze the results of the experiment and print the histograms (Hist.1) for

C1–C4 or copy them on Form 5, Exercise 6. Are the results of this experiment the same as in Experiment 5.2?

- Is the shape of the sampling distribution in C1 the same as the shape of the population distribution from which it was selected?
- Are the sampling distributions of C1–C4 balanced around the population mean?
- As the sample size increases, does the shape of the sampling distribution look more and more like a normal curve?

7. Repeat Experiment 5.2 using V10 (number of deaths in 1984) of the U.S. Cities population. Use Form 5, Exercise 7, to record the results of this experiment. Check the answers to each part of Exercise 7 before continuing.

A. Analyze V10 (parameters and histogram) and record the results on Form 5, Exercise 7.

B. Specify an experiment like Experiment 5.2 using V10 of population 4.

C. Conduct the experiment as specified in 7B. Analyze the results of the experiment and print the histograms (Hist.1) for C1–C4 or copy them on Form 5, Exercise 7. Are the results of this experiment the same as in Experiment 5.2? In what way, if any, are the results of this experiment different from the results of Experiment 5.2?

- Is the shape of the sampling distribution in C1 the same as the shape of the population distribution from which it was selected?
- Are the sampling distributions of C1–C4 balanced around the population mean?
- As the sample size increases, do the sampling distributions cluster more around the population mean?
- As the sample size increases, does the shape of the sampling distribution look more and more like a normal curve?

8. A. For which of the variables in population 1, Population Models, can we use Rule III to help us determine the sample size required for a normal sampling distribution? Check the answer to 8A before going on to 8B.

B. What sample sizes are required in order to get normal sampling distributions for the variables in population 1, Population Models? Use Rule III where appropriate.

9. Test Rule III by repeating Experiment 5.3 using V6 of the U.S. Cities population. Use Form 5, Exercise 9, to record the results of this experiment. Check the answers to each part of Exercise 9 before continuing.

A. Analyze V6 (parameters and histogram) and record the results on Form 5, Exercise 9.

B. According to Rule III, what is the required sample size, n´, for V6 to have a sampling distribution with a normal shape?

C. Specify an experiment like Experiment 5.3 using V6 of population 4. Set the sample size for C2 at the required sample size, n´, as determined in 9B.

D. Conduct the experiment as specified in 9C. Analyze the results of the experiment and print the histograms (Hist.1) for C1 and C2 or copy them on Form 5, Exercise 9. Do the results of this experiment confirm Rule III?

10. There are three children in a household, ages 1, 2, and 6. What is the skew index (SKEW) for the distribution of the three ages?

6 The Payoff: Putting the Theory to Use

Introduction

In the previous two chapters we have discovered three rules that help describe the mean (expected value), the standard deviation (standard error), and the shape of a sampling distribution. In this chapter you will learn one of the most important uses of the three rules, something called a **confidence interval**.

In the first section of this chapter you will learn what a confidence interval is and how to generate it from the three rules you have learned about the sampling distribution. As you will see, a confidence interval is a very powerful way of adjusting your sample data when you want to estimate an unknown population parameter.

In the rest of this chapter you will learn four different ways to use the confidence interval. First, you will learn how to use a confidence interval in your own research when you want to estimate a population mean. Second, you will learn how to use a confidence interval to estimate a percentage or proportion. Third, you will see how to use your knowledge of confidence intervals to determine the right size sample to select when planning a study. Knowing the right sample size is important because it can protect you from selecting a sample that is larger or smaller than you need. If you select too large a sample you will waste time and money; if your sample is too small, your study will lack the precision you need.

Finally, you will see how to use your understanding of the confidence interval to evaluate reports of studies described in scientific journals or newspapers. As you will see, the reports you read about studies are often incomplete or misleading.

Confidence Intervals

We illustrate the use of the confidence interval with a very simple problem. Suppose we want to know the mean weight of all males in the United States who are between 30 and 35 years of age. Let's assume there are N = 10,000,000 males in this population. To determine their mean weight, we select a simple random sample of 100 males in this age group. The mean of our sample is 180 pounds, and the standard deviation of the sample is 20 pounds. Past experience shows that the population distribution for the weights of 30 to 35-year-old males is not quite normal but has a unimodal shape with a slight positive skew. We may therefore assume, based on Rule III, that the sampling distribution for our sample of size 100 will be normally distributed. We will call this example the Weight Study.

Point Estimates

In Chapter 2 we said the purpose of many studies was to estimate some unknown population parameter. In the Weight Study we want to know the mean weight of the 10,000,000 men between 30 and 35 years of age. When we complete a study, we take the information obtained and use it to generate an estimate of the desired population parameter. The most common way to generate an estimate of a population parameter is to use the sample statistic as the estimate. For example, in the Weight Study we might use the sample mean, mean = 180, as our estimate of the population mean (MEAN).

We call an estimate, such as using the sample mean as an estimate of the population mean, a **point estimate,** because we are specifying the exact value of the population parameter. In the Weight Study, the estimate of 180 pounds is a point estimate because it is a single, specific value. Using point estimates, such as using the sample mean as an estimate of the population mean, seems like a natural thing to do. Point estimates are simple to generate and very precise. In fact, you might think they are the only way we could generate an estimate. But in truth, nobody really believes a point estimate, and it easy to see how we can improve upon it.

Interval Estimates

Given the sample mean of 180 pounds for n = 100 cases in the Weight Study, would you be willing to bet $100 that the mean weight for the population of all 10,000,000 men is exactly 180 pounds? That is, do you really believe the point estimate is perfect and that the mean weight of the population might not be 180.01 or 179.99 pounds?

You would probably not bet on the point estimate of 180 pounds, because you know that any study based on a small sample of the population, no matter how well conducted, has some margin of error. It wouldn't surprise you, given the results of the Weight Study, to find that the mean weight of all 10,000,000 males is 180.01 or 179.99 pounds. A point estimate does not take into account the margin for error, which is why you wouldn't place a bet on it.

We can generate an estimate that takes the margin of error into account if we allow ourselves to use a *range* of values as our estimate. For example, if we believe the margin of error in the Weight Study is about two pounds, we might use a ±2 pound range around the sample mean. Then our estimate for 10,000,000 males would be 180 − 2 = 178 to 180 + 2 = 182 pounds. An estimate that covers a range of values, such 178 to 182 pounds, is called an **interval estimate.**

Describing an Interval Estimate

There are two different ways to describe an interval estimate. First, we can use the range of values that the estimate covers—for example, 178 to 182 pounds. The second way is by using an equation. The general equation for an interval estimate of the MEAN is

$$\text{ESTIMATE(MEAN)} = \text{mean} \pm \text{INT.}$$

We read this equation, "Our estimate for the population mean is the sample mean plus or minus an interval." In the weight example, the sample mean was 180 pounds and we used a value of INT. = 2, so the equation would be

$$\text{ESTIMATE (MEAN WEIGHT ALL MALES)} = 180 \pm 2$$

Both ways of describing the interval say the same thing, but sometimes it is convenient to use one type of description and sometimes the other. The equation is particularly helpful for analytic purposes, because it focuses our attention on the two different elements in the estimate.

The first part of the interval estimate is the sample mean, which is fixed and anchors the interval. We have no control over the sample mean, since it comes from our sample. The second part of the interval estimate is INT., which determines the spread of the interval. Notice in the equation that we add INT. to the sample mean and subtract INT. from the sample mean. Therefore, the range of values covered by the interval estimate is actually twice the size of INT. In the weight example INT. = 2, but the range estimate is from 178 to 182. So, the range of the estimate is 182 – 178 = 4, which is twice the size of INT. The end points of the interval (178 and 182 in the example) are defined as being within the interval.

Size, Confidence, and Usefulness

We control INT. That is, we can make it whatever size we want. We can make INT. small, or we can make it large. The larger we make INT., the greater the range of values it will cover, and the more likely it is to be right. If we set INT. in the Weight Study at 2, we have a better chance of being right than if we set INT. at 1 (179 to 181 pounds). We would have an even better chance of being right if we set INT. at 4 (176 to 184 pounds). The larger we make INT., the more likely we are to be right, and the more we can trust the estimate. The larger the interval, the better it would be to bet on it (if you were a betting person). Let's call the degree to which we can trust an estimate our **confidence** in it. The larger we make INT., the greater is our confidence in the estimate.

If our confidence were the only criterion for evaluating an interval estimate, we would use the widest possible range of values and then we would surely be right. If we said the average weight of males 30 to 35 years of age was somewhere in the interval from 0 to 1000 pounds, we would almost certainly to be right. In fact, if we were willing to accept the 0-to-1000 pound interval, we could make this estimate without even conducting the study. The trouble is, a large interval isn't very useful. It doesn't help us very much to have such wide range of values for our estimate. What we need is as *precise* (or narrow) an estimate as possible.

So, there are two conflicting factors to consider when making an interval estimate: our confidence in it and its usefulness. In general, the larger we make INT, the greater our confidence in the estimate but the less useful it becomes. What we need is some way of deciding the appropriate size of INT. (which determines the range of the values). We need an interval that will give us as much confidence in the estimate as we need, yet keep the range as small as possible.

To set the right size for INT., we must first determine how much confidence we want to have in the estimate. Then, we must have a way of calculating the value of INT. that will give us the level of confidence we need.

The Three Standard Confidence Intervals

We can set INT. to give any degree of confidence we want. Past experience has led us to use confidence intervals of three different sizes. Most often we use an interval that gives us 95% confidence; we call it the 95% confidence interval. A 95% confidence interval offers 19 out of 20 chances of being right. We will explain shortly what we mean by this.

The 95% confidence interval works very well for most purposes, but sometimes we need even greater certainty. Suppose, for example, you conduct a market research study to determine the number of people who might buy a new type of CD player. Suppose the results of the study will determine whether a new plant costing $200,000,000 will be built. If your estimate of the market size is too large, the plant may be built and the company may lose a great deal of money. If your estimate of the market size is too small, the plant may not be built and the company may lose a very good business opportunity. In a case where such an important decision depends on the study, we often use a 99% confidence interval. As its name implies, the 99% confidence interval offers 99 out of 100 chances of being right.

On some occasions we do not require even 95% confidence in our estimate. For example, suppose you are conducting a market research study whose purpose is to drop from a list of ten new product ideas those with very little appeal. A second study will be conducted later to determine just how much appeal the more attractive product ideas have. In this case, you might use a 90% confidence interval. As its name suggests, the 90% confidence interval gives 9 out of 10 chances of being right.

It is easy to calculate the 90%, 95%, 99%, or any confidence interval you want to use. It is a little harder to understand exactly how it works. So we start by showing how to calculate the three standard confidence intervals and then show how they work.

The Equation for a Confidence Interval

To establish a confidence interval for the MEAN when the sampling distribution is a normal distribution (or very close to it), we break the value of INT. in the interval estimate equation into two parts, which we call Z and *ST.ERR.*

INT. = Z * *ST.ERR.*

ST.ERR. is the standard error of the sampling distribution. You know from Rule II that it is equal to ST.DEV./$\sqrt{n}$ when you select a simple random sample with replacement (or without replacement when n/N is less than .05.). The standard error is fixed by the sample size and the standard deviation of the population distribution. Once the sample is selected, you can calculate the standard error but you cannot control its size.

Z is a constant[1] that we can control. We can make Z any size we want. When we set the value of Z, we set the value of INT. and thus set the range of values covered by the estimate. This, in turn, sets the confidence we can have in the estimate. How do we know what value to give Z? Part of the beauty of probability theory is that other people have worked on this problem already. They have figured out what the value of Z is for different levels of confidence. They have recorded what they learned in a table of the normal curve. Using such a table, we can say that to create the three standard confidence intervals, you set the value of Z as follows:

For a 90% confidence interval, set Z = 1.65.

For a 95% confidence interval, set Z = 1.96 (some researchers use 2.00 because it is close and easier to remember).

For a 99% confidence interval, set Z = 2.57.

The following example shows how to calculate a 90%, 95%, or 99% confidence interval in the Weight Study. The general equation for a confidence interval is

confidence interval = mean ± (Z * *ST.ERR.*)

Suppose the sample in the Weight Study has a mean of 180 pounds. Suppose we calculate the standard error of the mean for the Weight Study, using Rule II, and find it is 2 pounds. By substituting the mean and standard error for the Weight Study in the general equation for a confidence interval, we have a general equation for the confidence interval in the Weight Study:

confidence interval (Weight Study) = 180 ± (Z * 2)

---

[1]A **constant** is a number that does not change.

We now set the exact confidence interval by inserting the value of Z we want to use in the equation for the Weight Study. We can get the three standard confidence intervals by using Z = 1.65, Z = 1.96, Z = 2.57.

90% confidence for Weight Study = 180 ± 1.65 * 2 = (176.70 to 183.30)

95% confidence for Weight Study = 180 ± 1.96 * 2 = (176.08 to 183.92)

99% confidence for Weight Study = 180 ± 2.57 * 2 = (174.86 to 185.14)

Notice that we get the confidence intervals by simply substituting the appropriate value of Z in the confidence interval equation. As you would expect, the greater the confidence, the wider the range of values it covers.

To move beyond these three commonly used confidence levels and get any level of confidence you want, you must be able to read a table of the normal curve. Most elementary texts in statistics will contain such a table and explain how to read it.

Now we define exactly what we mean by a confidence interval.

The Meaning of Confidence and Confidence Intervals

To define the term *confidence,* we must first define what we mean by an interval estimate being right or wrong. If we make an interval estimate and the population parameter falls within the interval, the estimate is right. If the population parameter falls outside the estimate, the estimate is wrong. In the Weight Study, if our interval estimate is 178 to 182 pounds and the mean weight of 10,000,000 males is 178.5 pounds, the estimate is right, because it falls within the range of our estimate. If the mean weight of all 10,000,000 men is 182.1 pounds, the estimate is wrong, because it does not fall within the range of values covered by the estimate. The end points of the interval are considered to be within the range of values covered by the interval. Therefore, if the mean weight of the 10,000,000 males is 182 pounds or 178 pounds, the estimate is right.

As you learned in Chapter 2, you will never know if the interval estimate is right or wrong when you make it, and in fact you may *never* know whether it is right or wrong. To know if the estimate is right or wrong, you must know the population mean. If you already knew the population mean, you would never need to make an estimate. You can, however, measure the probability or the chances that the estimate is right.

Suppose we were to select 1,000,000 simple random samples of size 100, with replacement, from the population of 10,000,000 males and calculate the mean of each sample. Suppose we then put an interval of ±2 around each of these 1,000,000 sample means. This would give us 1,000,000 interval estimates. Some of these interval estimates would be right and some would be wrong. As you will see shortly, our three rules can tell us *how many* of the 1,000,000 interval estimates would be right and how many would be wrong. Suppose 950,000 of the interval estimates would be right and only 50,000 wrong. That means that 19 out of 20 of the 10,000,000 estimates would be right.

Now we select one more sample, and this is the one that counts! After we select the 1,000,001st sample, we calculate its mean. Suppose the mean of the 1,000,001st sample is 180 pounds. Next we put an interval of ±2 around this sample mean and generate an estimate of 178 to 182 pounds.

Is our estimate of 178 to 182 pounds from sample 1,000,001 right or wrong? We don't know for sure, because we don't know the population mean. We do, however, know the results of the previous 1,000,000 samples, and the results we obtained from the first 1,000,000 samples tell us our 178 to 182 estimate is a good bet. In fact, our work with the first 1,000,000 samples tells us that the probability of being right is .95. Our estimate of 178 to 182 has 19 out of 20 chances of being right, so we say that we have 95% confidence in the estimate.

The amazing thing is that the three rules can tell us how many of the 1,000,000 samples would generate estimates that are right and how many of the samples would give wrong estimates, *even if we do not select the samples or know the population mean.* So when we use the term *confidence,* we mean the proportion of the samples we could select that would generate correct estimates. The rules will measure that proportion for us.

It would be helpful if you did Exercises 1 through 3 at the end of this chapter before proceeding further.

The next two sections show how the three rules reveal the proportion of samples that would give right or wrong estimates. Understanding why they work is helpful but not essential for using confidence intervals, so you may skip the next two sections if you wish and go on to Confidence Intervals for Population Means.

Measuring the Confidence: The Right Range

Now let's see how the three rules can measure the proportion of right estimates, when we do not select the 1,000,000 samples and do not know the population mean. First, we will establish the right range—that is, the range of sample means that would give us right estimates. Then, we'll see how many of the sample means fall in the right range. We start by defining the right range.

Suppose we use a value of INT. = 2, meaning we add and subtract 2 to whatever mean we get in our sample. In the Weight Study, the sample mean was 180 pounds. Suppose the population mean is 178 pounds. Then the estimate is right, because the end points in the interval are considered to be inside the interval.

Suppose, however, that our sample mean was larger than 180. Then our interval estimate would have been wrong, as it would not include the population mean of 178 pounds. For example, suppose the sample mean was 180.1 pounds. Then the interval estimate would be 180.1 ± 2, or 178.1 to 182.1 pounds, and it would not include the population mean of 178. This tells us that any sample mean that is greater than 180 pounds (or the population mean plus INT.) will give us an estimate that is wrong.

Suppose the sample mean was 176 pounds. That would give us an interval of 174 to 178, which is right because the population mean is 178 pounds and the end point of the interval is considered to be inside the interval. Now suppose the sample mean was less than 176 pounds. Then the interval estimate of mean ± 2 would be wrong. For example, if the sample mean were 175.9 pounds, then the interval estimate would be 173.9 to 177.9, which does not contain the population mean of 178 pounds. This tells us that any sample mean that is less than 178 pounds (or the MEAN − INT.) will give us a wrong estimate.

Now consider a sample mean within the range of 176 to 180 pounds. Any sample mean that falls within this range will give an estimate that is right. Take any sample mean within the range of 176 to 182 pounds, put the interval ±2 around it, and you will see that it contains the population mean of 178. For example, take a sample mean of 179, which falls within the range 178 to 182. The interval for a mean of 179 would be 177 to 181, which contains the population mean of 178 pounds.

In this example you have seen that you can divide all the sample means you might get in the Weight Study into three types: sample means smaller than 176, sample means greater than 180, and sample means between 176 and 180. Only the sample means in the last group, 176 to 180 pounds, will yield interval estimates of ±2 that are right. We will call the range of sample means that give the correct interval estimate the right range, and all other sample means the wrong range. In our example, the right range was 176 to 180 and the wrong range was less than 176 or greater than 180. The formula for the right range is

right range for sample mean = MEAN ± INT.

The equation says that the right range is equal to the population mean plus or minus the value of INT. that we use in the interval estimate. For example, suppose the population mean in the Weight Study was 174 pounds and the interval we used was ±4 pounds. Then the right range for the sample mean would be 174 − 4 = 170 to 174 + 4 = 178 pounds.

To evaluate the confidence in an interval estimate, we must know how many samples would have means in the right range and how many samples would have means in the wrong range. Once we know the number of samples with means in the right range, we can know how much confidence to have in the estimate.

Measuring Confidence: Determining the Number of Sample Means in the Right Range

Now we'll use the three rules to measure the number of samples with means in the right and wrong ranges, using the Weight Study. If you were to select 1,000,000 simple random samples of size 100 from the 10,000,000 males and calculate the mean weight for each sample, then the 1,000,000 sample means would be a sampling distribution. From Rule I you know that the mean of a sampling distribution is equal to the population mean from which the samples were selected. So the mean of the 1,000,000 sample means would be equal to the mean weight of the 10,000,000 males. We know this is true, by using Rule I, even if we don't actually select the 1,000,000 samples and even if we don't know the population mean.

To illustrate, assume we decide to set up an interval estimate with INT. = 3.3 pounds. Then we know the right range for the sample means would be the population mean ± 3.3 pounds. From Rule I we know the mean of the 1,000,000 samples (expected value) is equal to the population mean, so the right range for the sample mean would be the mean of the 1,000,000 samples (expected value) plus or minus 3.3 pounds (the value of INT.).

By applying Rule III, we know that the sampling distribution of the 1,000,000 sample means is normally distributed. So we have discovered that the number of samples in the right range would be the number of samples that falls under a normal curve from 3.3 below to 3.3 above the mean. We know this from Rules I and III and the equation for the right range, even if we do not select the 1,000,000 samples.

The 1,000,000 sample means are a sampling distribution. Thus, we can use Rule II to determine the standard deviation of the 1,000,000 sample means. Suppose the standard deviation (the standard error) of the 1,000,000 sample means was 2 pounds. Since the interval equals 3.3, which is equal to Z * ST.ERR., and the ST.ERR. according to Rule II was 2 pounds, we have:

INT. = Z * ST.ERR.

3.3 = Z * 2

Z = 3.3/2 = 1.65

We know, or could find from a table of the normal curve, that 90% of the area under the normal curve falls between the limits of $Z = \pm 1.65$, which tells us that 90% of the 1,000,000 samples would fall in the right range. From this we know that we can have 90% confidence in the estimate 180 ± 3.3 pounds, and we have learned it by applying Rules I, II, and III.

Is our estimate right? We don't know for sure but we know we have nine out of ten chances of being right. In the rest of this chapter you'll see how to actually use the confidence interval.

Confidence Intervals for Population Means

Needing to Know the Population Mean: The Agency Study

The goal of many studies is to determine the mean of some population distribution. In the field of marketing, for example, most companies know their own sales but do not know the total sales of all the products like theirs in the market. Knowing the total sales can tell them their market share, or how well they are doing relative to their competition. It can also tell them whether changes in their sales level are due to a fundamental increase or decrease in the market or to a change in their own or their competitors' marketing programs. To measure the total sales (both their own and those of competitors), many companies conduct market research studies in which they interview samples of consumers or industrial customers. From these market surveys the companies project average sales per customer, which then makes it possible for them to estimate the total size of the market (average sales per customer × population size = total sales). A confidence interval is an ideal tool for projecting the average sales in such marketing studies to the total market for the product.

In Chapter 1 we discussed the problem of a small social work agency that wanted to learn what had happened to the 3000 cases handled in the past ten years. The agency might want to know the average number of referrals these cases had to other agencies or the average number of court appearances for their clients. It might be too expensive to track all 3000 cases, but the agency might be able to track a simple random sample of 100 cases. Suppose they did track a simple random sample of former cases. They could use a confidence interval to project the average number of referrals or court appearances they found in the sample of 100 cases to the total population of 3000 cases.

How might the agency actually use the sample data to generate a confidence interval for the mean number of referrals to other agencies for the 3000 clients? We call this example the Agency Study. Let's assume we are the research team conducting the Agency Study.

Generating a Confidence Interval for a Mean

Based on the theory described earlier in this chapter, we use the following seven steps to generate a confidence interval:

1. Select a simple random sample.
2. Calculate the sample mean, the sample standard deviation, and the sample skew index.
3. Set the level of confidence to be used.
4. Determine, using Rule III, whether the sampling distribution has a normal shape.
5. Determine the value of Z required for the confidence level selected in step 3.
6. Use Rule II to calculate the standard error of the sampling distribution.
7. Calculate the confidence interval using values of the sample mean, Z, and the standard error (steps 2, 5, and 6) and the general formula for a confidence interval:

ESTIMATE(MEAN) = mean ± (Z * ST.ERR.)

Let's take these steps one at a time. Five of the steps are very straightforward applications of the theory.

1. *Select a simple random sample.* We begin by selecting a simple random sample of 100 cases from the agency's list of 3000 cases. The sample will be selected without replacement, because sampling without replacement has a smaller random error. We may have a real problem tracking the cases to get the required information, but let's assume we are able to do it. We have now satisfied the first step by selecting a simple random sample.

2. *Calculate the mean, standard deviation, and skew index for the sample.* Once we have selected our sample, we calculate the sample mean, standard deviation, and skew index.[2] Let's suppose our calculations tell us that mean = 4.50, st.dev. = 2.25, skew = 1.50.

3. *Set the desired confidence level.* The next step is to set the level of confidence for our estimate. We could use the default 95% confidence interval, but no important decisions are to be based on the study, so we might consider using the 90% confidence interval. Let's assume that we decide to use the 90% confidence interval.

4. *Make sure the sampling distribution is normal.* Now we must see if the sampling distribution of the mean forms a normal curve. This raises a new problem. In our past work we knew what the population distribution looked like and we could calculate its skew index. But in an actual study such as the Agency Study we do not know for sure what the population distribution looks like or what its skew measure is. We will have to depend on the general experience of the social workers in the agency and the data in the sample to judge this.

On the basis of past experience, the social workers in the agency might tell us that agency referrals are common for this population. That might lead us to expect to find a mean of about three or four referrals, with a few cases that have seven or more. From these conversations, we might expect the population distribution of referrals for the 3000 cases to be unimodal, with a moderate positive skew. It takes a great deal of experience in designing samples to make these preliminary estimates. But it can be done, based on information like

[2]See Chapter 3 to review how to calculate the mean and standard deviation; see Chapter 5 to review how to calculate the skew.

that provided by the social workers, after you have done it a number of times.

The sample data would confirm these expectations. We might find a sample mean of 4.5 referrals, a little higher than expected but fairly close to expectations, and a sample distribution with a moderate positive skew index of 1.5. Since the sample data and past experience generally agree, we will assume the skew index of the population is close to that of the sample. If the population skew index were about 1.5, then according to Rule III a sample size of $1.5^2 * 25 = 56.25$ or more would be large enough for the sampling distribution to be normal. (The number of referrals in the sample might have varied from zero to ten, so there are more than the five categories necessary for using Rule III.) Since our sample size of 100 is greater than the required number $n' = 56.25$, we have reason to believe the sampling distribution will be very close to a normal curve.[3]

5. *Get the value of Z.* In the fifth step we set the Z value required for the 90% confidence interval as $Z = 1.65$.

6. *Calculate the standard error.* Next we calculate the standard error according to Rule II:

$$ST.ERR. = ST.DEV./\sqrt{n}$$

We know that our sample size is n = 100, but we don't know the value of the population standard deviation (ST.DEV.) Once again we must depend on our sample data. In step 4 we found that the sample distribution seemed to give a reasonable picture of the population distribution, so we will assume that the population standard deviation (ST.DEV.) is very much like the sample standard deviation (st.dev.). The larger the sample size, the more reasonable this assumption is. In step 2 we found that st.dev. = 2.25, so our estimate of the standard error is:

$$ST.ERR. = st.dev./\sqrt{n} = 2.25/\sqrt{100} = 2.25/10 = .225$$

---

[3]If the sampling distribution is not a normal distribution, there are other statistical procedures that you can use for generating estimates. These procedures are described in more advanced statistics textbooks, particularly those that specialize in the theory of sampling and statistical inference.

Notice that we selected our sample without replacement but used the formula for sampling with replacement. We did this because $n/N = 100/3000 = .03$, which is less than .05. (If we had used the fpc to adjust for sampling with replacement, the standard error would be reduced to $.02 * 225 = .221$, which would not meaningfully change the confidence interval we will generate.)

7. *Calculate the confidence interval.* Since we know mean = 4.50, Z = 1.65, and *ST.ERR.* = .225, we can now calculate the 90% confidence interval:

ESTIMATE(MEAN) = $4.50 \pm (1.65 * .225)$

This provides an estimate of 4.24 to 4.76 referrals. Since the staff of the agency thought the mean would be between three and four referrals, they have learned that their former clients needed about 20% more assistance from other agencies than they expected.

It would be helpful to work on Exercise 4 before reading the next section.

Confidence Intervals for Population Proportions

Needing to Know a Proportion or Percentage

The purpose of many studies is to estimate a proportion or percentage. For example, Mrs. Martin wanted to know the proportion (or percentage) of blood donors who were infected with hepatitis B. In Chapter 1, the manufacturer of disks wanted to know the proportion of 50,000 disks that were defective. The midwife wanted to know the proportion of home births with midwives present that required emergency hospital visits. The social agency in the previous example might want to know the proportion of its former clients who were gainfully employed.

In this section you will learn how to generate a confidence interval for a proportion. You can get a confidence interval for a **percentage** by calculating the confidence interval for a proportion and then multiplying it by 100. For example, suppose the confidence interval for the number of home births requiring a hospital visit was .10 to .15. The same confidence interval for percentages would be 10% to 15% of home births.

Defining Some Terms

We begin by defining the following terms:

PROP. = the proportion of a population. For example, if 2000 of the 3000 former clients of the social agency are now employed, then PROP. = 2000/3000 = .67.

NOPROP. = 1.00 – PROP. = the proportion of the population that are not in the PROP. category. For example, if 2000 of the 3000 former clients of the agency are employed, then PROP. = .67 and NOPROP. = 1.00 – .67 = .33 (the proportion of all former clients who are not employed).

prop. = the proportion of a sample. For example, if 60 out of 100 members of a simple random sample of the agency's former clients are employed, then prop. = .60.

noprop. = 1.00 – prop. = the proportion of the sample that is not in the prop. category. For example, if .60 of the sample of 100 former clients are employed, then noprop. = 1.00 – .60 = .40 (the proportion of the sample who are not employed).

Modifying the Seven Steps in Generating a Confidence Interval for a Proportion

We can use the approach described in the previous section for generating confidence intervals for proportions or percentages, with the following two modifications:

1. There is a shortcut formula for calculating the standard deviation of a proportion (or percentage).

2. Rule III for determining the required sample size for a normal distribution is different.

The shortcut formula for computing the standard deviation of a proportion is:

$$\text{ST.DEV.(PROP.)} = \sqrt{(\text{PROP. * NOPROP.})}$$

$$\text{st.dev.(prop.)} = \sqrt{(\text{prop. * noprop.})}$$

In the agency example, PROP. = .67 and prop. = .60. Thus their standard deviations using the shortcut formula would be:

$$\text{ST.DEV.(PROP.)} \quad = \sqrt{(\text{PROP.} * \text{NOPROP.})} \quad = \sqrt{(.67 * .33)} = .47$$

$$\text{st.dev.(prop.)} \quad = \sqrt{(\text{prop.} * \text{noprop.})} \quad = \sqrt{(.60 * .40)} = .49$$

The second modification required for calculating the confidence interval of a proportion involves Rule III. We cannot use the skew index to help us decide if the sampling distribution is normal when we are estimating proportions.

For PROP. close to .50, a sample size of 30 or more will give a sampling distribution that is close to normal. As PROP. moves away from .50, becoming either larger or smaller, larger sample sizes are required for a normal sampling distribution. When PROP. = .3 or .7, then sample sizes of 80 are required to obtain a normal sampling distribution.[4]

Calculating the Confidence Interval for the Proportion Unemployed

Now let's see how to calculate a confidence interval for a proportion, using the Agency Study described above. You will remember that we selected a simple random sample of 100 of the 3000 former clients of the agency. Suppose we asked all members of the sample if they were currently employed. We would like to generate a confidence interval for the proportion of the total population who might have answered yes to this question. We would go through the same seven steps as we used for the confidence interval of the mean, with the two modifications just described.

1. Select a simple random sample of 100 cases without replacement.

2. Calculate the proportion who were employed. Let's say that 70 out of 100 sample members were employed. This gives prop. = .70 and noprop. = 1.00 − .70 = .30. We can calculate the standard deviation of prop. = .70 using the shortcut formula:

   $$\text{st.dev.(prop.)} = \sqrt{(.7 * .3)} = \sqrt{.21} = .46$$

   We would not calculate the skew index, because we do not use it in applying Rule III for a proportion.

3. We will set the confidence level at 90%, as we did when calculating the mean referrals in the previous section.

[4]A more detailed table of the sample sizes required for a normal sampling distribution for a proportion will be found in *Sampling Techniques,* 3rd edition, by William G. Cochran (New York: John Wiley and Sons, 1977), page 58.

4. Our experience has indicated that the sample gives reasonable estimates of the population, so we can assume that PROP. will be similar to prop. So PROP. will be around the .70 value we observed for prop. For PROP. = .7, we know that a sample size of 80 or more should give an approximately normal sampling distribution. The agency sample size of n = 100 therefore should give an approximately normal sampling distribution for the proportion of employed former clients (PROP. = .70).

5. The value of Z for the 90% confidence interval with a normal sampling distribution is 1.65.

6. Once again we will assume the sample is reasonable, so we can use the standard deviation of the sample (calculated in step 2) to represent the standard deviation of the population. Given this assumption, we can calculate the standard error using Rule II:

$$ST.ERR. = ST.DEV./ \sqrt{n} = st.dev./ \sqrt{n} = .46/ \sqrt{100} = .046$$

7. We now calculate the required confidence interval as follows:

$$ESTIMATE(MEAN) = prop. \pm (Z * ST.ERR.) = .7 \pm (1.65 * .046)$$

The required confidence interval tells us we can have 90% confidence in reporting the proportion employed as being between .62 and .78. If we wanted to report our results in percentages, we would multiply both the upper and lower limit by 100, which would give us a 62% to 78% current employment rate for the 3000 former clients.

It would be helpful to work on Exercises 5 and 6 at the end of this chapter before continuing with the next section.

Finding the Right Sample Size

Precision, Cost, and the Right Sample Size

Research is a process that moves through time. At each point in time we make certain decisions and conduct our study based on those decisions. So far in this chapter we have assumed we were at the point where the sample had already been selected and we were generating estimates from data that had already been collected. Thus the sample size was given, and the confidence interval was determined solely by the confidence level we chose, which fixed the value of Z.

At an earlier point in the research process, before we collect the data, the sample size is not fixed. We can choose the sample size we want to use. This choice of sample size is very important. Here you will learn how the confidence interval can help to determine the right sample size.

Two conflicting factors influence our decisions about the sample size: the precision required and the cost. In general, the larger the sample size, the smaller the random error in sampling and the greater the precision achieved in the study. However, the greater the sample size, the higher the cost in time, money, and effort. In selecting the right sample size, we have to achieve a balance between our need for precision and cost.

If you select a sample that is too small, your confidence interval will be too large. If you select too large a sample, you will waste your time, money, and effort. So you have to know the right sample size—that is, the sample size that gives you enough precision for your purposes, but no more.

Determining the Right Sample Size

The following five steps are used to determine the right sample size:

1. Specify the specific objective of the study.
2. Set the confidence level and INT.
3. Get the value of Z.
4. Estimate the population standard deviation.
5. Calculate the right sample size.

We'll illustrate how to determine the right sample size using the Agency Study described above. Assume now that we are in the planning stage of the Agency Study and we want to determine the right sample size.

1. *Specify the objective of the study.* The first step in determining the sample design in general and the sample size in particular is to set a specific objective in terms of the most important parameters to be estimated. In the case of the Agency Study, there were many things the agency wanted to know about its former clients. These included the mean number of other agency referrals, the proportion of clients who had court appearances, and the proportion of clients who were employed.

If we can select one of these objectives as the criterion for designing the sample, it is relatively easy to determine the right sample size. If we cannot select a single objective for the study, it may require a very complex process to determine the right sample size. We may find that the right sample size for one objective—for example, the mean number of referrals—is not the right sample size for a second objective—for example, the proportion employed. We would then have to work out some compromise that might not be perfect for any single objective but would be the best compromise among the multiple requirements of the different objectives.

Let's assume the agency decides that the most important objective is to measure the proportion of former clients who are currently employed. We can now select the sample size with this objective in mind. This procedure sets the degree of precision desired for the one parameter that we select as the objective of the study, but it gives us no control over the precision of the other parameters that we might measure in the study.

2. *Set the confidence and INT.* Next we must determine how much confidence we want for our confidence intervals and how large an interval we can tolerate in the completed study. We might decide to use the 95% default level of confidence. However, because no major decisions will be affected by the results of the study, we can probably use a 90% confidence interval. So let's decide to use a 90% confidence interval when we generate our confidence interval for the proportion employed.

Next we must specify how large we want our confidence interval to be. Do we want the confidence interval to be ±.01, ±.02, ±.03, or what? This is not an easy decision. But suppose we say that we could tolerate an interval of ±.05. So we set INT. = .05.

3. *Get the value of Z.* Once we have determined the confidence we want to have in our estimate, we can set the value of Z. For the 90% confidence interval we have decided to use, the value of Z is 1.65.

4. *Estimate the population standard deviation.* Next we make a preliminary estimate of the population standard deviation. Since we are estimating a percentage, the standard deviation will depend on the value of PROP., the proportion currently employed in the population. Once we fix the value of PROP., we can calculate NOPROP. =

1.00 – PROP. We can then calculate the value of the standard deviation using the shortcut formula:

ST.DEV.(PROP.) = $\sqrt{\text{PROP. * NOPROP.}}$

Once again, we do not know the value of PROP. and we have not collected the data from the sample. So we can do one of two things. We can use our past experience and that of the social workers in the agency to get a preliminary estimate of PROP., or we can take the worst possible case, which is always PROP. = .50. (When we set PROP. at .50, it will give the largest standard error, which in turn will force us to select the largest possible sample size.) This will ensure we have sufficient precision, though it may generate a larger sample size than necessary.

Suppose past experience leads us to believe that PROP. = .6. A .6 will give sample sizes very close to but a little smaller than PROP. = .5. We could use past experience or take the worst case, which is PROP. = .5, or make an estimate halfway in between. Suppose we decide to take the worst case and risk selecting a few cases too many in order to be sure we have the required level of precision.

We get our estimate of the standard deviation by putting PROP. = .5 into the shortcut formula for the standard deviation of a proportion. (If PROP. = .5, then NOPROP. = 1.00 – .5 = .5.)

ST.DEV. = $\sqrt{\text{PROP. * NOPROP.}}$ = $\sqrt{(.5 * .5)}$ = .50

5. *Calculate the standard error.* By doing a little algebra, we can now calculate the right sample size. The formula for INT. is

INT. = $Z * ST.ERR.$ = $(Z * ST.DEV.) / \sqrt{n}$

From working with this equation you can see that

$\sqrt{n}$ = Z * ST.DEV. / INT.

To get an equation that tells us the required sample size, we square both sides of this equation, which gives us

n = (Z * ST.DEV. / INT.)^2

In the earlier steps we set the values of Z = 1.65 (for 90% confidence), ST.DEV. = .50, and INT. = .05. By inserting these values in the equation, we can calculate the required sample size:

n = (1.65 * .50 / .05)^2 = 272

This exercise shows that a sample size of about 272 cases would be required if we want to estimate the proportion of currently employed former clients, with a 90% confidence interval, assuming the proportion is around .50.

Note that the sample size of 272 cases will be large enough for the sampling distribution of the proportion to have a normal distribution. As mentioned earlier, a sample size of 30 is sufficient for a normal sampling distribution when PROP. is around .50. This is an important consideration, as we need a normal sampling distribution to generate a confidence interval using the procedure described above.

Also note that we will really have a little more precision than we specified because we will select our sample without replacement, which will reduce the standard error by .05 (fpc = .95). So the actual value of INT. will be .0475, not .05. We could factor the fpc into our calculations of the required sample size, but it would greatly complicate the mathematics involved.

From the equation for the right sample size, you can see that three factors determine the right sample size:

- the required degree of confidence. The greater the confidence required, the larger the value of Z, and the larger the sample size will have to be.

- the specified size of INT. The larger the value of INT. that is acceptable, the smaller the sample size can be.

- the standard deviation of the population. The larger the standard deviation, the larger the sample size will have to be.

It would be helpful to do Exercise 7 before continuing.

Reading Research Reports

You will see confidence intervals many times, both in the mass media and in technical publications. For example, newspapers, magazines, television, and radio news often report the results of opinion polls. Often they report a "margin of error" in connection with their poll results. You may read, for example, that 60% of the public supports some policy and that the margin of error for this 60% is 3%. The 3% "margin of error" is a confidence interval.

In Chapter 1 we mentioned health professionals who must keep up with a constant stream of new discoveries reported in technical journals and at conferences they attend. Many of the new developments health officials hear about will be reported in terms of confidence intervals. You will find that no matter what profession you may be in, you will have the same experience as health professionals. You will see a steady stream of new developments in your field reported in terms of confidence intervals.

Your understanding of confidence intervals will help you to evaluate the reports you read in both the mass media and technical journals. You will see that these reports can easily be misunderstood and are sometimes misleading. In this section, we discuss some features to look for when you see a confidence interval reported in either the mass media or technical sources.

From this chapter you can see that the report of a confidence interval is meaningless unless it is accompanied by the level of confidence that goes with it. A 3% error could be generated that gives you 99% confidence or only 50% confidence. If you read that a poll has a 3% error, you must also be told what level of confidence goes with that 3% error. You should disregard any confidence interval that is given without a report of the level.

You should also realize that confidence intervals such as those reported in the press or in technical publications do not cover all types of errors, but only the random errors due to sampling. The confidence interval does not cover errors in measurement or systematic errors caused by sampling.

In Chapter 2 we said that we would not be concerned with measurement errors in this text so we could concentrate on sampling errors. Unfortunately, measurement errors do occur in all types of studies. They occur in surveys because the questions may not be clear or the respondents may not wish to reveal their true feelings. In fact, you can usually assume the measurement error in a survey will be greater than the random error from sampling, once the sample size is larger than 300 or 400 cases.

Systematic error from sampling also occurs for a variety of reasons. The list we use for selecting our sample may not cover all the cases in the population, which can lead to a systematic sampling error. Often, we are unable to collect information for each case we select for our random sample. We may not be able to reach some of the respondents we have randomly selected, and other respondents may refuse to talk. Systematic errors are not included in the potential for error that is measured by a confidence interval, and they are often much larger.

From this discussion, you can see it is important not to interpret the report of a confidence interval as the total error in a study, which we described in Chapter 3 as the root mean error. It is very useful to know how large the random error of sampling might be, which the confidence interval may tell us, but you must assume that there are some measurement and systematic errors of sampling as well. Technical reports often include sections describing the methods used in the study, which you should read very carefully. These technical descriptions, often in an appendix, will help you evaluate how large the measurement and systematic errors of sampling might be. Without access to a technical report about the methods used, you simply do not know how large the measurement and systematic errors of sampling might be. In general, you can safely assume they will be as large or larger than the random error of sampling that is reported in the confidence interval. So you must be very cautious in using the results of any study if you do not fully understand how it was conducted. In the next chapter we cover some of the points you should look for in a technical report with regard to how the sample was selected.

One final point, which is very distressing, is that researchers frequently report a confidence interval when it is not appropriate. A precondition for generating a confidence interval is that the sample is a probability sample. In the examples we used, simple random samples were selected. More complex types of probability samples could have been selected, though the formulas for the standard error would be different. But strictly speaking, you cannot generate a confidence interval for nonprobability samples. In Chapter 1 we outlined a number of nonprobability samples that are often used in studies, including pseudo census, self-selected, typical case, convenience, and quota samples. Many studies are conducted using one of these nonprobability samples and the results then reported in the form of a confidence interval. There is no basis for calculating a confidence interval for nonprobability samples. Therefore, you should discount any level of confidence that is attached to an interval estimate generated from a nonprobability sample.

EXERCISES

The answers to these exercises are in Appendix C.

1. A. Suppose the sample mean in the Weight Study was 170 pounds and we used an interval estimate of 160 to 180

pounds for the population mean. Would our estimate be right or wrong if the population mean was 165 pounds? 190 pounds? 160 pounds? 155 pounds? 180 pounds?

B. What is the value of INT. in the interval estimate given in Exercise 1A?

C. Suppose the sample mean in the Weight Study was 175 and we wanted to generate an interval estimate using INT. = 5 pounds. Write the equation for the interval estimate. What range of values would be in the interval estimate?

2. A. What are the three most frequently used confidence intervals, and what values of Z go with these confidence intervals?

B. Suppose the sample mean for the Weight Study was 180 pounds and the standard error for the sample mean was 5 pounds. Give the confidence intervals for estimating the population mean if we set the value of Z at 1.96, 2.57, and 1.65. Express the confidence interval for each value of Z using the equation for the confidence interval and as a range of values.

3. Suppose the sample mean in the Weight Study was 170 pounds and the standard deviation of the population was 10 pounds. Give the following confidence intervals:

A. The 90% confidence interval if n = 100

B. The 95% confidence interval if n = 100

C. The 90% confidence interval if n = 400

4. Suppose we select a simple random sample of males for the Weight Study and have reason to believe that the sampling distribution of the mean is normally distributed. We also believe we can use the standard deviation of the sample as an estimate of the standard deviation of the population. Under the assumption just stated, give the 95% confidence intervals for the population mean for the following sets of results:

A. n = 144, mean = 175, st.dev. = 24

B. n = 81, mean = 175, st.dev. = 24

C. n = 144, mean = 175, st.dev. = 12

5. A. There is a class with 50 students. Of these, 10 are male. What proportion of the students are male? What percentage of the students are female?

B. What are the values of PROP. and NOPROP. for the proportion of males in the class described in 5A?

    C. What is the standard deviation for the proportion of males in the class described in 5A?

Check your answers to Exercise 5 before doing Exercise 6.

6. Suppose we select a simple random sample of former clients for the Agency Study and have reason to believe the sampling distribution of the proportion of employed is normally distributed. We also believe we can use the standard deviation of the sample as an estimate of the standard deviation of the population. Under these assumptions, give the 95% confidence intervals for the population proportion of employed for the following sets of results:

    A. $n = 100$, prop. $= .50$

    B. $n = 100$, prop. $= .40$

    C. $n = 400$, prop. $= .70$

7. Determine the right sample size for the Weight Study under the following sets of conditions:

    A. The 95% confidence interval should have INT. $= 2$ when ST.DEV. $= 10$.

    B. The 99% confidence interval should have INT. $= 2$ when ST.DEV. $= 10$.

    C. The 95% confidence interval should have INT. $= 4$ when ST.DEV. $= 10$.

    D. The 95% confidence interval should have INT. $= 2$ when ST.DEV. $= 20$.

7 Making It Work

So far in this book you have explored the kinds of problems statistical sampling can help you solve and you have gained an understanding of the ideas underlying sampling theory. This chapter moves in a different direction, away from theory and into practicalities. If you are going to unleash the power of the theoretical ideas you have encountered, you need to put them into practice. To do this, you need to learn how to translate the theory into research decisions and operations. If you want to be able to study a sample of cases instead of an entire population (and thus save a great deal of time, money, and energy), you need to be able to draw a sample in such a way that the theoretical ideas you have learned can be applied to it. The goal of this chapter is to introduce you to some relevant research practicalities that determine whether you can put sampling principles to work.

Sample Design and Implementation

Selecting a sample is a process in which you make a series of decisions. Each decision is then followed by the activities required to carry them out. For example, in Chapter 4 we selected simple random samples of size four, without replacement, from a 12-store population. The decisions we made in the process of selecting the sample included the decision to use the 12 stores as a population, the decision to select a simple random sample without replacement, and the decision to select a sample of size four. The activities we engaged in to implement these decisions included creating the deck of 12 cards, one for each store in the population, shuffling the deck of 12 cards, and selecting the top four cards as the sample.

In the remainder of this chapter we use the term **sample design** to refer to the total set of decisions used in selecting a sample. We use the phrase *implementing the sample design* to describe all the activities engaged in to execute the decisions.

Implementing a probability sample design involves three steps:

1. Setting up a **frame** that lists or organizes the population so that the sample may be randomly selected from it

2. Random selection, in which sample members are randomly selected from that frame

3. Data collection, in which the data required for the study are actually collected from the sample members selected in the previous step

Some sample designs are easy to implement and you can complete all three steps by yourself in an hour or two. Other sample designs are very difficult to implement and require many months of work by a team of statisticians and interviewers.

The three steps in implementing a sample design are interdependent. Each step affects the steps that follow it and in turn is influenced by them. The three stages thus fit together into an overall pattern. If the three steps fit together smoothly, implementing the sample design will go well and the potential for error will be minimized. If the three steps are not properly coordinated, the implementation will go badly and the potential for error may be huge.

We start with an example to illustrate the three steps. Then we cover the first two steps in greater detail.

Implementing the Sample Design for the Agency Study

The Sample Design

In the last chapter we described the Agency Study. Its purpose was to learn what happened to the former clients of a social agency. The sample design called for selecting a simple random sample of 100 former clients, without replacement, from all the former clients of the agency. How might we implement this sample design?

Setting Up the Frame

First we must create a frame of the population that lists every member in it. We do this by printing a list of all former clients. But first we must find out who the former clients are. Most agencies keep files of former clients, in a "closed cases" file. Thus we could create our frame by going through the agency's file of closed cases and listing the name and file number of each former client. The file numbers would help us locate the sample members after the sample is selected.

After we have listed every name in the closed cases file, we will assign a number to each line in the list, starting with 1 and going up to the last former client listed. Assuming that we find 3000 former clients, our assigned numbers will run from 1 to 3000. The number assigned each former client on the list is the same as the number of the line on which he or she is listed. These line numbers will be used to randomly select the sample.

Exhibit 7.1 illustrates the list we might set up as our frame for selecting this sample. The series of dots after line 4 indicates that we are skipping the listing of all the population members between Ester Brown (0004) and Hamit Abdul (2999).

Exhibit 7.1

The Frame for the Agency Study

Line number	Name of client	File number
0001	Peter Parker	4423
0002	Leslie Orawa	4425
0003	Kin Pan	4427
0004	Ester Brown	4467
.	.	.
.	.	.
.	.	.
2999	Hamit Abdul	8821
3000	Sean Mara	8823

Notice that the line numbers in Exhibit 7.1 are four-digit numbers: 0001, 0002, and so on. The numbers 1 and 0001 mean the same thing, but using the four-digit number 0001 facilitates the random selection, which we do next.

Randomly Selecting the Sample From the Frame

To randomly select a simple random sample of 100 former clients, without replacement, from the frame illustrated in Exhibit 7.1, we use a table of random numbers. You will find a table of random numbers in most elementary statistics books and in many research methods texts. Exhibit 7.2 is the table of random numbers we will

Exhibit 7.2

Table of Random Numbers

Row number					Column number					
	1–4	5–8	9–12	13–16	17–20	21–24	25–28	29–32	33–36	37–40
01	4010	5760	2318	4575	6224	1399	7161	6904	6414	1792
02	5957	3127	4896	2861	6714	0677	0636	7399	3420	7827
03	2116	1573	0632	5594	1150	9321	2288	7635	6465	2378
04	6759	1735	1063	2849	6489	8751	1189	5490	7827	0818
05	9196	4586	4792	1260	6523	1040	9930	7971	2092	8076
06	5687	2599	8687	7479	9436	0700	8264	1736	6533	0861
07	6313	7006	7045	1184	5183	6473	8021	5717	7223	7774
08	5886	3034	8901	2385	8256	9014	1210	8898	2828	1461
09	7400	8927	3789	2030	1993	1095	7274	3555	2440	4361
10	1901	9658	4784	9365	3381	7815	8950	7231	3033	9175
11	7524	9350	5140	2135	8663	8578	5394	8523	7079	4224
12	2514	9333	1594	6791	9689	5988	2382	0477	0652	9478
13	1760	3373	8785	1910	1166	9949	0763	4814	1280	7974
14	2628	8792	6215	0216	9192	1250	6229	7757	5179	2703
15	0603	7909	2948	0803	4836	2153	4725	8701	4885	0841
16	2598	1946	5217	7612	8893	3776	8070	2895	0573	3275
17	3036	6778	9780	3483	7158	4305	4941	3189	1890	3453
18	3665	6001	1596	0486	3371	9474	2386	8908	8234	6319
19	7784	4135	5297	7004	9047	9890	8998	0940	1752	5533
20	6721	7080	2209	3867	0794	6977	3721	1511	2765	4075

use for selecting the Agency Study sample. Simply think of each random number in the table as though it were the number on the top card in a well-shuffled deck. In effect, the table does the same thing that we did in Chapter 4 when we randomly selected the four-store sample by shuffling the 12-store deck.

If you look at the left side of Exhibit 7.2, you will see that each row is numbered, starting with 01 for the first row and ending with number 20 for the last row. You will also see that the numbers on each row, after the line number, are grouped into sets of four numbers. The first set of four numbers on row 01 is 4010. The second set of numbers on row 01 is 5760. The numbers on each row beyond the row numbers are the random numbers we will use for selecting the sample. Across the top of the table are column numbers. At the top of the first four columns of random numbers (above the first random number 4010 on row 01) are the numbers 1–4, which indicates columns 1–4.

The row and column numbers are used for reference purposes when we want to talk about the random numbers in the table. For example, if we specify the four-digit random number in row 04, columns 37–40, we are talking about the random number 0818, found in the fourth row (04) under the columns numbered 37–40. (The random number 0818 is the number 818.)

A simple random sample of 100 former clients can be selected from the list (frame) illustrated in Exhibit 7.1 by using the Table of Random Numbers (Exhibit 7.2) as follows:

- Close your eyes and point with a finger at any place on the table of random numbers. Suppose you point to the number on row 04 in columns 9–12. The random number at this location is 1063. This random number is our start point.

- The random number at the start point selects the first sample member—in this case, the former client listed on line number 1063 in the frame.

- We record the selection of 1063 in two ways. First, we put a check mark on line 1063 of the frame to indicate that the former client on that line has been selected. Second, we mark a blank piece of paper to tally the number of sample members we have selected.

- We move down columns 9–12 to the next four-digit random number, which is 4792. The number 4792 is larger than the last number on the frame (3000) so we skip it.

- We continue down columns 9–12 in this way, skipping four-digit random numbers larger than 3000 and recording the selections for random numbers smaller than (or equal to) 3000. When we finish with row 20 at the bottom of columns 9–12, our tally sheet will show that we have selected five sample members, and check marks on the frame will show that we have selected the former clients on lines 1063, 1594, 2948, 1596, and 2209 of the frame.

- Next we go up to the top (row 01) of the next four columns (13–16) and proceed down those columns in the same manner, skipping random numbers that are too large and selecting the respondents that correspond to random numbers under 3000. When we reach the bottom of columns 13–16, we go on to the top of columns 17–20, and so on. If necessary, we return to the beginning of the table and work down columns 1–4, 5–8, and 9–12 until we return to our starting point. We will stop whenever our tally sheet shows us we have selected 100 sample members.

- If we have not yet selected the 100 sample members when we return to the start point, we begin again with a new start point. However, this time we select a four-digit random number made up of four rows under one column. For example, the four-digit random number in column 7, rows 05–08, is the random number 8903. We then move from left to right across rows 05–08, then across rows 09–12, and so on, until we have selected the required 100 sample members.

- If we select a random number of 3000 or less and find that line number is already checked in our frame (meaning that population member has already been selected), we skip that random number just as we would a random number larger than 3000. However, if we were selecting a sample with replacement, we would make a second check mark on the frame for that line number and add a tally mark for another sample selection.

If you actually completed the procedure just described, you would have selected a simple random sample of size 100, without replacement, from the frame that listed the 3000 former clients. You would know exactly which clients were selected by the check marks on the frame for the selected sample members.

Collecting Data From the Sample

The third step in the selection procedure is getting the required information for each case. The first step would be to go to the file folders for the 100 former clients who were selected. The file numbers listed on the frame facilitate locating those files. We might take an index card for each sample member and write on it the last known telephone number and address in the file for that client.

After making the index cards, we could begin contacting and interviewing the former clients in the sample. We might make a telephone call and, if necessary, a home visit to interview the 100 sample members. We would find that, despite our best efforts, we could not reach all 100 randomly selected sample members. (The inability to reach randomly selected members of a sample is called a **nonresponse.**) We would summarize our data collection stage by saying we had a **response rate** of 65% (that is, we interviewed 65 out of 100 randomly selected sample members), or a **nonresponse rate** of 35% (100% minus the response rate). The higher the nonresponse (or missing data) rate, the larger the potential error that might affect the results of our study in the data collection stage.

The Three Steps in the Agency Study

Notice in the Agency Study example how we took all three steps in implementing the sample design: (1) listing the population from the closed cases file (the frame); (2) using a table of random numbers to randomly select sample members from the frame (random selection); and (3) using the closed cases file to get the telephone numbers and addresses of the selected sample members, then using a telephone call or home visit to obtain the required data (data collection).

Notice, too, how the three steps were connected. The line numbers on the frame tied the random selection to the frame, and the file numbers tied the frame and random selection to the data collection. All three steps fit together smoothly into a single overall process. Now we examine the first step more closely.

Frames

Different Types of Frames

The first step in implementing a sample design for a probability sample is to set up a frame. Sometimes this is very easy to do. In the Agency Study we constructed the frame by means of a simple clerical operation conducted in an office. This might take a day or two. Sometimes, however, it is very difficult to set up a frame. For example, in the Weight Study, where we wanted to select a probability sample of 10,000,000 males, it would be very difficult to set up the frame, although it could be done.

A frame can take many different forms. Some of the more common types of frames are printed lists (as in the Agency Study), computer lists (a list in the form of computer files), physical lists (like the twelve cards used for randomly selecting Mr. Martin's sample), implicit lists (described later), staged lists (described later), and multiple lists (described later). The particular type of frame used depends partly on the sample design and partly on the available resources. In the Agency Study the frame was created in response to the demands of the sample design, which specified a population of former clients, with the resources available, which consisted of the closed cases file.

The function of the frame is the same regardless of the form it takes, namely to put the population into a usable form, from which a sample may be randomly selected. The frame must also identify each randomly selected member of the sample so that data may be collected from that member. Consider some of the more common types of frames.

Printed Lists

One of the most common frames is a printed list like the one we used in the Agency Study. Printed lists of many populations are readily available. Businesses, social agencies, voluntary, professional, and charitable organizations have lists of their employees, clients, customers, or subscribers. There are companies that specialize in developing and selling lists of business establishments, registered voters, doctors, lawyers, and so forth. When a printed list is available, it can be used as a frame, and the sample can be randomly selected from it using a table of random numbers, as in the Agency Study.

Computer Lists

Many organizations have their lists in computer files. For example, most magazines have their subscriber list in computer files, and many schools have their list of students in computer files. Organizations are increasingly creating and saving their databases in the form of computers files rather than paper files. A computer list can be used as a frame in the same way we used the printed list in the Agency Study. There is one advantage in using a computer file for the frame. Computer programs exist (or can easily be written) that enable the computer to make the random selection. If the population size and/or the sample size is large, the use of computers to randomly select the sample from a computer file frame can save considerable time and effort.

Physical Lists

In Chapter 4, for Mr. Martin's study, we selected samples of size four from a deck of 12 cards. The deck of 12 cards was the frame. In a sense the deck of cards can be considered a list, except each entry in the list is a physical object (a card) rather than a printed line. There are many situations in which a physical list can be used as a frame. For example, suppose Mrs. Martin has the name of each blood donor in her district on an index card. Then we do not have to set up a list as in Exhibit 7.1, but can use the set of index cards as the frame. All we need to do is number the cards 1, 2, and so on. If the social agency had numbered its closed files from 1 to 3000, then we could have used the file folders themselves as our frame.

Physical frames are often helpful when we sample material objects, particularly those that come off a production line. Consider, for example, the problem of the software manufacturer discussed in Chapter 1, who wanted to measure the proportion of defective disks in a set of 50,000 disks. Suppose the sample plan calls for testing a simple random sample of 200 disks. Suppose the disks are stacked in 50 piles of 1000 each. The piles of disks can serve as a frame (physical list) if we mentally assign numbers to the disks. The top disk in the first pile is given the number 00001, the one underneath it is assigned the number 00002, and so on, to the last disk in the first pile, which is given the number 01000. We start the second pile with the next number, 01001, and assign numbers to each disk in the second pile in the same way, and so on through all 50 piles. We do not have to write the assigned numbers on the disks. All we must do is order the piles so we are sure which is the first pile, which is the second, and so on.

Next we select 200 different random numbers from 00001 to 50000, using a table of random numbers. We then locate the disks that have been mentally assigned the numbers that correspond to the random numbers selected. If the first random number were 04010, we would go to the fifth pile (the fifth pile starts with 04001 and goes to 05000) and count down to the tenth disk. The tenth disk in the fifth pile would be the sample member selected by the random number 04010.

Physical frames are also useful when we sample a process that takes place in time. For example, suppose we want to sample customers who made purchases in a supermarket during a week in June. We can specify a frame that consists of customers as they leave the checkout counters. We might select a sample of every tenth customer. In this example, the customers themselves provide a physical frame, which is ordered by the sequence in which they left the checkout counters.

Implicit Lists

Sometimes the frame we use is not actually spelled out but is completely implicit. For example, many telephone surveys use telephone numbers that are randomly generated from a table of random numbers or by a computer. The table of random numbers may give us the telephone number 664-2317. We would then call that number. We never actually generated the frame, but it was implicit. The frame for that exchange consisted of the numbers 664-0000, 664-0001, and so on up to 664-9999.

Staged Frames

Many of the most difficult problems in implementing a sample design occur when we have a list that puts clusters of population members together in a single listing. For example, suppose we are conducting a public opinion poll of all adults in a certain city, using a telephone survey. We would start the sample selection procedure by selecting a sample of telephone numbers from a frame such as a telephone directory (printed list) or by means of randomly generated telephone numbers (the implicit list of random telephone numbers). The population for the study consists of individuals but the frame lists telephone numbers that reach households containing one or more individuals within them.

When a frame, such as the telephone directory, lists groups of population members under a single entry, we must generate the frame in two or more stages. In the first stage, we randomly select the groups of population members (for example, the telephone numbers). In the second stage, we create a frame of all the population members in each of the groups of population members selected from the first-stage frame. We then randomly select the sample members from the frames (for example, the lists of individuals living in the telephone households) set up at the second stage.

In the telephone survey, we could set up the second-stage frames by asking the person who answers the randomly selected telephone number to list all members of that household who are 18 years or older; we could then randomly select one of them as the respondent for our survey. Another procedure is to interview the person whose birthday is closest to the time of the interview. In this case, the respondent creates an implicit frame of household members ordered by date of birth. The closest-birthday procedure assumes that birthdays are randomly distributed throughout the year. This is not strictly speaking correct, but experience with the procedure indicates that it works very well.

Exit polls reported on election night frequently use a frame that is set up in stages. The first frame might be a list of voting locations. A random sample of voting locations is selected from a list of all locations. Interviewers are then sent to the selected voting places, where they randomly sample the voters as they leave the voting place. In this two-stage example, the first stage is the printed list of voting places, and the second stage is a physical list (like the one used in the supermarket example) that is generated for each of the voting places selected in the first stage.

Multiple Frames

Sometimes a frame will consist of two or more first-stage lists. For example, suppose we wanted to sample the population of individuals in a certain city who are interested in classical music. There may be no single list to use for this frame. We may, however, be able to construct several different lists of classical music lovers. For example, we could generate a list of persons listed in the classified telephone directory as music teachers. We might get a second list of persons who have written to a classical radio program requesting that they play a particular piece of music. We might also be able to get a list of customers who have made purchases from a store that sells classical CDs and sheet music. Finally, we might be able to get a list of members of the local philharmonic society. The frame for this study would be constructed from the four lists.

Problems in Creating a Frame

While we can always create a frame, the frame we create usually does not perfectly reproduce the population specified in the sample design. Frames that are not exact replicas of the population can introduce systematic error into the results of a study. The greater the difference between the frame and the specified population, the greater is the potential for error in the results of the study.

Four general problems make it difficult for us to create a perfect frame:

1. Missing cases—that is, members of the population are left out of the frame.

2. Excess cases—that is, listings are included in the frame that are not part of the population.

3. Duplicate listings—that is, one or more members of the population are listed more than once.

4. Cluster listings—that is, the listing in the frame leads to a cluster of one or more members of the population.

By understanding these four problems you can take steps to minimize their effects, even though you may not be able to eliminate them completely.

Coverage (Missing Cases)

Most frames will leave out some members of a population. In the Agency Study, for example, some cases may have been closed recently and their files may still be in the open cases file. The folders for some cases may have gotten lost over time. A social worker may have forgotten to return a closed case folder, or closed case folders may have been misfiled in the open cases file.

In conducting a public opinion poll by telephone, our frame will exclude all persons who do not live in telephone households. Such persons include the homeless, persons living in temporary quarters such as hotels or boarding houses, poorer people who cannot afford a telephone, persons living in newly erected buildings without phone service, and people who live in remote places. If we use the telephone book as the frame, that will eliminate persons who live in telephone households with unlisted numbers. The unlisted households include both persons who have recently moved and whose new number is not yet in the book and persons who wish to keep their telephone numbers private.

We use the term **coverage** when we talk about the inclusion of population members in a frame. We measure coverage by the proportion of the population that is included in the frame. In the telephone poll example, we might expect to find that 5% of the public live in nontelephone households and another 30% live in unlisted households. We would say that the telephone directory frame covers 100% − 5% − 30% = 65% of the population, or that 100% − 65% = 35% of the population is not covered.

Measuring the Potential Error From
Not Covering the Entire Population

If a member of the population is not included in the frame, then that member of the population has no chance of being selected for the sample. We call such cases **zero probability cases**. If the zero probability cases differ from the nonzero probability cases in the characteristics we want to study, then a systematic error will be introduced into the results of our study. You can see how this would follow from Rule I, which says that the expected value of the sampling distribution for a simple random sample is equal to the mean of the population from which it is selected.

Suppose we select a simple random sample from a frame that contains 65% of the population we want to study. Then the expected value of the sampling distribution will be equal to the mean of the 65% of the population that is in the frame—that is, the mean of that part of the population that is covered. If the 65% of population members who are in the frame are different from the 35% who are not in the frame, the mean of the 65% who are covered will be different from the mean of the total population. So, the expected value will also be different from the mean of the total population. If the expected value is different from the mean of the total population, bias will occur when we use the mean of our sample to estimate the mean of the population.

From this discussion you can see that the size of the bias will depend upon the proportion of the population that has zero probability of being selected, and the degree to which the zero probability cases differ from the cases that do have a chance of being selected. The greater the proportion of zero cases and the greater the difference, the larger the bias will be.

Increasing Coverage

The first step toward maximizing coverage is to assume that the initial frame is incomplete. No matter how good the frame may be, assume it is faulty. Next try to identify the possible ways population members might be excluded from the frame. You may find that the frame is complete, but you will often find that some categories of population members are excluded.

Once you have identified a source of excluded cases, you may also find a way of adding them to the frame. For example, in the Agency Study we identified several reasons why the frame of closed cases might be incomplete. To deal with these potential problems in coverage, before we create our frame we would suggest that the agency have all social workers report recently closed cases, verify that all closed cases have been transferred to the closed cases file, check the open cases file to ensure that no closed cases are there, and circulate the list obtained from the closed cases file so that agency staff can add any closed cases they know of that are not on the list.

Even if no former clients were added to the list as a result of these four steps, they would be worth the time and effort they took as a form of insurance. (Remember that insurance is one payment we usually hope never to collect on.) The chances are, however, that we will add a number of population members to the list, thus increasing our coverage. Even after we make every effort to get a complete list, there may still be some former clients who are not on the list, but we assume the number would be small, so the potential bias due to missing cases would also be small.

Excess Cases

Many frames include cases that are not part of the population. In our public opinion poll, the telephone directory frame may include commercial and nonworking telephone numbers, which do not provide access to members of the public. We may also find nonmembers of the population who are reached at the residential numbers we select. Such nonmembers of the population might include persons under 18 or residents of other cities who are visiting a household in the city whose population we are studying. Some of the telephone numbers in the directory may be for households outside the city. Such excess cases in the frame can cause logistical problems and increase the cost of the study, but if properly identified they need not introduce a serious bias into the results. If we use random-digit telephone numbers, we will encounter even more cases of excess population members because a very large proportion of the numbers we call will be nonworking numbers.

To deal with excess cases in the frame, we have to do four things:

1. Adjust the sample size to take the excess cases into account.
2. Screen for excess cases in the data collection stage.
3. Keep a careful record of how many excess cases occur.
4. Adjust the population size for excess cases in projecting population totals.

If 10% of the frame are excess cases and we select a simple random sample of 100 cases from the frame, we will probably get a sample of 90 population members and 10 excess cases. If we want a sample size of 100 population members, we must adjust for the reduction in sample size due to excess cases when we select from the frame. The adjustment is made by dividing the desired sample size by the proportion of the frame which we believe are not excess cases. In our example, if we want a sample of 100 population members when 10% of the list are excess cases, we should select $100/.9 = 111$ cases from the frame. The 111 cases randomly selected from the frame will probably give us 100 population members and 11 excess cases.

Nonmembers of the population who are selected from the frame must be identified. In the telephone directory example, we may be able to identify some nonresidential numbers by examining the telephone listing itself. We would assume a listing such as Third Precinct Police Station or Waldbaum's Supermarket is nonresidential and mark these as excess cases without making any telephone calls. Nonworking numbers would be identified by calling the number. Random-digit telephone samples have even more excess cases in the frame as they include many more nonworking numbers than the directory and may make it impossible to exclude commercial numbers.

It is also possible in telephone surveys to reach someone at a residential number who is not part of the population. For example, we may reach someone who is under 18 or who does not live in the city. For this reason, it is necessary to screen all respondents to qualify them as population members.

In every study, a good general rule to follow is to check (screen) every sample member to make sure that he or she is a member of the population, before collecting data from that sample member. Note how the screening ties the data collection stage back to the first step of creating the frame. The presence of excess cases in the frame will not affect our estimates of means or proportions, as long as we screen them out in the data collection stage. It can, however, bias our projection of totals. When we project totals, we frequently use the number of cases in the frame as the population size. We then project totals by multiplying the population size by the sample mean or proportion. For example, suppose we have a frame that lists 20,000 cases. Suppose we select a simple random sample of n cases from the frame and find that 90% of the cases we select from the frame are in the population, while 10% are excess. Suppose we interview the 90% of the sample that is in the frame and find that 20% of them are college graduates. If we want to project total college graduates in the population from the results of our sample, we would use the adjusted frame size of $.9 * 20,000 = 18,000$ for projecting totals and our projected total would be .2 * 18,000 = 3600 college graduates, not .2 * 20,000 = 4000.

To make this adjustment it is necessary for us to keep a very accurate count of the number of cases we select from the frame that are population members and the number that are excess cases. It is a good idea to keep such a record even when you are not projecting totals, as it helps guide and control the data collection stage.

Duplicate Listings

Many frames contain multiple listings for some but not all population members. The duplicate listings change the probabilities of selection, which can lead to a bias in the results of a study. In effect, the duplication results in varying probabilities of selecting the sample. If the population members with a higher probability of selection are different from the population members with a lower probability of selection, a bias may be introduced into the results of the study. The size of the bias depends on the variability of the probability of selection and the degree to which the probability of selection is related to the observations made on the sample.

Three procedures deal with multiple listings. First, we can try to remove the duplication from the frames before we select the sample. Second, we can identify those members of the sample who have duplicate listings after the sample is selected, but before the data are collected, and remove those duplicates from the sample. Third, we can collect data from the duplicate cases but measure the number of times they were in the frame and use this measure of duplication to adjust our estimates.

The problem of duplicate listings is particularly important when we use a frame made up of two or more lists. The same population member may often be found on several lists. A classical music fan, in the multiple listings example described previously, may be a music teacher who has purchased CDs, has requested a song on the radio program, and belongs to a local philharmonic society. This person would therefore be on all four of the lists we are using for the frame.

Duplication in multiple lists can be reduced by comparing the lists and eliminating as many duplicate cases as possible before selecting the sample. Special computer programs exist for the task of comparing lists and removing duplicates, if each of the lists is in machine-readable form. Remember to adjust the size of each list to take into account the duplicate cases that may be dropped from it.

Duplicates can also be eliminated from multiple lists by first selecting samples from each list and then comparing the samples selected from each list against the other lists. If the lists are large and not in a computer, it may be simpler to compare the samples against the other lists, rather than comparing the total lists with each other. There are several different ways of conducting the sample-versus-list comparisons. One of the easiest is as follows:

- Before selecting the samples from each list, put the lists in order from the largest list to the smallest list.

- Each list except the last list must be put in some kind of order, such as alphabetical order by last name. This is necessary in order to check for duplication.

- Decide on a sample size for each list.

- Select a random sample of the specified size from the first list. This sample need not be compared to the other lists.

- Select a random sample of the specified size from the second list. Compare the sample members selected from the second list with the first list for duplication. Drop any sample member selected from the second list whose name is found on the first list.

- Adjust the size of the second list to take into account the cases that have been dropped because of the overlap with the first list. For example, suppose the second list has 400 names on it and you select a sample of 20 names from this list. If you drop 4 names from the sample of 20 names selected from the second list because they were on the first list, then you have dropped $4/20 =$ .20 or 20% of the sample. This means you will use 80% or .8 of the selected sample. To adjust the size of the second list for the overlap with the first list, multiply the number of entries on the second list by the proportion of cases in the sample from the second list that are not overlap cases. In this example, the adjusted size of the second list would be $.8 * 400 = 320$.

- Select a random sample of the specified size from the third list and drop any sample member selected from the third list whose name appears on the first or second list. Then adjust the size of the third list for cases dropped because of the overlap.

- Continue in the same way through all the lists that will be used for the frame.

Duplication can also be found when using a single list for a frame. For example, most households have one telephone, but many households will have two or more telephone numbers. Some families have more than one place of residence with telephone numbers. For example, families with summer homes may have telephones in both their main and summer residences. Households with two telephone numbers (in the same or multiple houses) will have twice the chance of being selected as those with one telephone number. A few households will have three telephone numbers, and they will have three times the chance of being selected as a household with one listing.

In some studies you cannot eliminate the duplication in the frame or in the sample lists before data are collected. It is, however, possible to measure the duplication in the data collection stage and use the estimated duplication to adjust the sample results. In the telephone survey, for example, we can ask each household we interview how many telephone numbers they have and use this as a measure of duplication for that sample member.[1]

Clustered Listings

Some frames do not list the population members as individuals but list clusters of population members. For example, in our discussion of staged frames, we saw that a telephone poll of the general public uses a frame of telephone numbers but more than one member of the population may be reached through each telephone number. We would encounter the same problem of clustered frames if we wished to conduct a survey of purchasing agents in companies and selected a sample of companies from a frame of business establishments. Because there may be more than one purchasing agent in a company, the frame must be considered a frame that lists clusters of population members.

In general, when we encounter a clustered listing we must use a multistage frame. In the telephone survey and purchasing agent examples just described, we would simply generate a list of all population members for each listing selected from the first-stage frame, and then randomly select one population member from each of the second-stage listings.

The second stage of selection can result in selecting sample members who have varying probabilities of being selected. For example, in the second stage a member of a two-person household has half the chance of being selected as a member of a one-person household. As a result, the sample is no longer a simple random sample, and we would have to adjust the results to take the varying probability of

---

[1]It is possible to remove any bias due to duplicate listings in the frame if you weight by the inverse of the probability of selection. The topic of weighting will not be covered in this text, but it is discussed in other texts (for example, Cochran) devoted to the subject of sampling.

selection into account. You may have noticed that this problem, caused by the varying probability of selection, is similar to the problem associated with duplication in the frame.

The design and implementation of multistage frames can be handled in many different ways, with very different cost and error implications. Deciding on the best of the many alternate ways to set up a multistage frame is very complex and requires a very detailed understanding of sampling theory. Therefore, it is usually a good idea to consult a statistician before designing a study using a clustered frame.

Summary: Frames

We have outlined a number of different ways that frames can be created and four problems that may arise when using a frame. We can summarize our discussion as follows:

- You must set up a frame as the first step in implementing a sample design.
- There will always be some way to set up a frame.
- No matter how simple and straightforward a frame may seem, always assume that it is incomplete and that it contains excess cases, duplication, and clustered listings.
- Try to identify the sources of the missing cases and take whatever steps you can to get them into the frame.
- Always try to estimate the proportion of cases that are missing.
- To deal with duplicate cases, screen each case in the sample to make sure it belongs in the population.
- Keep a careful record of the number of sample cases selected that are in or out of the population.
- Adjust the frame size for excess cases before using it to project population totals.
- Check for the possibility of duplicate listings when using more than one list for the frame. Try to remove all duplicates by comparing the lists, or screen the samples selected from the lists for duplication.
- Screen for duplication within a single list and, if necessary, measure the number of ways each sample member might be selected.
- Check the frame to see if there is a one-to-one correspondence between the items in the frame and the members of the population.

If more than one member of the population could be selected for the sample through a single entry in the frame, you must use a multistage frame.

- You may need the help of a statistician if you are going to use a multistage frame.

Random Selection

Two Ways of Selecting a Random Sample

The second step in selecting a probability sample is to randomly select a sample of the items listed in the frame. There are two different ways in which random selection can be done. First, we can put the frame in random order and then take the top n items in the frame. This was the procedure used when we selected the sample of four stores in Chapter 4. In this example, the frame was the 12-store deck. We put the frame in random order by shuffling it and then took the top four cards in the deck as the sample.

The second way of randomly selecting from a frame is to number the frame and use random numbers for the selection. This is the procedure we used in the Agency Study. There the frame was a printed list which we numbered sequentially. We then selected the sample by using a table of random numbers.

Both procedures, if properly executed, will randomly select a sample from the frame, but randomization of the frame is usually inefficient when the population is large. So for most studies you will select a probability sample by numbering the frame and using random numbers.

Random Numbers

A **random number** is a number that is generated by a process in which every possible number in some set of numbers has the same probability of being generated, and which is unrelated to any other number. Note the four parts of the definition:

- A random number is a number that is generated—that is, produced or created by a process.
- There is a set of numbers that could be produced by the process that generates the random number.

- The process is such that it gives every number in the set of possible numbers the same probability of being the specific number that is generated.

- The number that is produced by the process is unrelated to any other number.

For example, suppose you wish to generate a single random number between 1 and 10. The numbers 1, 2, 3, . . . , 10 provide the set of numbers. To actually generate the random number between 1 and 10 you can use the 12-store deck. The deck contains 12 cards. Examine the cards in the deck, and you will see each one carries an identification number, starting with 1 and going up sequentially to 12. The identification number appears just before the name of the purchasing agent. Drop the two cards with the identification numbers 11 (Timm E.) and 12 (Velt R.) from the 12-store deck. This leaves you with ten cards. Consider their identification numbers. Each number in the range for our random number appears on one and only one card. There is one card with the identification number 1, one card with the identification number 2, and so on, up to one card with the identification number 10.

Take the deck of ten cards, turn the deck face down, and give the deck a very thorough shuffle. Make sure you shuffle it so well that you are no longer sure where any of the ten cards is in the deck. Now turn the top card over and note its identification number. Suppose the identification number on the top card is 8. That number 8 on the top card can be considered a random number in the set of 1 to 10 because:

- it is a number (8) generated by a process (shuffling the ten-card deck and taking the top card).

- the process could have generated any of the numbers from 1 to 10 in the set.

- the process gave each number in the set the same chance of being the number that was generated.

- the random number 8 could not have been predicted from any number, and the number 8 does not help us predict any other number.

There are a variety of ways for generating a random number. It can be generated by shuffling a deck of cards, spinning a roulette wheel, rolling dice, or flipping a coin. A random number can be generated by any physical process that has a number of possible outcomes to which we can assign each number in the set from which the random number is selected and which gives each possible numbered outcome the same chance of being the actual outcome.

Random numbers, or the equivalent of a random number, can be generated by a computer. The computer generates a random number from a starting number, such as the time in hours, minutes, and seconds that it reads from its clock. It then subjects the starting number to a variety of mathematical functions, the outcome of which is a number that has the characteristics of a random number.

A table of random numbers is set up so that each digit in the table is a random number from 0 to 9. The random numbers in the table could be generated by a physical process or by computer. To illustrate what we mean by a random number, how a table of random numbers could be set up, and the logic underlying the use of the table, we will conduct one final experiment.

Experiment 7.1: Constructing a Table of Random Numbers

In this experiment you will use the 12-store deck and Form 7.1 to generate your own table of random numbers. Begin by removing from the deck the cards with identification numbers 11 (Timm E.) and 12 (Velt R.). This leaves a deck of ten cards, with the identification numbers 1 to 10. We will read the identification number 10 (Ralt V.) as 0 (zero), so the identification numbers go from 0 to 9.

Look at Form 7.1, found in Appendix B. Note that there are five rows, numbered 1 to 5, and ten columns, labeled 1 to 10. You will select 50 random numbers between 0 and 9, using the ten-card deck, and put one random number in each of the ten columns in each of the five rows of Form 7.1.

Take the ten-card deck. Turn it face down, give it a thorough shuffle, and then turn the top card face up. The identification number on the top card is your first random number. Write the identification number in column 1 of row 1 on Form 7.1. Remember, if the identification number on the top card is 10, you write a 0 on Form 7.1.

Turn the top card face down and give the deck another very thorough shuffle. Then turn the top card over and write its identification number in column 2 of row 1. Continue the same process of turning the top card face down, shuffling the deck, turning the top card up, and copying the identification number of the top card in Form 7.1, until you have filled in each of the 10 columns in rows 1 through 5 with random numbers. When you finish, your table of random numbers will look like Exhibit 7.3. The numbers in your Form 7.1 will be different from the numbers in Exhibit 7.3, but both tables were generated in the same way.

Exhibit 7.3

A Table of Fifty Random Numbers

	1	2	3	4	5	6	7	8	9	10
1	7	9	8	1	8	5	3	1	5	0
2	5	0	9	4	5	6	1	6	3	8
3	6	0	1	2	3	4	4	4	4	2
4	0	9	6	2	6	8	4	7	9	8
5	1	6	7	3	4	0	6	1	7	5

Analyzing the Table of Random Numbers

Now we'll analyze this table of random numbers. First, let's prove that each of the 50 digits in the table is a random number.

- Each digit in the table was produced by a process—namely, shuffling the ten-card deck and taking the top card.

- The process that produced each number in the table might have produced any single digit from 0 to 9 (the card numbered 10 is 0). Therefore, there is a set of digits (0 to 9) that might have been produced by the process that produced each of the 50 digits in the table.

- Each digit in the set 0 to 9 had the same chance of being selected for each of the 50 digits in the table.

- The specific digit that was generated in each position in the table is unrelated to any other digit in the table or any other number produced by any other process.

Each of the 50 digits in the table satisfies the four criteria for a random number; therefore, each digit is a random number in the set 0 to 9. Now consider how the table can be used to randomly select samples from frames.

Using the Table of Random Numbers to Select Samples From Frames

The table of random numbers is a very flexible tool that can be used to select many different types of probability samples from many different kinds of frames. Since each digit is a random number, we can use the table for selecting random digits within any set of numbers we want. For example, we can use the table of random numbers for generating numbers in the range 1 to 5, 134 to 6789, .001 to 3.236, or odd numbers between 1 and 1119. You can use the table to randomly select a single case from a frame numbered 1 to N, giving equal probability to each case in the frame.

Suppose you have a frame that lists 100 names (N = 100), numbered 1 to 100. Suppose you want to randomly select one name in the frame, giving each name in the frame the same chance of being selected. Close your eyes and point to any two-digit number in Exhibit 7.3 (remember, Exhibit 7.3 was set up the same way you set up your table of random numbers in Experiment 7.1). Suppose you point to the two digits in row 3, columns 3 and 4, which are a 1 and a 2. We can make the following three points about the two digits you have selected:

- The first digit you selected (1, in row 3, column 3) is a random number in the set 0 to 9, so it gives each digit in the set 0 to 9 the same chance of being the first digit selected.

- The second digit you selected (2, in row 3, column 4) is a random number in the range 0 to 9, so it gives each number in that set the same chance of being selected.

- Since both the first and second digits selected are random numbers, they are unrelated to each other.

Now read the two digits you have selected as a single two-digit number, 12. Given the previous points about the two digits that go into making up the number 12, we know the following:

- The number was produced by a process that includes the way in which numbers were put in the table and the way in which you selected the two numbers from the table.

- The process that produced the number 12 could have produced any number in the set 1 to 100 (read the two-digit number 00 as 100).

- Each number in the set 1 to 100 had the same chance of being the random number produced by the process.

- The two-digit number, 12, produced by the process is unrelated to any other number.

Notice that we could have read the two-digit number we selected in either direction, forward as 12 or backward as 21. We could also have selected two single digits in different parts of the table, rather than two digits next to each other in the table. The only rule we must follow is to specify in advance what we are going to do. That is, we must start out with the decision to pick two digits next to each other or two separate digits, or to read the numbers forward or backward. We must not select the numbers and then decide what we are going to do after we select them.

A table of random numbers can also be used to select a sample from a subset of the frame, which helps us select stratified samples. For example, from the frame of 100 names you could select a case from the first 20 names, giving equal probability to each of the first 20 names listed by using the procedure just described. The only difference is that you would skip the random number you select if it is not in the range 1 to 20. You would keep selecting until you get a number that is in the range 1 to 20.

The table can also be used to select cases from the frame in such a way as to give some cases a greater chance of being selected than others. We will illustrate this by the procedure called selecting with probability proportionate to size. This type of selection can be very useful when selecting from a multistage frame if you know the number of population members in each first-stage frame.

For example, suppose we want to select one city out of four cities, A, B, C, and D, which have populations of 10,000, 20,000, 30,000, and 40,000, respectively. We might want to select the city in such a way as to give each member of the population the same chance of being selected. If we select the city giving each city the same chance of being selected, we will be giving a greater chance to the people living in A, which has the smallest population, and the least chance to the people in D, with the largest population. To give each population member the same chance, we must select the cities giving one chance to A, two chances to B, three chances to C, and four chances to D. We can make the selection of the city with the probabilities 1 to 2 to 3 to 4 as follows:

- Select a single digit at random from the table of random numbers.
- If the selected digit is 1, select City A.

- If the selected digit is 2 or 3, select City B. (This gives B two chances to one chance for A.)
- If the selected number is 4, 5, or 6, select City C. (This gives C three chances to one for A.)
- If the selected number is 7, 8, 9 or 0 select City D. (This gives D four chances to one for A.)

We can randomly select two or more numbers from the table in such a way that the second or later number will or will not be affected by the earlier numbers that are selected. This makes it possible to use the table for selecting samples with or without replacement. To select each number so that it is not affected by any other number we select, we simply use a rule for selecting each number that makes the selection independent of any other number we select. If we want to select the cases so that the later case is affected by the earlier cases selected, we specify a rule for the later cases that makes them conditional on the earlier cases selected. For example, to select without replacement, the rule is to not use a number from the table that has already been selected.

Seemingly Random Selection

There is little potential error introduced into the results of a study if you randomly select your sample using a shuffled deck or a table of random numbers, as described in this chapter, or if you use computer-generated random numbers. These procedures, when properly applied, are known to generate random or very nearly random samples.

Another approach that is sometimes used for selecting a sample seems as though it randomly selects a sample, but actually it may not. The basis for this is the belief that a selection procedure is random if one cannot think of a reason why the procedure is not random. This negative approach to random selection is very dangerous and should be avoided.

For example, many people believe they can generate the equivalent of a random sample by haphazardly checking off cases for the sample as they go through a list. They may or may not be able to generate a random sample that way, but there is a good chance there will be something of a pattern in their selection. Such a pattern would result in sampling errors that cannot be measured. Strictly speaking, you could not use the three rules you have learned in this book, which apply only to random samples. The pattern in haphazard selection might lead to a systematic error that would increase the total error in the estimate.

The same problem would occur if you tried to generate a set of random numbers by just putting down the numbers that come into your head. The numbers you would generate this way might, and probably would, be characterized by some kind of pattern and would not yield the type of sampling distribution that is generated by random selection. The pattern might also introduce bias into the result.

The same type of seemingly random selection can occur when we are presented with a list that we believe is in random order because we can't think of a reason why it shouldn't be. We might be tempted to take the first n cases, as we did with the shuffled deck. The list may or may not be in random order, however. You cannot be sure, therefore, that you can use the three rules for measuring the potential error if you use such a seemingly randomly selected sample.

Therefore, if you want to use the powerful theory of probability to help you when you report the results of your study, avoid the use of seemingly random selection and always use a proven procedure for randomly selecting the sample from a frame.

Summary: Random Selection

To summarize the points made in this section, remember that random selection from a frame is the second step in selecting a probability sample. There are two different ways to randomly select cases from a frame:

- Put the frame in random order.
- Use random numbers.

The use of random numbers is more efficient when the frame and/or sample size is large. Random numbers or near random numbers can be generated by a physical process that meets the requirements for generating random numbers or by computer computation. A table of random numbers or computer-generated random numbers can be used for randomly selecting any type of probability sample.

Avoid using seemingly random procedures for selecting the sample from the frame. Seemingly random procedures include haphazardly checking off cases in the frame, generating numbers out of your head, or assuming that a list is randomly ordered because you cannot think of a reason why it should not be.

A Final Note

This brings us to the end of our journey. In this book you have learned how to think about and measure the potential for error in the results of research based on samples. You have seen how the theory works and how it can help you to plan and conduct a better study. The theory you have learned can help you in your own research as well as in evaluating the results of other studies. Although there is much more you can learn about sampling, research design, and the conduct of research, you have already taken an important step toward advancing your knowledge of sampling by conducting the experiments in this book.

REFERENCE

Cochran, William G. *Sampling Techniques.* 3rd ed. New York: Wiley, 1977.

Appendix A
Installing, Loading, Using, and Exiting the ISEE Program

The ISEE program allows you to see what happens when you select probability samples and to conduct experiments selecting different types of samples. Here we describe how to:

- Install the program on a hard disk.
- Load and exit the program.
- Use the Setup option to customize the program for your PC.
- Activate the modules required for the exercises in this book.
- Load population data for conducting experiments.
- Use the options and commands within each module.
- Print results.

We use the term ENTER for the key that is sometimes referred to as the ENTER key and sometimes referred to as the RETURN key.

If the PC you are using is running Windows, go to DOS by double-clicking on the MS-DOS icon before installing and using the ISEE program.

Installing, Running, and Exiting the ISEE Program

Copying the ISEE Diskette

Before doing anything else, you should make a copy of the ISEE disk that accompanies this book and store it in a safe place. See your DOS manual for the procedure to use in copying a floppy disk.

Installing the Program on a Hard Disk

Parts of the ISEE program can be run from a floppy disk, but the preferred way to run it is from a hard disk. To do this, you need to install it first. Begin by turning on the PC and getting to the DOS prompt (usually C:\). Then do the following:

1. Check to see that you have at least one megabyte of free space on the hard disk. Do this by typing **dir** at the DOS prompt. In the lower right corner you will see a number followed by "bytes free." That tells you how much space is left on the hard disk. One megabyte is one million bytes. You need at least that much.

2. Create a directory called ISEE on the hard disk by typing **MD\ISEE** and then press the ENTER key.[1]

3. To enter the ISEE directory you have created, type **CD\ISEE** and then press the ENTER key.

4. Put the copy of the 3.5-inch ISEE disk into a floppy disk drive (usually A: or B:).

5. Type the command **copy A:*.* C:\ISEE,** or **copy B:*.* C:\ISEE** if the ISEE disk is in the B: drive, and press the ENTER key.

This will copy the ISEE program files into the ISEE directory of the hard disk.

Loading the ISEE Program From a Hard Disk

To load the ISEE program from the hard disk:

1. Go to the ISEE directory on the hard disk that contains the ISEE program.

2. Type the command **ISEE** or the command **ISEE /NOMOUSE**. (The latter will disable the mouse.)

3. Press the ENTER key.

The program will load, and the MAIN MENU will be displayed in the lower left corner of the screen.

Running the ISEE Program From a Floppy Disk

If you don't have a hard disk available, you can run two of the three ISEE modules from the ISEE diskette. To run these two modules from the floppy disk, put the *copy* of the ISEE program in the A: or B: disk drive and type **A:ISEE** (or **B:ISEE**), or **A:ISEE /NOMOUSE** (**B:ISEE /NOMOUSE**) to disable a mouse.

---

[1]In this appendix, **boldface** indicates a computer command to be typed by the user.

Exiting the ISEE Program

To exit the program at any time (whether loaded from a hard disk or floppy disk):

1. Press the ALT and X keys at the same time.
2. Answer the question that appears on the screen by typing Y (for yes), and you will exit.

Installing ISEE on a Network

If you will be running ISEE on a network—for example, in a PC laboratory at a college or university—you should find out who the network administrator is for the space where you will be using the program. Take a *copy* of ISEE to the network administrator and ask him or her to install it on the network. Then the program will be available to everyone using the network.

The MAIN MENU

When you load the ISEE program by typing **ISEE**, the upper portion of the first screen you see contains the title and authors. The lower left corner contains the MAIN MENU for ISEE. The MAIN MENU offers four options:

1. SAMPLE DESIGN
2. SIMPLE SAMPLE
3. UNIVARIATE
4. SETUP

The first three options (1–3) activate the three working modules of the program, which you will use for loading and analyzing populations or conducting experiments. The first two options (SAMPLE DESIGN and SIMPLE SAMPLE) can be run from either a hard or a floppy disk, but the third option (UNIVARIATE) can be run only from a hard disk. Option 4, SETUP, is used to customize the ISEE program.

Selecting an Option in the MAIN MENU

To select one of the options in the MAIN MENU:

1. Move the cursor (the box enclosing an option in the MAIN MENU) by pressing the up or down ARROW keys, or moving

the mouse, until the cursor (box) encloses the option you want to select.

2. Press the ENTER key, or click the mouse button.

You can also select options from the MAIN MENU by typing the number of the option you wish to activate.

Returning to the MAIN MENU

You can return to the MAIN MENU when you are in any of the four options by typing the ALT and M keys at the same time, then the typing Y (for yes). In addition, you can return to the MAIN MENU from the Setup option by simply pressing the ESC key.

Exhibit A.1 illustrates how to load the ISEE program and move from one option to another. Remember, you can exit the program at any time by pressing the ALT and X keys and then typing Y (for yes).

Exhibit A.1

Loading and Moving Around the ISEE Program

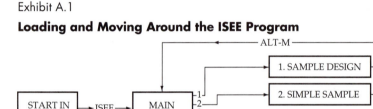

The SETUP Option

If you select option 4, SETUP, from the MAIN MENU, the Setup Menu will appear in the lower right corner of the screen and the cursor will move from the MAIN MENU window to the first item in the Setup Menu (the NO following the Music option). You can change the settings for the program, using the Setup Menu and the cursor, as follows:

1. Move the cursor, using the up and down ARROW keys or the mouse, to the setting you wish to change.

2. Press the SPACE bar until the screen displays the setting you want.

3. Move the cursor to the Update option.

4. Press the ENTER key.

The settings can be changed as many times as you want. The last change you make will stay in effect after you activate the Update option, even when you exit the program. The available settings are:

Music	YES	Will play music when the program is loaded or any of the working modules is activated.
	NO	Will not play music.
Sounds	YES	Will generate a beep within a module to call the user's attention to something on the screen.
	NO	Will not generate a beep.
Printer	EPSON	For printing results with an Epson-like dot-matrix printer.
	LASERJET	For printing results using a laser printer.
Port	LPT1	Uses Port 1 for the printer.
	LPT2	Uses Port 2 for the printer.
	LPT3	Uses Port 3 for the printer.
Numbers		Sets the format for numbers that appear on the screen.
	Fixed 0	No numbers to right of decimal point.
	Fixed 1	One digit to right of decimal point.
	Fixed 2	Two digits to right of decimal point.
	Fixed 3	Three digits to right of decimal point.
	Fixed 4	Four digits to right of decimal point.
	Generic	Maximum number of digits to right of decimal point.
	Exponent	Scientific format: X.XXXX±XX

Press the ESC key to return to the MAIN MENU.

Printing an ISEE Computer Display

You can print any ISEE computer display by pressing the ALT and P keys at the same time and then answering Y (yes) to the question. Print output of an ISEE computer display can also be obtained using the Print option in the menus for the SIMPLE SAMPLE and UNI-VARIATE modules. The ALT + P command must be made from the keyboard; it cannot be made with the mouse. The print commands in the menus can be made either from the keyboard or with a mouse.

It may take several minutes to print the display. Make sure you have selected in the SETUP menu the type of printer you are using before you try to print a screen display.

The SAMPLE DESIGN Module

This module illustrates five different ways of selecting a probability sample and also generates sampling distributions. This module can be run from either the hard disk or floppy disk. Screen displays for this module can be printed using the ALT + P command, but they cannot be saved.

When the SAMPLE DESIGN module is activated, your screen display will be divided into four sections. The lower left corner of the screen contains a SAMPLE DESIGN menu listing the options in this module. Options 1–5 illustrate five different methods of selecting a sample. Option 6 illustrates how a sampling distribution is generated.

The upper left part of the screen displays 32 boxes, representing a population from which samples will be selected. Each box has a number inside and a second number on top. Think of the number inside the box as a measure of size in cubic inches. The top number is an identification number. The boxes in the population change color as they are selected for the sample.

The upper right part of the screen explains what happens when a sample is selected. Once a sample is selected, the sample results appear here.

The lower right part of the screen explains the options in the SAMPLE DESIGN menu. Once an option is selected, this area contains some information about the options selected and lists available commands.

Options 1–5 in the SAMPLE DESIGN Menu

Proceed as follows to study any one of the five sample types (options 1–5) listed in the SAMPLE DESIGN menu:

1. Make sure the cursor box is surrounding one of the options in the SAMPLE DESIGN window. If it is not, press the ESC key.

2. Select one of options 1–5 by moving the cursor to the desired option and pressing the ENTER key.

3. Read the messages in the upper right and lower right portions of the screen.

4. Press the ENTER key to select the sample and watch the upper left part of the screen as the sample is selected. Note the pattern, if any, in the sample members that are selected.

5. After the sample is selected, read the message in the lower right.

6. Then study the results in the Sample Results window. It lists identification numbers (Box Num) of the selected population members, their sizes (Box Value), the population and sample averages, and the error (Absolute Diff.) when the sample average is used as an estimate of the population average.

You can now press the ENTER key to select another sample of the same type, or the F6 key for further information about the sample type just selected. If you press F6, the information will appear at the top of the screen and the cursor will return to the SAMPLE DESIGN menu. Or, you can return directly to the SAMPLE DESIGN menu by pressing the ESC key.

The visual displays in options 1–5 can be supplemented by sound and music if you set the Music and Sound options in the Setup (option 4 on the MAIN MENU) to YES. The Music option assigns a specific note to each box and plays that note when a box is selected for the sample. Thus, each sample selected plays its own characteristic tune.

Exploring Sampling Distributions

Option 6, Sampling Dist., of the SAMPLE DESIGN menu shows how a sampling distribution is generated. When you select this option, the screen display changes. Histograms of five population distributions with different shapes appear at the top of the screen. Right below the histograms a message describes this option. Read this message.

A list naming the five population distributions according to their shapes appears in the lower right portion of the screen. The cursor will move to the name of the first population distribution in the list.

To generate a sampling distribution, first select one of the five distributions by placing the cursor on it and pressing the ENTER key. The samples are selected from this population distribution.

After a population distribution is selected, the screen display will change. The top of the screen will show the selected population distribution on the left and a scale marked with values from 24 to 72 on the right. A histogram of the 2000 sample means will be displayed above this scale. The sample means come from simple random samples of size n = 8, selected with replacement from the population distribution displayed on the left side of the screen. The population mean is marked by an arrow under the scale.

The program selects the first sample of size eight from the population distribution portrayed on the left side of the screen and marks the mean of this sample with a box above the scale. The eight sample values will be displayed in the lower right part of the screen. Note: you must complete this procedure before you can exit the program or return to the MAIN MENU or SAMPLE DESIGN menu.

Press any key, and the program will select a second sample (n = 8) from the population distribution and mark it with a second box placed over the scale. The eight sample values for the second sample will be displayed in the lower right part of the screen. Press any key. The program will now select 1998 more samples of size eight and display the means of each of these samples as small boxes above the scale.

Press any key, and the screen display showing the five population distributions will reappear. You can now select a distribution to use in generating another sampling distribution or press:

- the ESC key to return to the menu in the lower left corner of the screen.
- the ALT and M keys to return to the MAIN MENU.
- the ALT and X keys to exit from the ISEE program.

The SIMPLE SAMPLE Module

The SIMPLE SAMPLE module (option 2 in the MAIN MENU) lets you load, edit, and analyze small population distributions with fewer than 13 cases, and conduct sampling experiments with these populations. All screen displays for this module can be printed, using either the ALT + P command or the print options in the menus, but the results cannot be saved.

When you activate the SIMPLE SAMPLE module, you see a screen display with four windows. The lower left corner contains a menu with eight options, numbered 1 to 8. Note the cursor box surrounding option 1. You move the cursor with the up and down ARROW keys or a mouse. You select an option by placing the cursor on it and pressing the ENTER key or clicking the mouse. You can also select an option from the menu by typing the option number.

The POPULATION window is in the upper left corner. It lists the names of 12 population members and four population distributions called V1, V2, V3, and V4. You may enter or change the values in these four population distributions at any time during a SIMPLE SAMPLE session. However, you are limited to using values between 36 and 60. These limits facilitate the graphic displays of the experimental results.

The upper right corner of the screen shows the results of the options executed by the program. When the SIMPLE SAMPLE module is loaded, the program carries out option 1 of the SIMPLE SAMPLE menu and displays the results of this option.

The lower right corner describes the options in the SIMPLE SAMPLE menu and displays additional options and commands. You use this window to conduct and analyze experiments.

The SIMPLE SAMPLE Menu

Look at the eight options in the SIMPLE SAMPLE menu, in the lower left part of the screen. The first four options (1–4) let you analyze the population distributions V1–V4 listed in the POPULATION window. Options 5 and 6 allow you to enter, delete, or change the values in population distributions V1–V4. Option 7 is used for conducting experiments in which you select samples from population distributions V1–V4. Option 8 will print the current screen display.

The POPULATION Window

Look at the POPULATION window. You will see 12 rows, numbered 1 through 12. Each row stands for a member of the population, whose name follows the row number. At the top are four column headings: V1, V2, V3, and V4. These column headings are the names of four population distributions that are available for you to sample.

Under V1 you will see a column of numbers. This population distribution is loaded by the program. Under V2, V3, and V4 you will see a column of asterisks, which means missing data. There are no population distributions for V2–V4 when the SIMPLE SAMPLE module is loaded.

Loading and Editing Population Distributions V1–V4 (Option 6, Data)

You can load and edit population data by using option 5 or 6 in the SIMPLE SAMPLE menu. To load a new population distribution or change an existing population distribution, move the cursor to option 6, Data, and press the ENTER key.

The cursor will move onto the first row under V1. You can move the cursor to any row under V1, V2, V3, or V4 by using the ARROW keys. To change any value in the cursor box:

1. Press the BACKSPACE key until an asterisk appears.
2. Type in the values you want (within the range of 36 to 60).

When you finish changing or entering data in the POPULATION window, press the F6 key to save the changes made. Pressing the ESC key will move the cursor to the SIMPLE SAMPLE menu in the lower left corner of the screen.

Loading and Editing Population Distributions V1–V4 (Option 5, Variables)

You can also use option 5, Variables, in the SIMPLE SAMPLE menu to load a new or edit an existing population distribution. To use this option, place the cursor on option 5, Variables, and press the ENTER key. A new menu, listing the four population distributions (V1, V2, V3, and V4), will appear to the right of the SIMPLE SAMPLE menu, and the cursor will surround V1. Select the population distribution you wish to add or edit by placing the cursor on the listing for that population and pressing the ENTER key. You can also select a population by using a mouse or typing the number of the population distribution. (Press the ESC key to return to the SIMPLE SAMPLE menu.)

If you select one of the four population distributions on the list, the EDIT window will appear in the upper right corner of the screen. This window will display:

- the list of names assigned to the 12 population members followed by the population distribution you have selected.
- six parameters of the population distribution you have selected.
- a histogram of the population distribution you have selected.

The cursor will move to the EDIT window, where it will surround the value for the first case in the population distribution you have selected. (Remember, an asterisk means no data for that case.) You can now change or enter a new value for any case in the population distribution you have selected, as follows:

1. Place the cursor on the value you wish to change or enter.
2. Clear out an existing value by pressing the BACKSPACE key as many times as necessary until an asterisk appears.
3. Type in the value you wish to use for this case (values are limited to integers from 36 to 60).

If you wish to see the effect of the changes you have made on the parameters and histogram of the population distribution, press the F5 key.

You save all changes by pressing the F6 key. If you do not press the F6 key, any changes you make in a population distribution will disappear when the cursor leaves the results window.

To edit a new variable, press the ESC key and the cursor will return to the list of the four population distributions. Select the population distribution to be edited as described above. To return to the SIMPLE SAMPLE menu, press the ESC key.

Exhibit A.2 illustrates the use of Option 5, Variables.

Note: Although ISEE was not designed for this purpose, the F5 command in the EDIT window allows the user to conduct exercises

Exhibit A.2

Option 5, Variables, in the SIMPLE SAMPLE Menu

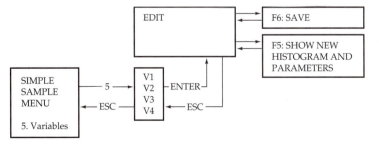

calculating the parameters and drawing histograms. Some students have found this application of the F5 command very useful in learning about these statistical procedures.

Analyzing Population Distributions V1–V4 (Options 1–4)

To analyze the four populations (V1–V4), place the cursor on option 1, 2, 3, or 4 of the SIMPLE SAMPLE menu and press the ENTER key. The analysis you selected will appear in the window in the upper right part of the screen.

For each of the four population distributions, the analysis will show

1. Parameters: the count (number of cases with data), mean, median, standard deviation (division by count), maximum and minimum values.

2. Frequencies: the frequency distributions.

3. Histograms: in the histograms the thin vertical line marks the population mean. (The term EMPTY SET is used to designate a population distribution with no data.)

4. Icharts: plots the value of each individual case in the population distribution in order from 1 (Arrow B.) to 12 (Velt R.). The thin horizontal line marks the mean of the population distribution. The Ichart is useful for identifying patterns that might affect the sampling distribution of systematic samples.

Conducting and Analyzing Sampling Experiments (Option 7, Experiments)

To conduct and analyze an experiment, place the cursor on option 7, Experiments, and press the ENTER key. Two menus will appear in the lower right part of the screen. The menu on the left, which we refer to as the Experiment menu, is used to specify an experiment. The menu on the right, which we call the Analysis menu, is used to analyze the results of the last experiment conducted by the program.

When you activate the Experiments option, the cursor moves to the Select option at the top of the Analysis menu. You can move the cursor to any option in the Analysis or the Experiment menu by using the ARROW keys or mouse.

Using the Experiment Menu to Specify an Experiment

Look at the Experiment menu. You will see four rows, labeled C1, C2, C3, and C4. Each row stands for an experimental condition (C1 = Condition 1, C2 = Condition 2, and so forth) that you may use, depending on the experiment you wish to conduct. To use a condition:

1. Go to the first column in the menu, labeled Var. Type in the variable number of the population distribution from which samples will be selected. Use 1 for V1, 2 for V2, 3 for V3, and 4 for V4.

2. Select the type of sample (second column in the menu, labeled Type). You can choose one of three types of samples by pressing the SPACE bar until the sample type you want is displayed. The three sample types are

    SRSW = simple random sample with replacement

    SRSN = simple random sample without replacement

    SYS = systematic random sample (size n = 3)

3. Type the size of the sample to be selected in the third column, labeled Size. Note: The sample size must be less than 13 for SRSN and is fixed at 3 for SYS.

    The fourth column of the menu, labeled Mis. for missing data, is optional. It is used to specify a population member that will be excluded from any sample and replaced by another population member. The Mis. feature can be used to study the effect of missing data on sampling distributions. Note: Always make sure there is an asterisk in the Mis. column for each condition you use in your experiments unless you are using the Mis. feature for that condition.

    To complete the specification of an experiment, you must type in the last row of the menu the number of samples (from 1 to 9999) you want to select. That number of samples will be selected for each condition specified. Different samples are selected for each condition.

    Always check to see that there is an asterisk in the Var column for any condition you do not want to include in an experiment.

Conducting an Experiment

To conduct an experiment, place the cursor on the Select option that heads the Analysis menu and press the ENTER key.

An Example Showing How to Specify and Conduct an Experiment

To illustrate the procedure for specifying and conducting an experiment, we will specify an experiment in which we select 1000 simple random samples, with replacement, of sizes two and four from population distribution V1. We will use Condition 1 (C1) for samples of size two and Condition 2 (C2) for samples of size four. To specify this experiment:

- Put the cursor in the first column (Var) of the C1 row. If the number 1 does not appear under the cursor, clear the cursor box by pressing the BACKSPACE key until an asterisk appears, and then type 1. This specifies V1 as the population distribution from which samples will be selected for Condition 1.

- Move the cursor to the second column (Type) on the C1 row. If the entry SRSW (simple random samples with replacement) does not appear, keep pressing the SPACE bar until it does.

- Move the cursor to the third column (Size) on the C1 row. If the number 2 does not appear, keep pressing the BACKSPACE key until an asterisk appears, and then type 2 (for samples of size two). If the last column on the row for C1 (Mis.) does not contain an asterisk, move the cursor to the fourth column and keep pressing the BACKSPACE key until one appears. This completes the specification of C1.

- Move the cursor to the first column in the row for C2, and specify the following for the C2 experimental condition: sample from the V1 variable, select simple random samples with replacement (SRSW), and select samples of size four. If necessary, use the SPACE bar to change the entry in the Type column. Make sure there is an asterisk in the last column of C2 and asterisks in the Var column on the rows for C3 and C4. An asterisk in the Var column eliminates that condition from an experiment.

- To complete the specification of the experiment, you must tell the program to select 1000 samples for each experimental condition that is specified. Do this by moving the cursor to the bottom row of the Experiment menu, pressing the BACKSPACE key until the Number of Samples box contains an asterisk, and then typing the number 1000. When you finish, the Experiment menu should look like Exhibit A.3.

To conduct the experiment, move the cursor to the Select button in the upper left corner of the Analysis menu and press the ENTER

Exhibit A.3

The Specification of an Experiment

	Var	Type	Size	Mis.
C1	1	SRSW	2	*
C2	1	SRSW	4	*
C3	*	SRSN	*	*
C4	*	SRSN	*	*
Number of Samples: 1000				

key. The program will now conduct the experiment you have speci-fied. First, it will select 1000 simple random samples of size two, with replacement, from V1; calculate the mean of each sample; and store the means in its memory under C1. The program will then re-peat the process, selecting 1000 simple random samples of size four, with replacement, from V1; calculating the means of these samples; and storing the means under C2 in its memory.

When you press the ENTER key, four rectangles will appear in the EXPERIMENTS window, one for each of the four experimental conditions (Condition 1, Condition 2, and so forth). There is a mes-sage in each rectangle. If you have specified a condition, the message will read PREPARING SET, which tells you it is preparing for the se-lection you have specified. If you have not specified the details for a condition, the message will read EMPTY SET, which means nothing is done for these conditions.

After the preparation is complete, the program will generate the sampling distribution for each experimental condition. Then it will draw a histogram of the sampling distribution in the rectangle for that condition. In this example, it will draw a histogram of the means of the 1000 samples of size two, selected with replacement from V1, in the rectangle for Condition 1. It will draw a second his-togram of the means of the 1000 samples of size four, selected with replacement from V1, in the rectangle for Condition 2.

Note the thin vertical line in the center of each histogram. This line shows the value of the population mean (48).

For small experiments, the preparation time will be minimal. In more extensive experiments, it may take several minutes or longer to complete the preparation. If you wish to abort an experiment while the preparation message appears on the screen, hit the F2 key and answer the question by typing Y (for yes).

Using the Analysis Menu to Analyze the Most Recent Experiment

The Analysis menu in the lower right corner of the screen can be used to analyze the most recent experiment. Place the cursor on the type of analysis you wish to conduct, and press the ENTER key or click the mouse. You will see the results of the analysis in the upper right window. The following types of analysis can be performed:

List
Lists the first 113 means for an experimental condition. You must select the experimental condition by placing the cursor on the label for the experimental condition (right side of the Analysis menu) and pressing the EN-TER key.

Freq.
Generates the frequency distribution of all means selected for an experimental condition. You must first select the experimental condition, as described above. In addition to the frequency distribution, the histogram of the population distribution from which the samples were selected and the sampling distribution will be displayed.

Param.
Shows a table of the expected value, bias, standard error, and root mean error for all experimental conditions. The table will show both the theoretical (Th.) value of these measures and the actual observed (Ob.) measure for the means selected in the experiment.

Ichart
Displays an Ichart of the first 113 means for each experimental condition.

Hist.1
Displays a histogram of all means selected in each experimental condition on a scale that corresponds to the value of the sample mean itself.

Hist.2
Same as Hist.1, except the scale shows the difference between the sample mean and the population mean.

Returning to the SIMPLE SAMPLE Menu

To return to the SIMPLE SAMPLE menu, press the ESC key.

Printing Screen Displays in the SIMPLE SAMPLE Module

To print the screen displays showing the results of an experiment, use the ALT + P command or the Print option in the Analysis menu rather than the Print option in the SIMPLE SAMPLE menu. To use the Print option in the Analysis menu, place the cursor on the word Print and press the ENTER key.

To print any other screen display, use ALT + P command or Option 8, Print, in the SIMPLE SAMPLE menu.

The UNIVARIATE Module

The UNIVARIATE module will conduct and analyze sampling experiments (similar to those conducted in the SIMPLE SAMPLE module) with larger populations. The populations are limited to 17 variables and as many cases as the memory of the computer will hold. Experiments may be conducted on populations loaded by a user or on the six resident populations that were loaded with the module. The program holds a maximum of 17 resident populations at any one time.

All screen displays for this module can be printed using either the ALT + P command or the Print option in the menus. All the populations loaded and the results of all experiments are automatically saved by the program and stored in the ISEE directory on the hard disk. The UNIVARIATE module can be run only from the hard disk.

The UNIVARIATE module can be used in three different ways. First, it can be used to reanalyze a previously conducted experiment that is currently stored by the program. We call this use the *reanalysis mode*. Second, the program can be used to repeat a previously conducted experiment. We call this the *repeat mode*. Third, the program can conduct a new experiment—that is, one not currently stored by the program. We refer to this as the *new mode*.

To activate the UNIVARIATE module, place the cursor on option 3, UNIVARIATE, in the MAIN MENU and press the ENTER key. You may also use the mouse or type the number 3 to activate the UNIVARIATE module when the cursor is in the MAIN MENU.

After you activate the UNIVARIATE module, a screen display appears. It has three parts:

- The lower left corner of the screen contains the UNIVARIATE menu with four options, numbered 1 to 4. This menu remains on the screen until you exit the UNIVARIATE module.

- The lower right screen is used to describe options in the UNIVARIATE menu, list commands that can be issued by the user, and provide menus for specifying and analyzing experiments.

- The upper portion of the screen displays the results of options activated by the user.

The UNIVARIATE Menu

The UNIVARIATE menu contains four options:

1. Population: used for adding, deleting, labeling, or selecting a population to analyze or use in an experiment.
2. Variables: used to label and analyze the variables in any resident population selected by the user. The analysis displays the parameters and histograms of all variables in the selected population.
3. Experiments: used to conduct, analyze, or label experiments. It can be used in the reanalysis, repeat, or new modes, defined above.
4. Print: prints the current screen display.

You can select an option in the UNIVARIATE menu in the same way as you did in the MAIN MENU by using the cursor, mouse, or by typing its number. The ESC key takes you from any option back to the UNIVARIATE menu.

Note: When the UNIVARIATE module is activated, the program activates option 1, Population, and the cursor moves into the Population List described below. To select another option from the UNI-VARIATE menu, you must first press the ESC key to return to the UNIVARIATE menu.

Option 1. Population

When option 1, Population, is activated, the Population List will appear at the top of the screen and the cursor will move to the first line in the Population List. The list shows all the populations currently stored by the program. Each population is assigned the line number on which it is listed as its number. The population list displays:

- the population number.
- the name of the population (to help the user remember its content).
- the number of records stored for the population (Cases).
- the number of variables stored for the population (Var.).
- the number of experiments using this population that are currently stored by the program on the hard disk (UniVar.).

The following commands can be issued in this module:

ENTER   Selects a population for analysis or for an experiment. To issue this command, place the cursor on the line containing the population to be selected and press the ENTER key. There will always be a selected population while this module is resident. The selected population is indicated by the population number found in the upper right corner of the UNIVARIATE menu. Note: After you press the ENTER key, the cursor moves to the UNIVARIATE menu.

ESC   Returns the program to the UNIVARIATE menu. To issue this command, press the ESC key.

F8   Changes the name of a population. To issue this command, place the cursor on the line in the Population List containing the population whose name you wish to change. Next press the F8 key, type the name you wish to use for the population, and press the ENTER key.

F9   Activates option 2, Variables, in the UNIVARIATE menu and displays the Variable List for the selected population. The Variable List is described in a later section of this appendix. To issue this command, place the cursor on the line in the Population List containing the population whose variables you wish to display. Then press the F9 key.

INS   Loads a population into the ISEE program. This option is described in the next section of this appendix.

DEL   Deletes a resident population from the ISEE program. All populations except Population 1 can be deleted using this command. To issue the command, place the cursor on the row in the Population List containing the population you wish to delete. Next press the DEL key, answer the question by typing Y (for yes), and press the ENTER key. Note: All experiments using a population will be deleted if the population is deleted.

You can also use the ALT and X command to exit the program or the ALT and M command to return to the MAIN MENU. Note: All populations that were loaded and not deleted, as well as the results of all experiments conducted and not deleted, are saved when you exit the UNIVARIATE module.

Loading Populations Into the UNIVARIATE Module

Large populations can be loaded into the UNIVARIATE module using the INS command when you are in option 1, Population, of the UNIVARIATE menu. To load a population:

1. Press the INS (insert) key.
2. Type the path required to reach the file for the population you wish to load.
3. Press the ENTER key.

The program will then load the specified population and assign it the lowest available line number in the Population List. It will assign the name Population X (when X equals the line number) to the population just loaded. If you wish to change the name of the population you have loaded, you can use the name changing option (F8) described in the previous section.

The program can add a population only when a line is open in the Population List. If no line is open, you must delete a resident population (by using the DEL command described in the previous section) before you can add a new one.

The population files to be loaded into the UNIVARIATE module must be in ASCII format with the values separated by spaces. Missing data must be noted with an asterisk. The program will not load a file that contains a letter or symbols other than numbers or asterisks. The file should be ordered by record and by variable within records.

The program does not limit the number of records in a file but limits the number of variables in the file to 17.

Option 2. Variables

Option 2, Variables, in the UNIVARIATE menu displays the Variable List, parameters of the variables, or histograms of the variables for the selected population. This option can also be used for changing the name assigned to any variable in the Variable List for the selected population.

To use this option, first select a population by using the ENTER command in option 1, Population, described above. The selected population's number will appear in the upper right corner of the UNIVARIATE menu.

To activate option 2, Variables, place the cursor on that option and press the ENTER key. (You can also activate this option using a mouse or by typing the number 2. You can activate option 2, Variables, from option 1, Population, by pressing the F9 key.)

When you activate the Variables option, the Variable List for the selected population appears at the top of the screen. The Variable List displays the following information for every variable in the selected population:

Line number
: The line number on which the variable is displayed. The program designates variables by their line numbers.

Name
: The name of the variable, to help users remember its content

Count
: The number of cases for which there are data on this variable (the total number of records in the file minus the number of records in the file that have an asterisk for the variable)

Mean
: The arithmetic mean for the variable

St.Dev
: The standard deviation of the variable, using the count and not the count minus one in the denominator.

Skew
: R. A. Fisher's G^2 measure of skew for the variable. The formula for this measure of skew is:

$$G^2 = \frac{\sum_{i=1}^{N}(X_i - \bar{X})^3}{N * \sigma_X^3}$$

Min.
: Minimum value for any record on this variable

Max.
: Maximum value for any record on this variable

Once the Variable List appears at the top of the screen, you can issue the following commands:

ESC
: Returns the cursor to the UNIVARIATE menu. To execute this command, press the ESC key.

F8
: Changes the name assigned to any variable in the variable list. To execute this command, place the cursor on the row for the variable whose name you wish to change and press the F8 key. Type the new name you wish to use for the variable and press the ENTER key.

F9
: Returns to option 1 and the Population List. To issue this command, press the F9 key.

F10   Displays the histograms of the variables in the Variable List. To issue the command, press the F10 key. A description of the Histograms option follows.

The Histograms Option

After you issue the Histograms command (F10), the display at the top of the screen divides into two parts. On the left is the list of variable names and numbers for the selected population. Above the list is the title Variables, followed by the population number of the selected population. The cursor is on the first row of the list. To the right is a window labeled Histograms which contains four boxes, each of which contains the words EMPTY SET. Histograms for the selected variables will appear in these boxes.

To see a histogram, place the cursor on the row in the Variables list for the variable whose histogram you want to see and press the ENTER key. The histogram for the selected variable will appear in one of the boxes in the Histograms window. The name and number of the selected variable will appear above the box in which the histogram is displayed. The mean for the selected variable is displayed in the histogram as a thin vertical line. The value of the mean is given on the scale under the histogram. The scale for each histogram is based on the standard deviation of the variable. Therefore, the histograms show the shape of each variable but do not show the dispersion of any variable relative to any other variable.

You can view as many histograms as you want, though only four will appear on the screen at the same time. You can exit the Histograms option in four different ways:

ALT-X   Exits the ISEE program

ALT-M   Returns the program to the MAIN MENU

ESC   Returns the program to the UNIVARIATE menu

F10   Returns the program to the Variable List for the selected population

Moving Between the Population List and the Variable List

There are several different ways to move back and forth between the Population List and the Variable List. Exhibit A.4 shows the various ways of moving between these lists.

Exhibit A.4

Moving Between Population and Variable Lists

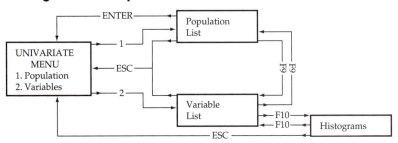

Option 3. Experiments

To conduct or analyze experiments, first select the population you want to use in the experiment (see previous section), then select Option 3, Experiments, in the UNIVARIATE menu (type 3 when the cursor is on one of the options in the UNIVARIATE menu.

When you activate option 3, Experiments, the upper part of the screen displays the Experiment List for the selected population. This list shows the following information for each prior experiment using the selected population and currently stored in the program:

Experiment number	The number used by the program to designate the experiment and the line number where the experiment is listed
Experiment name	The name used to describe the experiment
Samples	The number of samples selected for each experimental condition
Cond 1, 2, 3, 4	The variable number (V), type of sample (T), and sample size (n) used in each experimental condition (see SIMPLE SAMPLE, specification of an experiment)

When the Experiment List appears, you can use four commands:

ENTER   Used to reanalyze, repeat, or conduct a new experiment (described further in the next section). To reanalyze or repeat an experiment, place the cursor on the row in the Experiment List for the experiment you want to reanalyze or repeat, and press the ENTER key. To conduct a new experiment, place the cursor on an open line in the Experiment List and press the ENTER key.

ESC   Exits option 3, Experiments, and returns the cursor to the UNIVARIATE menu. To execute this command, press the ESC key.

F8   Changes the name of an experiment. To execute this command, place the cursor on the row that lists the experiment whose name you wish to change and press the F8 key. Type the new name you wish to give the experiment and then press the ENTER key.

DEL   Deletes an experiment. To execute this command, place the cursor on the row that lists the experiment you want to delete, press the DEL key, and answer the question YES.

Note: The program will store a maximum of 17 experiments for a given population at any one time.

The ENTER Command

The ENTER command is used to reanalyze or repeat an experiment currently stored by the program for the selected population or to conduct a new experiment (an experiment not currently stored by the program for the selected population). When the ENTER key is pressed, the screen display changes as follows:

- The upper portion of the screen divides into two parts. On the left is a list of the variable numbers and names for the selected population. Above the list is the name Variables X (with X being the number of the selected population). To the right is a window labeled EXPERIMENT X (X being the line number in the Experiment List on which the cursor was resting when you pressed the ENTER key. The experimental results will be displayed in this window.

- In the lower right portion of the screen, two menus appear. We call the left menu (next to the UNIVARIATE menu) the Experiment menu and the right menu the Analysis menu. These menus are used to specify, conduct, and analyze experiments. The Experiment and Analysis menus closely resemble those in the SIMPLE SAMPLE module.

Note: The Experiment menu in the UNIVARIATE mode does not contain the Mis. option. The Select, Hist.1, and Hist.2 options in the UNIVARIATE module differ in certain respects from the comparable commands in the SIMPLE SAMPLE module.

The Select command in the UNIVARIATE module affects experiment results stored under the line number on which the cursor is resting when the ENTER key is pressed. It will erase the results of any experiment currently stored under this line number and store the results of the new experiment it is about to select. Therefore, if you plan to conduct a new experiment, be sure before you press the ENTER key that the cursor is not resting on a line in the Experiment List containing experimental results you want to save.

The Hist.1 option in the UNIVARIATE module displays histograms of the experimental conditions that are based on the standard deviation of the experimental condition being displayed. As a result, these histograms give a good picture of the shape of the sampling distribution for each condition, but may not offer a good picture of the dispersion of these histograms relative to one another. The Hist.2 option uses the largest standard deviation of the distributions generated in the experiment as the basis for scaling the results of all experimental conditions. Hence, Hist.2 enables you to compare the relative dispersion of the sampling distributions in all experimental conditions used in the experiment, but may not give a good picture of the shape of one or more of these sampling distributions. Use Hist.1 to see the shapes of the sampling distributions generated by the experiment and Hist.2 to compare the dispersion of the sampling distributions relative to one another.

Note: The histograms that appear when the Select command is activated are Hist.1 type histograms, showing the shapes of the sampling distributions. These histograms will not show the relative dispersion of those sampling distributions.

The Reanalysis Mode

To reanalyze the results of an experiment currently stored in the program:

- Select the population used in the experiment.
- Select option 3, Experiments, in the UNIVARIATE menu.
- Place the cursor on the row in the Experiment List where the experiment you wish to reanalyze is listed.
- Press the ENTER key.

- Move the cursor to the type of analysis you wish to conduct in the Analysis menu. (Note: If you choose the Select command, the program will erase the existing results for an experiment, conduct the experiment again, and store the new experimental results.)
- Press the ENTER key.

The Repeat Mode

To repeat an experiment:

- Select the population used in the experiment.
- Select option 3, Experiments, in the UNIVARIATE menu.
- Place the cursor on the row in the Experiment List where the experiment you wish to repeat is listed.
- Press the ENTER key.
- Move the cursor to the Select command in the Analysis menu.
- Press the ENTER key.

Note: If you issue the Select command, the program will *erase* the existing results for an experiment, conduct the experiment again, and store the results of the new experiment. If you wish to repeat an experiment but *save* the results of the earlier experiment, follow the New Experiment procedure described below.

To analyze the experiment, use the Analysis menu (as in SIMPLE SAMPLE).

The New Experiment Mode

To conduct an experiment that is not currently stored by the program, or to repeat an experiment that is currently stored without erasing the results of the previous experiment:

- Select the population to be used in the experiment.
- Select option 3, Experiments, in the UNIVARIATE menu.
- Place the cursor on any empty row in the Experiment List.
- Press the ENTER key.
- Use the Experiment menu (as in SIMPLE SAMPLE) to specify the experiment you want to conduct.
- Move the cursor to the Select command in the Analysis menu.
- Press the ENTER key.

To analyze the experiment, use the Analysis menu (as in SIMPLE SAMPLE).

Note: The program automatically stores the results of the experiment conducted after the Select command is activated and lists the experiment just conducted on the line in the Experiment List on which the cursor was resting when the ENTER key was pressed.

Printing Screen Displays in the UNIVARIATE Module

Use the ALT + P or the Print command in the Analysis menu to print the screen display when you are in option 3, Experiments. Use ALT + P or option 4, Print, in the UNIVARIATE menu to print all the other screen displays.

Appendix B

Cards and Forms

The 12-Store Deck
(Page 1 of 2)

1. ARROW B. 52	2. BRAUN M. 40	3. BROWN G. 48
4. ELF G. 36	5. GRAY C. 56	6. HART R. 52

The 12-Store Deck
(Page 2 of 2)

7. JONES J. 48	8. KRAUS K. 60	9. KRIM E. 44
10. RALT V. 48	11. TIMM E. 48	12. VELT R. 44

Form 4.1

For Recording the Results of Experiment 4.1
(n = 4: 5 SRSW & SRSN samples from 12-Store Deck
& SIMPLE SAMPLE)

NAME   V1

N		ST. DEV		
MEAN		MINIMUM		
MEDIAN		MAXIMUM		

1. Arrow B. _____
2. Braun M. _____
3. Brown G. _____
4. Elf G. _____
5. Gray C. _____
6. Hart R. _____
7. Jones J. _____
8. Kraus K. _____
9. Krim E. _____
10. Ralt V. _____
11. Timm E. _____
12. Velt R. _____

HISTOGRAM V1

36   40   44   48   52   56   60

	WITHOUT REPLACEMENT			WITH REPLACEMENT		
	12-STORE DECK ....CASE....	SIMPLE SAMPLE	12-STORE DECK ....CASE....	SIMPLE SAMPLE
SAMPLE	1 : 2 : 3 : 4 mean	mean	1 : 2 : 3 : 4 mean	mean
1	: : :		: : :	
2	: : :		: : :	
3	: : :		: : :	
4	: : :		: : :	
5	: : :		: : :	
	EXP. VAL.		EXP. VAL.	
	BIAS		BIAS	
	ST. ERR.		ST. ERR.	

HISTOGRAM: SIMPLE SAMPLE MEANS: WITHOUT REPLACEMENT

36   38   40   42   44   46   48   50   52   54   56   58   60

Form 4.2

For Recording the Results of Experiment 4.2
(n = 1: 9999 SRSW or SRSN samples from V1–V4)

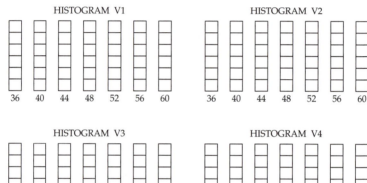

	NAME	V1	V2	V3	V4
1.	Arrow B.	52	36	36	36
2.	Braun M.	40	36	36	36
3.	Brown G.	48	36	40	36
4.	Elf G.	36	36	40	40
5.	Gray C.	56	36	44	40
6.	Hart R.	52	36	44	44
7.	Jones J.	48	60	52	52
8.	Kraus K.	60	60	52	56
9.	Krim E.	44	60	56	56
10.	Ralt V.	48	60	56	60
11.	Timm E.	48	60	60	60
12.	Velt R.	44	60	60	60

	V1	V2	V3	V4
N				
MEAN				
MEDIAN				
ST. DEV				
MINIMUM				
MAXIMUM				

HISTOGRAM V1   HISTOGRAM V2

HISTOGRAM V3   HISTOGRAM V4

	C1	C2	C3	C4
EXPECTED VALUE				
BIAS				
STANDARD ERROR				

Form 4.3

For Recording the Results of Experiment 4.3
(n = 1, 2, 4, 8: 9999 SRSW samples V2 on Form 4.2)

MEAN = 48.00

STANDARD DEVIATION = 12.00

	n	EXPECTED VALUE	BIAS	STANDARD ERROR	TEST OF DOUBLING RULE	TEST OF 4-TIMES RULE
C1	1					
C2	2					
C3	4					
C4	8					

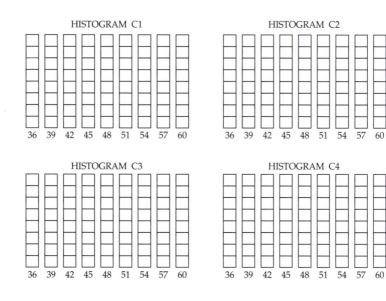

HISTOGRAM C1

36 39 42 45 48 51 54 57 60

HISTOGRAM C2

36 39 42 45 48 51 54 57 60

HISTOGRAM C3

36 39 42 45 48 51 54 57 60

HISTOGRAM C4

36 39 42 45 48 51 54 57 60

Form 4.4

For Recording the Results of Experiment 4.4
(n = 1, 2, 4, 8: 9999 SRSN SAMPLES from V2 on Form 4.2)

MEAN = 48.00

STANDARD DEVIATION = 12.00

	n	EXPECTED VALUE	BIAS	STANDARD ERROR	EXP. 4.3 STANDARD ERROR from Form 4.3
C1	1				
C2	2				
C3	4				
C4	8				

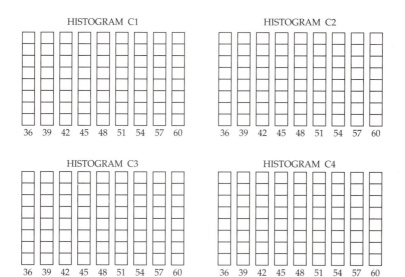

HISTOGRAM C1

36 39 42 45 48 51 54 57 60

HISTOGRAM C2

36 39 42 45 48 51 54 57 60

HISTOGRAM C3

36 39 42 45 48 51 54 57 60

HISTOGRAM C4

36 39 42 45 48 51 54 57 60

Form 4, Exercise 1

For Recording the Results of Exercise 1
(analysis of population distributions V2 and V3)

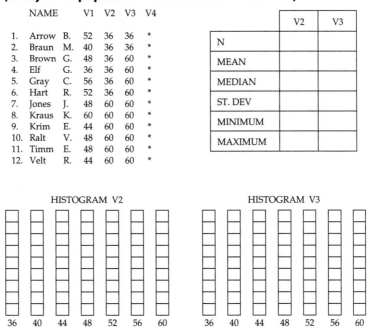

	NAME		V1	V2	V3	V4
1.	Arrow	B.	52	36	36	*
2.	Braun	M.	40	36	36	*
3.	Brown	G.	48	36	60	*
4.	Elf	G.	36	36	60	*
5.	Gray	C.	56	36	60	*
6.	Hart	R.	52	36	60	*
7.	Jones	J.	48	60	60	*
8.	Kraus	K.	60	60	60	*
9.	Krim	E.	44	60	60	*
10.	Ralt	V.	48	60	60	*
11.	Timm	E.	48	60	60	*
12.	Velt	R.	44	60	60	*

	V2	V3
N		
MEAN		
MEDIAN		
ST. DEV		
MINIMUM		
MAXIMUM		

HISTOGRAM V2

36   40   44   48   52   56   60

HISTOGRAM V3

36   40   44   48   52   56   60

Form 4, Exercise 2

Repeating Experiment 4.2 With a New Population Distribution (n = 1: 9999 SRSW or SRSN samples from V2)

NAME	V2
1. Arrow B.	____
2. Braun M.	____
3. Brown G.	____
4. Elf G.	____
5. Gray C.	____
6. Hart R.	____
7. Jones J.	____
8. Kraus K.	____
9. Krim E.	____
10. Ralt V.	____
11. Timm E.	____
12. Velt R.	____

	V2
N	
MEAN	
MEDIAN	
ST. DEV	
MINIMUM	
MAXIMUM	

	C1
EXPECTED VALUE	
BIAS	
STANDARD ERROR	

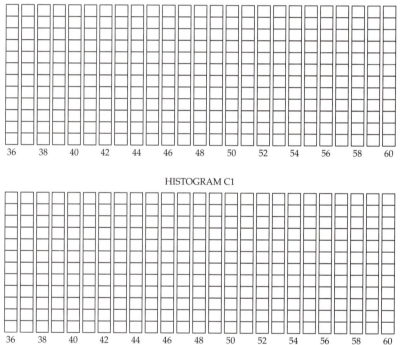

HISTOGRAM V2

36   38   40   42   44   46   48   50   52   54   56   58   60

HISTOGRAM C1

36   38   40   42   44   46   48   50   52   54   56   58   60

Form 4, Exercise 5

Repeating Experiment 4.3 With Different Sample Sizes Selected from Population Distribution V4 (Experiment 4.2) (n = 1, 3, 6, 9: 9999 SRSW samples from V4 on Form 4.2)

MEAN = 48.00

STANDARD DEVIATION = 9.79

	n	EXPECTED VALUE	BIAS	STANDARD ERROR
C1	1			
C2	3			
C3	6			
C4	9			

Form 4, Exercise 6

Repeating Experiment 4.3 With Different Samples Sizes Selected From a New Population Distribution

(9999 SRSW samples from V2)

	NAME		V2
1.	Arrow	B.	___
2.	Braun	M.	___
3.	Brown	G.	___
4.	Elf	G.	___
5.	Gray	C.	___
6.	Hart	R.	___
7.	Jones	J.	___
8.	Kraus	K.	___
9.	Krim	E.	___
10.	Ralt	V.	___
11.	Timm	E.	___
12.	Velt	R.	___

	V2
N	
MEAN	
MEDIAN	
ST. DEV.	
MINIMUM	
MAXIMUM	

	n
C1	
C2	
C3	
C4	

	n	EXPECTED VALUE	BIAS	STANDARD ERROR
C1				
C2				
C3				
C4				

Form 4, Exercise 7B

N	n	fpc
12	1	
12	2	
12	3	
12	4	

N	n	fpc
12	5	
12	6	
12	7	
12	8	

N	n	fpc
12	9	
12	10	
12	11	
12	12	

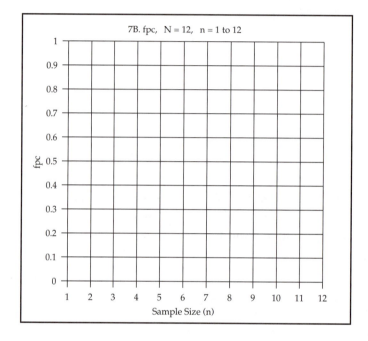

7B. fpc, N = 12, n = 1 to 12

Form 4, Exercise 9

Repeating Experiment 4.4 Using Population Distribution V4 (Experiment 4.2)
(n = 1, 2, 4, 8: 9999 SRSN samples from V4 on Form 4.2)

MEAN = 48.00

STANDARD DEVIATION = 9.79

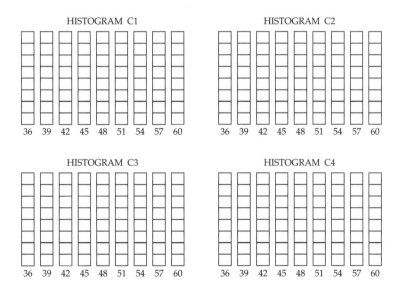

	n	EXPECTED VALUE	BIAS	STANDARD ERROR
C1	1			
C2	2			
C3	4			
C4	8			

HISTOGRAM C1

36 39 42 45 48 51 54 57 60

HISTOGRAM C2

36 39 42 45 48 51 54 57 60

HISTOGRAM C3

36 39 42 45 48 51 54 57 60

HISTOGRAM C4

36 39 42 45 48 51 54 57 60

Form 5.1

For Recording the Results of Experiment 5.1
(n = 1, 4, 16, 64: 5000 SRSW samples from V17 of
population 4)

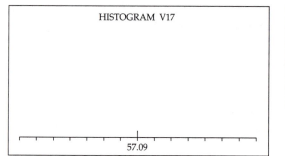

	PARAMETERS V17
COUNT	
MEAN	
ST. DEV.	
SKEW	

	n	EXPECTED VALUE	BIAS	STANDARD ERROR
C1	1			
C2	4			
C3	16			
C4	64			

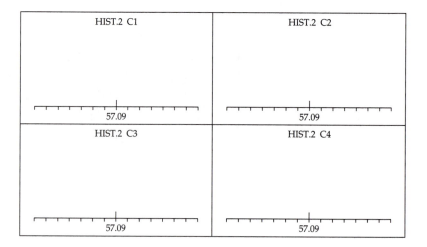

Form 5.2

For Recording Experiment 5.2
(n = 1, 2, 4, 40: 5000 SRSW samples from V5 of population 4)

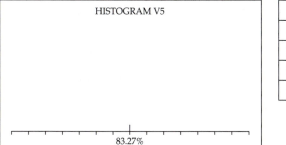

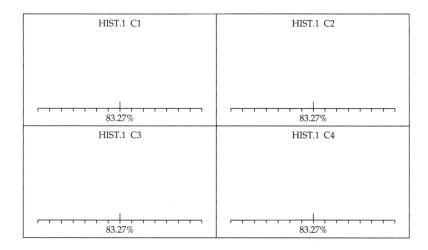

Form 5.3

For Recording the Results of Experiment 5.3
(n = 1, 25: 9999 SRSW samples from V14 of population 4)

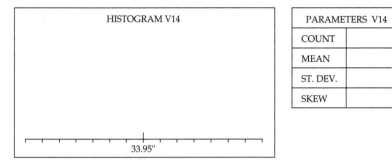

HISTOGRAM V14

PARAMETERS V14	
COUNT	
MEAN	
ST. DEV.	
SKEW	

33.95"

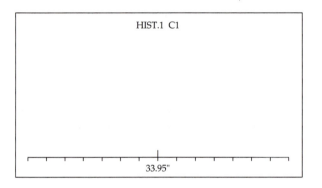

HIST.1 C1

33.95"

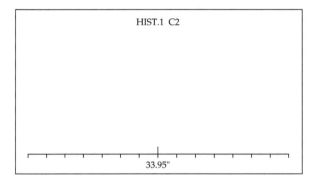

HIST.1 C2

33.95"

Form 5, Exercise 3

(n = 1, 4, 16, 64: 5000 SRSW samples from V17 of population 2)

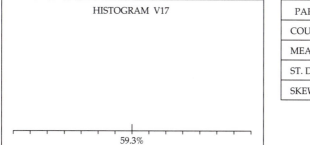

		HISTOGRAM V17		PARAMETERS V17	

	n	EXPECTED VALUE	BIAS	STANDARD ERROR
C1	1			
C2	4			
C3	16			
C4	64			

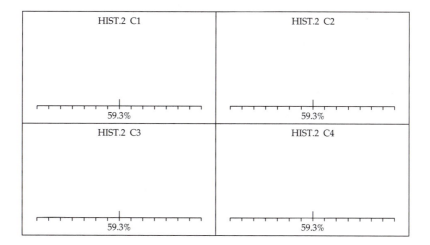

Form 5, Exercise 4

(n = 1, 4, 16, 64: 5000 SRSW samples from V__ of population __)

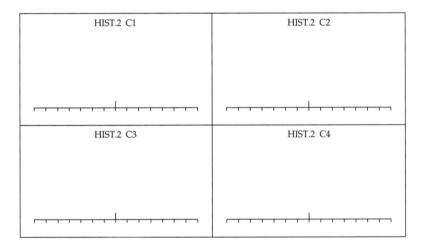

HISTOGRAM V__	PARAMETERS V__	
	COUNT	
	MEAN	
	ST. DEV.	
	SKEW	

	n	EXPECTED VALUE	BIAS	STANDARD ERROR
C1	1			
C2	4			
C3	16			
C4	64			

HIST.2 C1	HIST.2 C2
HIST.2 C3	HIST.2 C4

Form 5, Exercise 5

(n = 1, 4, 16, 64: 5000 SRSN samples from V17 of population 4)

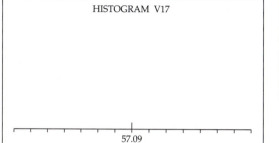

HISTOGRAM V17

PARAMETERS V17	
COUNT	947
MEAN	57.09
ST. DEV.	11.19
SKEW	–0.08

57.09

	n	EXPECTED VALUE	BIAS	STANDARD ERROR
C1	1			
C2	4			
C3	16			
C4	64			

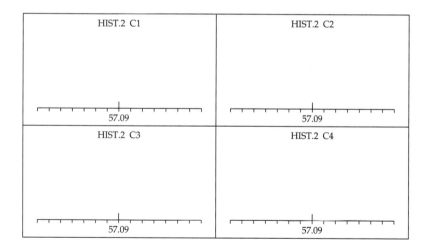

HIST.2 C1	HIST.2 C2
57.09	57.09
HIST.2 C3	HIST.2 C4
57.09	57.09

Form 5, Exercise 6

(n = 1, 2, 4, 40: 5000 SRSW samples from V9 of population 4)

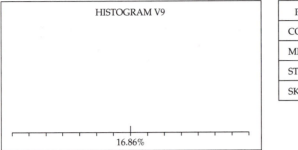

PARAMETERS V9	
COUNT	
MEAN	
ST. DEV.	
SKEW	

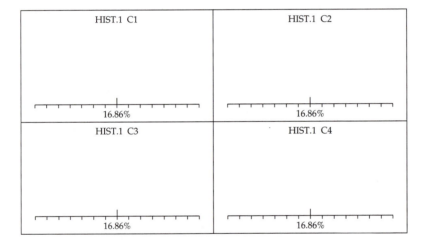

Form 5, Exercise 7

(n = 1, 2, 4, 40: 5000 SRSW samples from V10 of population 4)

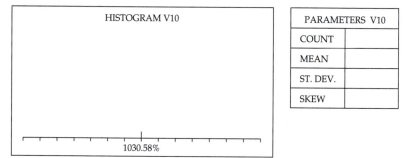

HISTOGRAM V10

1030.58%

PARAMETERS V10	
COUNT	
MEAN	
ST. DEV.	
SKEW	

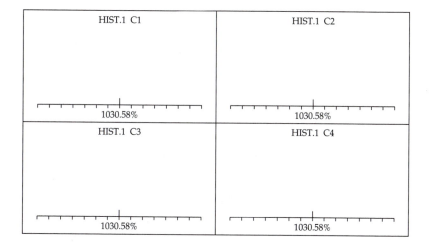

HIST.1 C1

1030.58%

HIST.1 C2

1030.58%

HIST.1 C3

1030.58%

HIST.1 C4

1030.58%

Form 5, Exercise 9

(n = 1, 96: 9999 SRSW samples from V6 of population 4)

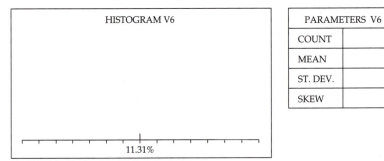

PARAMETERS V6	
COUNT	
MEAN	
ST. DEV.	
SKEW	

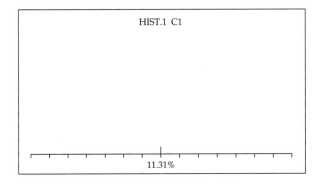

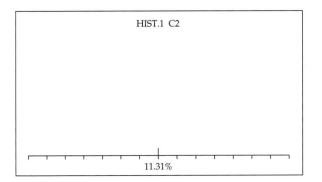

Form 7.1

Table of Fifty Random Digits

	1	2	3	4	5	6	7	8	9	10
1										
2										
3										
4										
5										

Appendix C

Answers to Exercises

Chapter 2

1. The sample types selected were:

   Helen Martin—census
   Mrs. Martin—convenience sample
   Mr. Martin—convenience sample

2. A. The population member would be a local sports store or its purchasing agent. The true score is the number of pairs of in-line skates a specific sports store would actually purchase.

   B. The population is the set of all local sports stores or agents—in this case, 12. The population distribution is the set of true scores associated with every member of the population. It would be a set of numbers that shows the number of pairs of in-line skates all 12 sports stores would buy.

   C. The parameter for this problem would be the total of the population distribution. It would be obtained by finding the sum of all the true scores in the population distribution.

3. A. The sample member is a purchasing agent for a local sports store who gave Mr. Martin information about the in-line skates they might purchase. The observation is the estimate given by the purchasing agent of the number of pairs of in-line skates that store would purchase.

   B. The sample is the two purchasing agents who were interviewed (Betty Arrow and Max Braun). The sample distribution is the two observed scores, 10 and 30, given by the two sample members.

   C. The sample statistic used by Mr. Martin was the sample mean.

   D. Mr. Martin's estimate was 240 pairs of in-line skates, which he obtained by multiplying the sample mean (20) by the population size (12):

   mean * N = 20 * 12 = 240

4. A. The population parameter is the total. We will use the symbol TOTAL for a population total. TOTAL = 120 for the population distribution given for Mr. Martin's problem.

    B. N = population size = 12

        TOTAL = the sum of all true scores = 120

        MEAN = mean of the population distribution = 10

        ST.DEV. = standard deviation of the population
                distribution = 5

        MEDIAN = median value of the population distribution = 10

        MODE = modal value of the population distribution = 10

        MAXIMUM VALUE = maximum value of the population
                distribution = 20

        MINIMUM VALUE = minimum value of the population = 0

        RANGE = MAXIMUM VALUE − MINIMUM VALUE = 20 − 0 = 20

5. A. The sample and sample distribution for Mr. Martin's problem are as follows:

Sample *(name of purchasing agent)*	*Sample Distribution* *(expected purchase)*
Betty Arrow	10
Max Braun	30

    B. n = sample size = 2.00

        total = the sum of all observed scores = 40.00

        mean = mean of the sample distribution = 20.00

        st. dev. = standard deviation of the sample distribution
            = 14.14

        (Remember, we use n − 1 in the denominator when we calculate a sample standard deviation.)

        median   = median value of the sample distribution
                      = 20

        maximum value = maximum value of the sample
                      distribution
                      = 30

        minimum value = minimum value of the sample
                      distribution
                      = 10

        range = maximum value − minimum value = 30 − 10 = 20

Chapter 3

1. If we shuffle the deck properly, it will put the deck in random order. Therefore, it makes no difference whether we select the sample from the top, bottom, or middle of the deck.

    To see this, we can list the samples that we could select if we select two cards from the bottom of the deck. The same six samples could be selected from the bottom of the deck as could be selected from the top of the deck (AB, AC, AD, BC, BD, and CD), and each of the six samples would have the same chance of being selected.

Since the samples are the same, the means of the samples will also be the same (45, 60, 75, 75, 90, 105). Thus, the sampling distribution is the same for samples selected from the top and bottom of the deck. Since the sampling distribution is the same for selecting from the top and bottom of the deck, the potential for error in the estimate is the same (–30, –15, 0, 0, 15, 30). Therefore, if we shuffle the deck thoroughly, it makes no difference whether we select the sample from the top or bottom of the deck.

2. You will find some differences between the results of your work in this exercise and the results we obtained in Experiment 3.1, but both experiments will show the following:

- The CON sample has a positive bias, while the SRS sample is unbiased.

- The SRS sample has a random error ($ST.ERR. > 0$), while the CON sample does not ($ST.ERR. = 0$).

- The root mean error for the CON sample is greater than the total error for the SRS sample ($RME_{CON} > RME_{SRS}$).

You can redo this exercise as many times as you like using whatever population distribution you choose, as long as the sales for C and D are greater than the sales for A and B. You will always find the CON sample will be biased with no random error and the SRS will be unbiased with random error. The total error will always be greater for the CON sample.

3. If we select a sample of three cards from the top of the deck, we can get four possible samples (ABC, ABD, ACD, and BCD). The four samples and the means of these four samples are as follows:

Sample	Sample Mean	
ABC	$(30 + 60 + 90)/3$	$= 60$
ABD	$(30 + 60 + 120)/3$	$= 70$
ACD	$(30 + 90 + 120)/3$	$= 80$
BCD	$(60 + 90 + 120)/3$	$= 90$

To calculate the total potential for error in the three-store sample, we must first calculate the bias measure for this sampling distribution. First, we need to calculate the expected value, or the mean of the sampling distribution:

$$EXP.VAL. = (60 + 70 + 80 + 90)/4 = 75$$

We can now calculate the bias (remember, the mean of the population distribution is 75):

$$BIAS = EXP.VAL. - M = 75 - 75 = 0$$

This tells us that the three-store SRS gives an unbiased estimate. (The potential for a positive error is balanced by the potential for a negative error; thus, there is no systematic error.) The total error (RME) will therefore be equal to the random error, or standard error:

$$ST.ERR. = \sqrt{\frac{(60 - 75)^2 + (70 - 75)^2 + (80 - 75)^2 + (90 - 75)^2}{4}} = 11.2$$

The total potential for error (RME) for the three-store SRS is equal to 11.2 pairs of in-line skates, while the total error for the two-store SRS is equal to 19.4. The potential error in using the mean of the three-store SRS is, as expected, much smaller than the potential for error in using the mean of the two-store sample.

4. A. The sampling distribution of the three possible samples is:

Sample	Sample Mean
BC	75
BD	90
CD	105

B. The expected value of the sampling distribution is

$$EXP.VAL. = (75 + 90 + 105)/3 = 90$$

C. The bias, or systematic error, in the estimate is

$$BIAS = EXP.VAL. - MEAN = 90 - 75 = 15$$

D. The standard error, or random error, in the estimate is

$$ST.ERR. = \sqrt{\frac{(75-90)^2 + (90-90)^2 + (105-90)^2}{3}} = 12.2$$

E. The total or root mean error is

$$RME = \sqrt{BIAS^2 + ST.ERR.^2} = \sqrt{15^2 + 12.2^2} = 19.3$$

Notice our estimate in this example has a potential for both systematic error and random error. The systematic error is due to the lack of cooperation by Store A, which introduces a nonrandom factor into the selection procedure. The random error is due to the random selection among the remaining three stores.

Inability to reach or interview randomly selected members of a sample is called *nonresponse*. It is one of the major sources of error in most sample surveys.

5. The 16 samples that could be selected, along with their means, are listed below:

AA	30	BA	45	CA	60	DA	75
AB	45	BB	60	CB	75	DB	90
AC	60	BC	75	CC	90	DC	105
AD	75	BD	90	CD	105	DD	120

The expected value (mean of the 16 sample means) is 75. Since *BIAS* = *EXP.VAL.* – MEAN = 75 – 75 = 0, the estimate is unbiased. The standard error (random error) is the standard deviation of the 16 means: *ST.ERR.* = 23.7. (Use 16 not 15 in calculating the standard error.) Since the estimate is unbiased, the total error (RME) will equal the random error: RME = *ST.ERR.* = 23.7. Thus, we see that the mean of the SRS, whether selected with or without replacement, is unbiased, but the mean of the SRS selected with replacement has a greater potential for error.

6. The 66 possible samples of size two selected from a deck of 12 cards (A, B, C, . . . , L) would be:

```
AB
AC   BC
AD   BD   CD
AE   BE   CE   DE
AF   BF   CF   DF   EF
AG   BG   CG   DG   EG   FG
AH   BH   CH   DH   EH   FH   GH
AI   BI   CI   DI   EI   FI   GI   HI
AJ   BJ   CJ   DJ   EJ   FJ   GJ   HJ   IJ
AK   BK   CK   DK   EK   FK   GK   HK   IK   JK
AL   BL   CL   DL   EL   FL   GL   HL   IL   JL   KL
```

Chapter 4

1. The parameters for the two distributions are:

	N	MEAN	MEDIAN	ST.DEV.	MINIMUM	MAXIMUM
V2	12	48	48	12.00	36	60
V3	12	54	60	10.39	36	60

The histograms for the two distributions are:

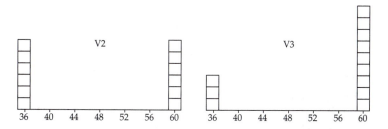

Both distributions are dichotomies of size 12 with scores of 36 and 60. V2 is a uniform symmetric curve that is balanced around its mean of 48. Note that the mean and median of V2 are both 48, which marks V2 as a symmetric distribution. V3 is a negatively skewed, unimodal curve with a mean of 54. The median of V3 is 60, which is greater than its mean of 54. Subtracting the median from the mean gives $54 - 60 = -6$, which is why V3 is called a negatively skewed distribution.

2. A. The specifications for this experiment are:

	Var	Type	Size	Mis.
C1	2	SRSW	1	*
C2	*	SRSN	*	*
C3	*	SRSN	*	*
C4	*	SRSN	*	*

Number of samples 9999

It does not matter how you specify Type for C2, C3, and C4 as long as there is an asterisk in the Var column for these conditions.

B. You should get the same results in this exercise as you obtained in Experiment 4.2.

- The sampling distribution for samples of size one selected from your distribution V2 should look very much like the population distribution from which the samples were selected.

- the expected value of your sampling distribution should be very close in value to the mean of your population (*EXP.VAL.* = MEAN).

- The standard error of your sampling distribution should be very close in value to the standard deviation of your population distribution V2 (*ST.ERR.*(1) = ST.DEV. = 12.00).

3. From the 4-times rule you found that increasing the sample size by a factor of k would reduce the standard error by a factor of $1/\sqrt{k}$. The sample size for each condition in Experiment 4.2 was 2 times larger than the sample size in the previous condition. Thus the increase in the sample size should reduce the standard error by $1/\sqrt{2}$ = .71. We can get the same results by using the equation $ST.ERR.(n) = ST.DEV./\sqrt{n}$.

$$\frac{ST.ERR.(2)}{ST.ERR.(1)} = \frac{ST.DEV./\sqrt{2}}{ST.DEV./\sqrt{1}} = \frac{ST.DEV. * \sqrt{1}}{ST.DEV. * \sqrt{2}} = \frac{1.00}{1.41} = .71$$

$$\frac{ST.ERR.(4)}{ST.ERR.(2)} = \frac{ST.DEV./\sqrt{4}}{ST.DEV./\sqrt{2}} = \frac{ST.DEV. * \sqrt{2}}{ST.DEV. * \sqrt{4}} = \frac{1.41}{2.00} = .71$$

$$\frac{ST.ERR.(8)}{ST.ERR.(4)} = \frac{ST.DEV./\sqrt{8}}{ST.DEV./\sqrt{4}} = \frac{ST.DEV. * \sqrt{4}}{ST.DEV. * \sqrt{8}} = \frac{2.00}{2.82} = .71$$

4. According to Rule II, the equation for measuring the standard error is $ST.ERR.(n) = ST.DEV./\sqrt{n}$. If the standard deviation for V4 is ST.DEV. = 9.79 and the sample sizes are 1, 3, 6, and 9, we should get standard errors as follows:

$$ST.ERR. (1) = ST.DEV./\sqrt{n} = 9.79/\sqrt{1} = 9.79/1.00 = 9.79$$

$$ST.ERR. (3) = ST.DEV./\sqrt{n} = 9.79/\sqrt{3} = 9.79/1.73 = 5.65$$

$$ST.ERR. (6) = ST.DEV./\sqrt{n} = 9.79/\sqrt{6} = 9.79/2.45 = 4.00$$

$$ST.ERR. (9) = ST.DEV./\sqrt{n} = 9.79/\sqrt{9} = 9.79/3.00 = 3.26$$

5. A. The specification for the experiment is:

	Var	Type	Size	Mis.
C1	4	SRSW	1	*
C2	4	SRSW	3	*
C3	4	SRSW	6	*
C4	4	SRSW	9	*

Number of Samples: 9999

B. The histograms for C1–C4 should all be balanced around the population mean, which supports Rule I. As you go from C1 to C4, the histograms should cluster more and more around the population mean of 48, which tells you that the potential for error is going down as the sample size increases.

The parameter table for this exercise should confirm Rules I and II. The bias measure for each condition should be close to zero (Rule I), and the standard errors should be similar to the values you calculated in response to Exercise 4 (Rule II).

6. You should find:

  • as the sample size increased, the sampling distribution clustered more around the mean of the population

  • the sample mean was an unbiased estimate of the population mean: *EXP.VAL.* = MEAN (Rule I).

  • The standard errors for conditions C1–C4 were nearly equal to the standard deviation of your population distribution divided by the square root of the sample size (Rule II).

7. A. The fpc is calculated in four steps: calculate $N - n$, calculate $N - 1$, calculate $(N - n)/(N - 1)$, and take the square root of $(N - n)/(N - 1)$.

   The fpc's for sample sizes 1 through 12 selected from the 12-store population are:

$n = 1$	fpc = 1.00	$n = 5$	fpc = 0.80	$n = 9$	fpc = 0.52
$n = 2$	fpc = 0.95	$n = 6$	fpc = 0.74	$n = 10$	fpc = 0.43
$n = 3$	fpc = 0.90	$n = 7$	fpc = 0.67	$n = 11$	fpc = 0.30
$n = 4$	fpc = 0.85	$n = 8$	fpc = 0.60	$n = 12$	fpc = 0.00

   B.

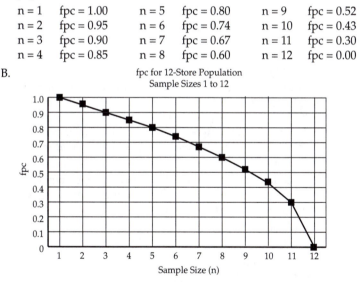

fpc for 12-Store Population
Sample Sizes 1 to 12

The fpc has a maximum value of fpc = 1.00 at sample size one. It declines in value for every increase in the sample size and reaches its minimum of fpc = 0 when $n = N$.

The results of this exercise illustrate the following two general rules:

  • The standard error for a simple random sample selected without replacement will be smaller than the standard error for the same size simple random sample selected from the same population with replacement except for the unusual case of n = 1. We draw this conclusion because the fpc is less than 1 for all values of n except n = 1.

- The larger the sample size, the greater the effect of the fpc on the standard error. We conclude this because the curve for the fpc drops at an increasing rate as the sample size increases from 1 to 12.

8. Given Rule II, the standard error for sampling without replacement is equal to the standard deviation of the population distribution, times the fpc divided by the square root of the sample size. The standard deviation of V4 is 9.79 so the standard errors for sample sizes of 1, 2, 4, and 8 with N = 12 are:

n = 1 $ST.ERR.(1) = 9.79*1.00/\sqrt{1} = 9.79$
n = 2 $ST.ERR.(2) = 9.79*0.95/\sqrt{2} = 6.57$
n = 4 $ST.ERR.(4) = 9.79*0.85/\sqrt{4} = 4.16$
n = 8 $ST.ERR.(8) = 9.79*0.60/\sqrt{8} = 2.07$

(The values of the fpc are taken from the answer to Exercise 7.)

9. A. The specification for this experiment is:

	Var	Type	Size	Mis.
C1	4	SRSN	1	*
C2	4	SRSN	2	*
C3	4	SRSN	4	*
C4	4	SRSN	8	*

Number of Samples: 9999

B. The values you find for the standard errors of C1–C4 should be very close to those calculated for Exercise 8, which would confirm the use of the fpc as an adjustment required in Rule II for sampling without replacement. The sample means should be balanced around the population mean and the bias measure should be near zero, which would confirm Rule I.

10. A. The standard deviation for a dichotomous population distribution 36, 60 is equal to 12 (ST.DEV. = 12). The fpc for n = 2 = N is zero. So the required standard errors are:

with replacement
$$ST.ERR.(2) = ST.DEV./\sqrt{n} = 12/\sqrt{2} = 8.48$$

without replacement
$$ST.ERR.(2) = ST.DEV. * fpc/\sqrt{n} = 12*0/\sqrt{2} = 0.00$$

B. When we sample with replacement, it is possible to select one or more members of the population more than once in a sample of size N. As a result, selecting a sample of size N with replacement does not guarantee that every member of the population will be selected in a sample. In this example, there are three possible samples of size two that can be selected from the population distribution 36, 60 with replacement:

- 36 and 36, with a mean of 36
- 36 and 60, with a mean of 48
- 60 and 60, with a mean of 60

The possibility of multiple selection creates variations in the sampling distribution, with the result that the standard error is not equal to zero.

When sampling without replacement, multiple selection cannot occur, and so there is only one possible sample of size n = N. In this case, the only possible sample of size n = 2 is the sample 36 and 60. Thus, there is no possibility for variation in the sampling distribution, and the standard error is equal to zero.

Chapter 5

1. To answer questions 1A–C you must activate option 1, Population in the UNIVARIATE window. The answers can be found in the Population List.

   A. The name assigned to population 2 is U.S. County Data.

   B. Lower East Side 1900 is population 6.

   C. There are 17 variables in the population called U.S. County Data.

   To answer questions 1D–H you must select the appropriate population (by placing the cursor on the required population and pressing the EN-TER key) and then activate option 2, Variables, in the UNIVARIATE window. The answers will be found in the Variable List for the selected population.

   D. Select population 2, U.S. County Data. The variable with the largest mean is 2, Population in 1986.

   E. Select population 2, U.S. County Data (same as in 1D). The variable with the smallest standard deviation is 6, Persons: Household 85 (0.23).

   F. Select population 1, Population Models. The range for variable 4, Skewed: Extreme, is 57.56 (145.77 – 88.21). (If you answer this question just after you answer question 1E, you will first have to return to the UNIVARIATE menu by pressing the ESC key. Then activate option 1, Populations, and select population 1. Finally, activate option 2, Variables, in the UNIVARIATE menu to get the Variable List for population 1.)

   G. The variables in population 3 are already ordered according to their skew (1, 2, 3, 4, 5, 6). Variable 1 has the largest skew index, and variable 6 the smallest.

   To check the skew of the six variables in population 3:

   - First select population 3, U.S. Places 2500.

   - Activate option 2, Variables, in the UNIVARIATE window.

- Give the Histograms command (press the F10 key).
- Generate the histograms for all six variables, V1–V6 by placing the cursor on each variable and pressing the ENTER key.

H. To answer this question, use the same procedure as in 1G and examine the resulting histograms, You will find that seven variables in population 4 have more than one mode. Variables 12, 13, 14, and 15 have two or more very clear modes. Variables 9, 16, and 17 have a second very small mode near the end of their tails.

2. A. Variable 2, Population in 1986, has the largest mean, so according to Rule I (*EXP.VAL.* = MEAN) it should have the largest expected value. Its expected value would be *EXP.VAL.*(V2) = 23,738.43.

   B. According to Rule I, the expected value for each of the six variables in population 3 should be equal to its population mean, so none of the six variables would have a biased sampling distribution.

   C. The sample size for the sampling distribution of the six variables is the same, so the size of their standard error relative to each other depends on the size of their standard deviations. Variable 2, Population in 1986, has the largest standard deviation, so it would have the largest standard error. Its standard error would be:

   $ST.ERR.(V2) = ST.DEV.(V2)/\sqrt{n} = 127{,}718.92/\sqrt{100} = 12{,}771.89$

   D. The root mean error (RME) measures the total potential for error. The RME is equal to the square root of the bias squared plus the square root of the standard error squared. Since each of the sampling distributions is unbiased, the RME is equal to the standard error. Since variable 2, Population in 1986, has the largest standard error, it also has the largest root mean error. In this example: RME(V2) = *ST.ERR.*(V2) = 12,771.89.

   E. Increasing the sample size by a factor of four should decrease the standard error by a factor of two, so we would need a sample size of n = 400 to cut the standard errors in half.

   F. The answers to 2A–2D would not be changed if the sample were selected without replacement.

3. A. The histogram of V17 in population 2 is bimodal. It has one mode one category above its mean and another mode one category below its mean. The parameters of V17, population 2, are: N = 3139, MEAN = 59.31, ST.DEV. = 12.50, SKEW = –0.21.

   B. The specification for this experiment is as follows:

Var	Type	Size
C1	17	SRSW	1
C2	17	SRSW	4
C3	17	SRSW	16
C4	17	SRSW	64

   Number of Samples: 5000

   C. If Rule II is true, $ST.ERR. = ST.DEV./\sqrt{n}$. With ST.DEV. = 12.50, the standard error for the four conditions in this experiment should be close to the following values:

C1	n = 1	$12.50/\sqrt{1}$	=	12.50
C2	n = 4	$12.50/\sqrt{4}$	=	6.25
C3	n = 16	$12.50/\sqrt{16}$	=	3.13
C4	n = 64	$12.50/\sqrt{64}$	=	1.56

   Note that the expected standard error for C1 with sample size one is the same as the standard deviation of V17. As we go from each condition to the next, the sample size increases by a factor of four and the expected standard error is cut in half.

D. The results of this experiment should be similar to the results obtained in Experiment 5.1.

- The sampling distribution of C1 should have the same bimodal shape as V17.

- The sampling distributions of C1–C4 should be balanced around the population mean. (Remember to use Hist.1 when analyzing the shape of the sampling distributions. The population mean is displayed as a thin line in the histogram.)

- The sampling distributions should cluster more and more around the population mean as we go from C1 (with the smallest sample size) to C4 (with the largest sample size). (Remember to use Hist.2 when comparing the spread of the sampling distributions.)

- According to Rule I, the expected value for each condition should be equal to the population mean of 59.31, and the bias measure should be equal to zero. Your results for this experiment should be very close to those predicted by Rule I.

- The standard errors for C1–C4 should be very close to those calculated in Part 3C.

4. A–F. Specific answers will vary according the Test Variable selected, but should parallel those in Exercise 3.

5. A. The histogram of V17, population 4, has three modes. The largest mode is at the mean, with secondary modes below and above the mean. The parameters of V17 from population 4 are: N = 947, MEAN = 57.09, ST.DEV. = 11.19, SKEW = –0.08.

B. The specification for this experiment is as follows:

	Var	Type	Size
C1	17	SRSN	1
C2	17	SRSN	4
C3	17	SRSN	16
C4	17	SRSN	64

Number of Samples: 5000

C. If Rule II is true, $ST.ERR. = ST.DEV. * fpc/\sqrt{n}$, with ST.DEV. = 11.19. The standard error for the four conditions in this experiment should be close to the following values:

		fpc	*ST.ERR.*		
C1	n = 1	1.0000	$11.19{*}1.0000/\sqrt{1}$	=	11.19
C2	n = 4	.9984	$11.19{*}0.9984/\sqrt{4}$	=	5.59
C3	n = 16	.9920	$11.19{*}0.9920/\sqrt{16}$	=	2.78
C4	n = 64	.9661	$11.19{*}0.9661/\sqrt{64}$	=	1.35

Note that the expected standard error for C1 with sample size one is the same as the standard deviation of V17. As we go from each condition to the next, the sample size increases by a factor of four and the expected standard error is cut in half and is reduced further by the fpc. The fpc has almost no effect at the smaller sample sizes (C1–C3), but it does start affecting the standard error of C4, where the sample size of 64 is 6.76% of the total population of 947. This illustrates the point made in Chapter 4 that sampling with and without replacement results in almost identical standard errors when the sample size is a very small part of N, but sampling without replacement will reduce the standard error when n/N (in this case 64/947) is not a small number.

E. The results of this experiment should be very similar to those of Experiment 5.1. The only difference is a slight reduction in the standard errors by the use of the fpc.

6. A. The parameters of V9 in population 4 are: N = 951, MEAN = 16.86, ST.DEV. = 5.14, SKEW = 1.56. The histogram for V9 (population 4) is unimodal, with its mode one category to the left of the mean. It has a positive skew, with its tail pointing off to the right.

B. The specification for this experiment is as follows:

	Var	*Type*	*Size*
C1	9	SRSW	1
C2	9	SRSW	2
C3	9	SRSW	4
C4	9	SRSW	40

Number of Samples: 5000

C. The results of this experiment should be similar to the results obtained in Experiment 5.2.

- The shape of the sampling distribution for C1 (n = 1) is the same as the shape of the population distribution of V9.

- The sampling distributions of C1 to C4 are balanced around the population mean.

- As the sample size increases (C1 to C4), the sampling distributions cluster more and more around the population mean and they look more like a normal curve.

7. A. The parameters of V10 in population 4 are: N = 951, MEAN = 1030.58, ST.DEV. = 3215.92, SKEW = 15.03. Note the extremely high skew index for V10. The histogram for V10 in population 4 is unimodal, with its mode at the mean and a large number of cases way out in the tail to the right of the mean. The many scores out in the tail are what give V10 its extremely large skew index. (The large skew index for V10 tells something about the sample size required before

the sampling distribution of V10 will become a normal curve. What does it tell us?)

B. The specification for this experiment is as follows:

	Var	Type	Size
C1	10	SRSW	1
C2	10	SRSW	2
C3	10	SRSW	4
C4	10	SRSW	40

Number of Samples: 5000

C. The results of this experiment should be similar to the results of Experiment 5.2 in all respects but one. The following results are the same for both experiments:

- The shape of the sampling distribution for C1 (n = 1) is the same as the shape of the population distribution from which the sample was selected.

- The sampling distributions of C1–C4 are balanced around the population mean.

- As the sample size increases (C1 to C4), the sampling distribution clusters more and more around the population mean.

- As the sample size increases, the sampling distributions become more like a normal curve.

The major difference in the results of the two experiments is the speed with which the sampling distribution becomes normal. In Experiment 5.2, the sampling distribution had already taken a normal-like shape in C4 (n = 40). In this experiment the sampling distribution does not yet look like a normal curve in C4 (n = 40). The difference in the results is due to the different amounts of skew in the V5 and V10 distributions. V5 has a moderate skew index of −1.58, and samples of size 40 begin to show an approximately normal sampling distribution. V10 has an extremely large skew index of 15.03, which requires sample sizes much larger than 40 before it will look like a normal curve.

8. A. To answer this question, select population 1, Population Models, and check the histograms of the eight variables in this population to see if they have five or more categories. For any that do, we can use Rule III to estimate the required sample size for a normal sampling distribution.

The histograms show that the first six variables V1–V6, all have more than five categories. We can apply Rule III to those variables. V7 and V8 have, as their names suggest, only two categories. Therefore, we should not use Rule III for V7 and V8.

B. V1, V2, V3, V5, and V6 have skew indexes within the range of +1 to −1. According to Rule III, a sample size of 25 or more should give normally shaped sampling distributions for these variables.

V4 has a skew index of 1.54, which is outside the range of +1 to −1. According to Rule III, it will have a normally shaped sampling distribution for a sample size of 25 * 1.54 * 1.54 = 59 or more.

Note that V3 has a skew index of 1.00. We could treat this variable as either in or out of the range of +1 to –1, and we would get the same result: a required sample size of 25.

Also note that V1 and V2, as their names suggest, are very close to being normal distributions. As a result, the required sample size for a normally shaped sampling distribution for these variables would be much smaller than 25, the size specified in Rule III. This illustrates one of the shortcomings of Rule III, which may overestimate the required sample size for distributions whose skew measure is near zero.

9. A. The histogram of V6 in population 4 is unimodal and positively skewed. Its mode is one category below its mean, and it has a tail pointing to the right. The parameters of V6 are: N = 951, MEAN = 11.31, ST.DEV. = 15.58, SKEW = 1.96.

B. The histogram for V6 shows it has more than five categories, so the required sample size n´ for V6 to have a normal distribution, according to Rule III, is

$$n´ = 25 * SKEW^2 = 25 * 1.96^2 = 96$$

C. The specification for this experiment is as follows:

	Var	Type	Size
C1	6	SRSW	1
C2	6	SRSW	96
C3	*	SRSN	*
C4	*	SRSN	*
Number of Samples:			9999

D. The results of this experiment should be very similar to the results of Experiment 5.3. The sampling distribution of C1 (n = 1) should look like the distribution of the variable (V6) from which it was selected. The sampling distribution of C2 (n = n´ = 96) should look very much like a normal curve, which would verify Rule III.

10. MEAN = 3, MEDIAN = 2, ST.DEV. = 2.16

MEAN – MEDIAN = 3 – 2 = 1, so the distribution is positively skewed, so SKEW is greater than 0.

SKEW	$= (A – B + C)/ST.DEV.^3$		
A	$= (1^3 + 2^3 + 6^3)/3$	= 225/3	= 75
B	$= 3 * 3 * (1^2 + 2^2 + 6^2)/3$	$= 3 * 3 * 41/3$	= 123
C	$= 2 * 3^3$	= 2 * 27	= 54
ST.DEV.^{3}	$= 2.16^3$		= 10.08
SKEW	= (75 – 123 + 54)/10.08		= .60

Chapter 6

1. A. The interval is 160 to 180 pounds.

If MEAN = 165, the estimate is right: 165 is in the range.
If MEAN = 190, the estimate is wrong: 190 is out of the range.

If MEAN = 160, the estimate is right: end points are in the range.
If MEAN = 155, the estimate is wrong: 155 is out of the range.
If MEAN = 180, the estimate is right: end points are in the range.

B. The interval is 160 to 180 pounds, the range of values covered is 180 – 160 = 20. INT. is half the range covered, so INT. = 10. The equation for this interval estimate is

ESTIMATE(MEAN) = 170 ± 10

C. If mean = 175 and INT. = 5, the range of values covered is 170 (mean – INT.) to 180 (mean + INT.). The equation for the interval is

ESTIMATE(MEAN) = 175 ± 5

2. A. The three most frequently used confidence intervals are the 90%, the 95%, and the 99% confidence intervals. The values of Z for these three confidence intervals are 1.65, 1.96, and 2.57, respectively.

B. The equation for a confidence interval is

ESTIMATE(MEAN) = mean ± (Z * ST.ERR.)

If Z = 1.96, ESTIMATE(MEAN) = 180 ± (1.96 * 5), range 170.2 to 189.8

If Z = 2.57, ESTIMATE(MEAN) = 180 ± (2.57 * 5), range 167.15 to 192.85

If Z = 1.65, ESTIMATE(MEAN) = 180 ± (1.65 * 5), range 171.75 to 188.25

3. A. For 90% confidence, Z = 1.65. If n = 100,

$ST.ERR. = ST.DEV./\sqrt{n} = 10/\sqrt{100} = 1$

ESTIMATE(MEAN) = mean ± (Z * ST.ERR.) = 170 ± (1.65 * 1)

range = 168.35 to 171.65 pounds

B. For 95% confidence, Z = 1.96. If n = 100,

$ST.ERR. = ST.DEV./\sqrt{n} = 10/\sqrt{100} = 1$

ESTIMATE(MEAN) = mean ± (Z * ST.ERR.) = 170 ± (1.96 * 1)

range = 168.04 to 171.96 pounds.

C. For 90% confidence, Z = 1.65. If n = 400,

$ST.ERR. = ST.DEV./\sqrt{n} = 10/\sqrt{400} = .5$

ESTIMATE(MEAN) = mean ± (Z * ST.ERR.) = 170 ± (1.65 *.5)

range = 169.175 to 170.825 pounds

4. A. For 95% confidence, Z = 1.96. If n = 144 and st.dev. = 24, then $ST.ERR. = 24/\sqrt{144} = 2$. With mean = 175, the confidence interval will be

ESTIMATE(MEAN) = 175 ± 1.96 * 2 (171.08 to 178.92 pounds)

B. If n = 81 and st.dev. = 24, then $ST.ERR. = 24/\sqrt{81} = 2.67$

With mean = 175, the confidence interval will be

ESTIMATE(MEAN) = 175 ± (1.96 * 2.67), 169.77 to 180.23 pounds

C. If n = 144 and st.dev. = 12, then $ST.ERR. = 12/\sqrt{144} = 1$.

With mean = 175, the confidence interval will be

ESTIMATE(MEAN) = 175 ± (1.96 * 1) (173.04 to 176.96 pounds)

Notice that the sample size and standard deviation have opposite effects on the confidence interval. Compare the answers to 4A and 4B. In 4B the sample size was smaller, so the confidence interval was larger. Now compare the answers to 4A and 4C. In 4C the standard deviation was smaller, and the confidence interval was smaller. In general, the confidence interval will change in the same direction as the standard deviation and in the opposite direction to the sample size. An increase in the standard deviation will increase a confidence interval, but an increase in sample size will decrease the confidence interval.

5. A. The proportion of males is $10/50 = .20$.
        The percentage of females is $(40/50) * 100 = 80\%$.

    B. For males, PROP. $= .20$ and NOPROP. $= 1.00 - $ PROP. $= .80$.

    C. The shortcut formula is ST.DEV.(PROP.)
        $= \sqrt{(PROP. * NOPROP.)}$.

        In this exercise, ST.DEV.(PROP.) $= \sqrt{(.20 * .80)} = .40$.

6. A. For 95% confidence, $Z = 1.96$. If prop. $= .50$, then noprop. $= .50$ and ST.DEV. $= .50$.

        If $n = 100$, then $ST.ERR. = .50/\sqrt{100} = .05$.

        The 95% confidence interval is

        ESTIMATE(PROP.) $= .50 \pm (1.96 * .05)$ (.402 to .598)

    B. If prop. $= .40$, then noprop. $= .60$ and ST.DEV. $= .49$.
        If $n = 100$, then $ST.ERR. = .49/\sqrt{100} = .049$.

        The 95% confidence interval is

        ESTIMATE(PROP.) $= .40 \pm (1.96 * .049)$ (.304 to .496)

    C. If prop. $= .70$, then noprop. $= .30$ and ST.DEV. $= .46$.
        If $n = 400$, then $ST.ERR. = .46/\sqrt{400} = .023$.

        The 95% confidence interval is

        ESTIMATE(PROP.) $= .70 \pm (1.96 * .023)$ (.655 to .745)

7. A. For 95% confidence, $Z = 1.96$. With INT. $= 2$ and ST.DEV. $= 10$, the right sample size would be

        $n = (1.96 * 10/2)^2 = 96$

    B. For 99% confidence, $Z = 2.57$. With INT. $= 2$ and ST.DEV. $= 10$, the right sample size would be

        $n = (2.57*10/2)^2 = 165$

    C. For 95% confidence, $Z = 1.96$. With INT. $= 4$ and ST.DEV. $= 10$, the right sample size would be

        $n = (1.96 * 10/4)^2 = 24$

    D. For 95% confidence, $Z = 1.96$. With INT. $= 2$ and ST.DEV. $= 20$, the right sample size would be

        $n = (1.96*20/2)^2 = 384$

If you compare your answer to 7A with the answers to B, C, and D, you will see:

- The right sample size varies directly with the confidence. The greater the confidence required, the larger the right sample size

Glossary/Index

A

Actual error The difference between the estimate and the population parameter, 19

B

Bias An estimate in which the potential for negative and positive errors is not balanced; if the potential for a positive error is greater, the estimate is **positively biased**; if the potential for a negative error is greater, the estimate is **negatively biased**, 7, 31, 44, 55, 66, 93, 165

C

Census Data collected on every member of a specified population, 4, 17, 83

Condition Used here to describe an experimental condition in the SIMPLE SAMPLE and UNIVARIATE modules of ISEE, in which a specified number of samples of a given size and type is selected from a specified population, 51

Confidence The probability that an interval estimate will be correct, 116, 119, 132

Confidence interval An interval that has a certain probability of being correct, 7, 113–114, 117–119, 135–136

Constant A number that does not change, 118

Convenience sample A sample of cases that can be collected in the easiest way possible, with little cost or effort; it does not try to cover every member of the population, 4, 28–29, 164–165

Cost, as a factor in sample design, 5

Count The number of cases with data in a particular population or sample, 87

Coverage The proportion of the population that is included in a sampling frame, 150–152

D

Distribution A set of numbers or symbols, such as the ages of all persons in a household, 6

E

Error, potential, 28, 30, 140. *See also* **Actual error**

Estimate The picture of a population parameter we get from doing some kind of research, 8, 16

Expected value The mean of any kind of a sampling distribution, 32, 55, 77, 104

F

Finite population correction factor (fpc) A mathematical formula used to adjust the sampling rule $ST.ERR. = ST.DEV. / \sqrt{n}$ when sampling is done without replacement; the numerator in the formula is the population size minus the sample size and the denominator is the population size minus one, 74–76

The formula for fpc is

$$fpc = \sqrt{\frac{N - n}{N - 1}}$$

Frame A way of listing or organizing the population, 140, 143, 145–146, 148–150, 157–158, 162

histogram describing the dispersion of cases across the range of values in a population or a sample, 6, 30, 89

A *rectangular distribution* has approximately equal numbers of cases in all the values.

Rectangular Distribution

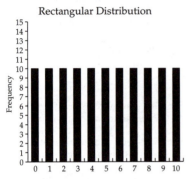

A *unimodal distribution* has one mode; that is, it has only one value with a greater frequency than all values that are adjacent to it.

Unimodal Distribution

In a *bimodal distribution*, the cases are distributed in such a way that they form two modes.

Bimodal Distribution

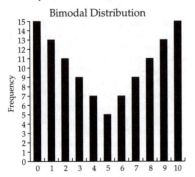

A *dichotomous distribution* has only two values.

Dichotomous Distribution

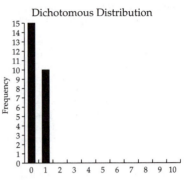

In a *symmetrical distribution,* the cases are evenly distributed above and below the mean value (*see* **normal distribution**). In a *positive skewed distribution,* the cases are unevenly distributed, with more at the lower values. In a *negative skewed distribution,* the cases are unevenly distributed, with more at the higher values.

Positive Skewed Distribution

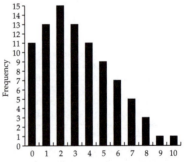

Negative Skewed Distribution

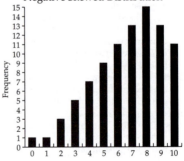